LYNCH STREET

End Of School

LYNCH STREET

The May 1970 Slayings at Jackson State College

Tim Spofford

THE KENT STATE UNIVERSITY PRESS
Kent, Ohio, and London, England

Frontispiece: From *Herblock's State of the Union* (Simon & Schuster, 1972).

The epigraph for chapter 1 is from "Strange Fruit" by Lewis Allan, c. 1939. Edward B. Marks Music Co., © renewed, used by permission. All rights reserved.

Photos from *The Kudzu* courtesy of David Doggett and Shannon Ferguson of *The Kudzu*. United Press International newsphoto courtesy of Bettmann Newsphotos, 48 East 21st Street, New York, N.Y. 10010. Associated Press wirephotos courtesy of Wide World Photos, 50 Rockefeller Plaza, New York, N.Y. 10020.

Library of Congress Catalog Card Number 87-21502
ISBN 0-87338-355-9 (cloth)
ISBN 0-87338-371-0 (paper)
Manufactured in the United States of America

The paper in this book meets the guidelines for permanence and durability of the Committee on Production Guidelines for Book Longevity of the Council on Library Resources.

Library of Congress Cataloging-in-Publication Data

Spofford, Tim.
Lynch Street.

Bibliography: p.
Includes index.
1. Jackson (Miss.)—Race relations. 2. Jackson State College. 3. Afro-Americans—Civil rights—Mississippi—Jackson. 4. Riots—Mississippi—Jackson. 5. Murder—Mississippi—Jackson. I. Title.
F349.J13S66 1988 976.2'51 87-21502
ISBN 0-87338-355-9 (alk. paper)
ISBN 0-87338-371-0 (pbk. : alk. paper)

British Cataloging-in-Publication data are available.

For Barbara

CONTENTS

1 Strange Roots 1
2 Mayday in Amerika 18
3 The Miniriot 33
4 By the Magnolia Tree 53
5 Jacktwo 80
6 Yoknapatawpha in Black 99
7 Crisis 115
8 Majesty of the Law 134
9 Showdown 141
10 Nixon's Court 154
Epilogue 175
Sources and Methods 181
Notes 184
Sources Consulted 196
Index 211

"Goodness gracious, anybody hurt?"
"No'm, killed a nigger."

Mark Twain, *Huckleberry Finn*

1

STRANGE ROOTS

Southern trees bear a strange fruit,
Blood on the leaves and blood at the root,
Black body swinging in the Southern breeze,
Strange fruit hanging from the poplar trees.

—Lewis Allan

They named it Lynch Street back when it was just a muddy roadway through a black neighborhood in Jackson. Not for the hanging Judge Lynch of Old Virginia, but for an emancipated slave who had done himself proud in Mississippi during Reconstruction.

His name was John Roy Lynch. He was a thin and light-skinned young man with a moustache, self-educated, and just twenty-four when the whites in the state legislature made him Speaker of the House of Representatives. At twenty-six, Lynch became Mississippi's first black congressman. But he had not come so far by playing Uncle Tom. At the capitol in Jackson, Lynch fought to repeal the "black codes" the Confederates had passed to create a new form of slavery after the Civil War. And in Washington he labored for passage of the 1875 Civil Rights Act. Later, after the whites had turned to the rope and the gun to drive blacks from office in Mississippi, Lynch urged President Grant to send federal troops to protect the freedmen. Grant never did send those troops, and soon Reconstruction and liberty for blacks came to an end in Mississippi. Not long afterwards, the political career of John Roy Lynch also drew to a close. But black Jacksonians remembered that he had never turned his back on them, so they named for Lynch one of the main streets in their city.

A century after John Roy Lynch held office in Jackson, the Second Reconstruction—the civil rights movement of the 1960s—transformed the politics of the Deep South. By 1970 black Mississippians could vote once again, though few held office. And while the street named after Lynch still ran through a black neighborhood, now it was a three-mile stretch of concrete that linked Jackson's business district with the suburbs to the west, where the whites lived.

For white commuters driving east each morning on their way downtown, the first two miles on Lynch Street seemed just another four-lane corridor through Neon Suburbia. They drove past gas stations, used-car lots, tire stores, and package stores. Past Miller's Discount Center, the Joy Car Wash, the Cotton Bowl Lanes, Cowboy Maloney's Appliances, and the Tipsy Kitty Lounge. But the last mile down Lynch Street was different. As the white drivers passed the black, seven-foot-tall letters of a sign that spelled W-O-K-J ("Ebony Radio"), they approached the campus of Jackson State, a black college. Down the dipping, then rising ribbon of white-dotted concrete, they glimpsed two blocks of athletic fields, tall brick dormitories, and classroom buildings. They saw black students carrying books and crossing the road on their way to classes.

Once they left the campus behind, the whites drove down the straight and sloping street through a black neighborhood. To white eyes it looked like a ghetto—five blocks of sleazy beer joints, grimy one-story storefronts, tottering shacks, and glass-strewn gutters. Stopping at a red light, the commuters noticed the old folks on the porches of their rickety wood-frame homes as they fanned away the muggy Mississippi heat. Many of the homes were "shotguns," long and narrow little cottages of just three rooms without partitions. The saying was that if you fired a shotgun through the open front door, and if the back one was open too, the shot would zip right through and hit nothing. Many blacks in the neighborhood lived in houses like these—with warped shingles and sagging roof peaks—each perched on red-brick piers that shifted in the damp and yellow clay.

In daylight, white drivers on the way home would stare and wonder about these things, and feel little discomfort. But some said that after nightfall it was unwise to drive slowly on Lynch Street.

Still, the blacks living here saw their neighborhood in a different light. To them Lynch Street was not a ghetto. There was little or no prostitution here, no dope-peddling, and no big brick tenements either. Although the poorest blacks lived in row after row of decaying shotguns in the alleys off Lynch Street, a few middle-class blacks owned the tidy white cottages on the street. They planted flowers, shrubs, and vegetable gardens in their small front yards, and kept their lawns mowed. Each Sunday they attended services at one of the neighborhood churches—the Lynch Street Methodist Church, the Mount Calvary Church, or the Pearl Street A.M.E.—where during tense times they could meet to plan civil rights strategy without worrying that police might barge in.

Over the years, small shops had sprung up among the churches, homes, and bars on Lynch Street. Not just because most residents were poor and lacked transportation, but because they preferred to shop in their own neighborhood. Also because some white merchants downtown had no use for black customers. Even in 1970 vestiges of segregation remained in downtown Jackson. True, blacks no longer had to sit in the colored waiting room in the Greyhound bus terminal. But some lunch counters in town still refused to seat black customers. The counter stools had been removed to thwart integration. At the Mayflower Restaurant there were three bathrooms: one for men, one for women, and one still labelled "colored."

To avoid such indignities and to buy the smaller items they needed, blacks patronized the stores on Lynch Street. At Dennis's Shoe Store, for instance, you could buy a hat or have a new pair of heels tacked to your shoes while you waited in stocking feet. In the Magnolia Food Store you could buy a pack of cigarettes so you could sit and smoke and while away some porch time. Over at Johnson's Barber Shop you could get a haircut and a good scalp massage, and leave feeling fresh and smelling fine. If they had the money, old folks who needed pills could pick them up at M-L-S Drugs, and anyone wanting to see a friend across town could get a ride up at the Deluxe Cab Company.

Lynch Street also had its own doctor and dentist offices, its own bank, an insurance company, a dry cleaner, and several gas stations, beauty parlors, corner stores, and bars. But the bars were what made Lynch Street an attraction. Some were for Jackson State students who went to dance and drink wine—dark, noisy, comfortable joints like the College Inn, the Tiger Lounge, the Psychedelic Shack, and the Doll's House, where on weekends the cigarette smoke dimmed the lights and jukeboxes sent the hip-swivelling, mellow-angry soul music of James Brown and Aretha Franklin rolling out to the street.

Older Lynch Street residents resented them, but there was nothing they could do about the black youths on the corners in front of the joints. They were the "cornerboys," nonstudents who either had dropped out of high school or never had gone on to college. They spent most of their time on the street and had names like Junebug, Tiny, Smiley, and Fats. Some had jobs. Some didn't. To kill time, they often went over to Cooper's to shoot pool, or squatted in the shadows behind a bar to roll dice. But mostly they stood on their corners, because that was cool.

"Those particular guys at that time—they would walk down the street and just break antennas off cars at night, or cut tires," N. Alfred Handy, a black photographer on Lynch Street, recalls. "In other words, they wanted to rule and control the neighborhood. And when people resisted them, they had something against you. I remember once, I had purchased a new car and parked it in front of my place. And when I looked out about two o'clock that afternoon, guys was laying all over the car. Without saying nothing, I walked out and got in the car to go to work. Later on I parked it on the other side of the street. One of them got so mad he went over there and got sat on it. But what happened about ten o'clock that night, a guy came to the house and said, 'Man, police lookin' for you.' I said, 'What?' He said, 'Well, some guys broke some windows out of your store.' This will give you an idea of the type guys that they were. They didn't have jobs—maybe some of them—I'm not sure. But I know several couldn't have jobs, because when you got here in the morning they were on the corner, and when you got here late at night they were on the corner."

Jackson State students feared the cornerboys because many carried knives or guns. Some used the weapons to persuade male students to part with their wallets or their ladyfriends. For that reason, most students traveled in groups on Lynch Street, but brawls between the two factions were common. The cornerboys resented the students for taking on airs and for having one toe in the middle class. The students feared the cornerboys, who were often stronger, older, and armed. Yet now and then a few members of the college football team would make a special visit to a bar to kick ass and even the score.

But Lynch Street was not just a place to brawl or barhop. It was part of the Jackson State College community. Both the college and the black neighborhood had sprung from the same pastureland at the turn of the century. In those days, the whites didn't cotton to the idea of coloreds learning to read and becoming schoolteachers. That is why Jackson College—as it was then called—was built on a rise a mile west of downtown. Originally, the campus had been closer to downtown on State Street. But in the late 1800s whites began building plantation-style mansions nearby. They resented the black students who rode mules and carried greasy lunch bags right past their new, white-columned palaces. And they didn't like it when the blacks mingled with the white boys from the school nearby that Major Reuben Millsaps had started. So the black college was forced to pull up stakes and head for the farmland just west of downtown. The college quickly sold some of that land as building lots to black families, and by the early 1900s, the campus was surrounded and protected by black neighbors.

Over the years, Jackson State students came to call their campus "the yard." But it was not beautiful. By 1970 Jackson State had become a state-supported college, and like most at the time, it spawned a hodgepodge of new buildings for the growing number of postwar baby-boom children in college. For example, looming above the four-lane traffic on the north side of Lynch Street were two new high-rise dormitories of red brick and green metal panels. One was Alexander Hall, a huge H-shaped dorm for women. In the commons park across the street was the library, another building of red brick and green panels. But nearby were Ayer Hall dormitory for women and Roberts Dining Hall, both of which were older, smaller, and painted white. On the lawn a block west was a pair of old white wooden barracks once used to house college athletes. Now they were used as offices by the ROTC staff.

Though there were no ivy walls at Jackson State, most students were proud of their school, which they saw as a black refuge from white Mississippi. It was a place where you could have a quiet, private talk with your girlfriend on a park bench under the oak trees. Or if she was across the street in her room in Alexander Hall, you could yell up to her and maybe she would come to the window and talk awhile.

To both the students and cornerboys, Lynch Street was their turf. Still, whites shuttled through each day and night, so conflict was inevitable. The crux of the problem was that nearly 60 percent of Jackson's population demanded the other 40 percent remain separate and unequal. Though segregation was no longer the law of the South, most whites in Jackson remained ardent segregationists. To them, Lynch Street meant nigger street.

• •

One of the first racial confrontations in the Lynch Street neighborhood took place in the spring of 1961.

It had been more than a year since the historic day of January 31, 1960, when four black students in Greensboro, North Carolina had taken seats at a segregated Woolworth's lunch counter. That move had inspired a wave of student sit-ins that had integrated public facilities in more than a hundred cities. But not in Mississippi. No one had dared a sit-in there until the

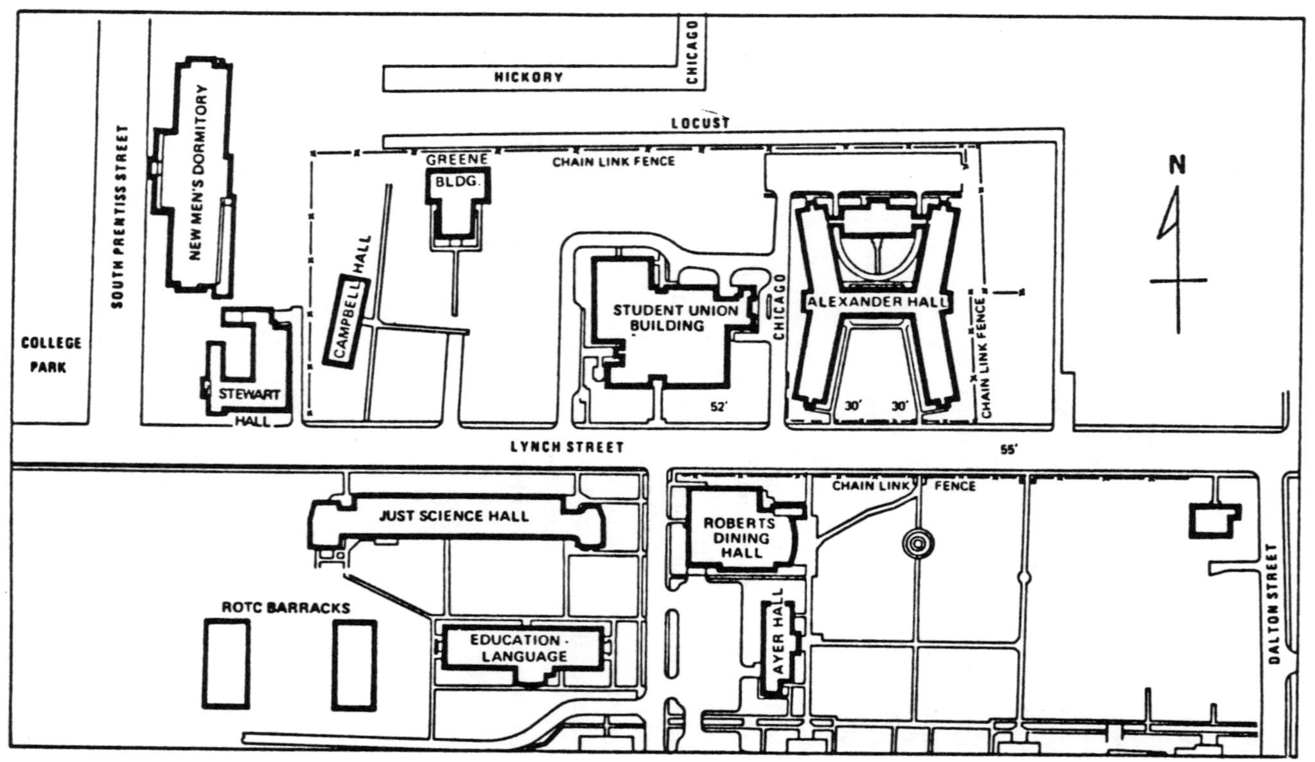

Map of the Jackson State Campus. (Copy: President's Commission on Campus Unrest)

drizzly, overcast morning of March 27, 1961. That day five young men and four women at Tougaloo College dressed in their Sunday best and left for the eight-mile drive south to downtown Jackson. Tougaloo was a private black college built on an antebellum cotton plantation just north of the Jackson city line. The students there resented the fact that the Jackson Municipal Library was for whites only.

Arriving in Jackson, the nine Tougaloo students broke the law by taking seats in the city library on State Street. Police in black jackets and white steel helmets threatened to arrest the students unless they left.

"Who is the leader, please?" asked Assistant Police Chief M. B. Pierce.

"Sir?" a female student replied.

"Who is the leader, please?" Pierce repeated.

"Leader of what, sir? There's no leader."

"You will all have to leave," he ordered them. "The colored library is on Mill Street."

When no one moved, Pierce arrested the nine students, hustled them off to the city jail and charged them with disturbing the peace. Finally, the sit-in had come to Mississippi.

On the Jackson State campus about a mile west of the city jail, a crowd of students gathered to protest the arrests. Marching around the aqua reflecting pools in front of the campus library, they chanted: "We want freedom! We want freedom!" One of these students was James Meredith, the Korean War veteran who would soon leave Jackson State to desegregate the University of Mississippi—an act that would result in a bloody clash between federal troops and white Mississippi. But at Jackson State that day, Meredith and his friends had planned their protests carefully to avoid violence.

> "When President Jacob Reddix came onto the campus near the library, our group was loose," Meredith remembers. "They were marching around the reflecting pools at first, but when he approached, they were tightening up into a small circle, everybody holding hands and one student praying. . . . So everybody kept listening to his prayer, and nobody paid any attention that the president was around, as far as responding to whatever he was saying. The president was visibly upset by the fact that no one paid him any attention, and he did what was part of the plan. He did some foolish things."

Reddix, conservative black patriarch of Jackson State, threatened to expel the students. Witnesses said he even shoved some in the crowd. The students dispersed quickly, and soon Chief Pierce and the city police were on campus with guns, clubs, tear gas, and two attack dogs. Though the protesters had gone and the demonstration was over, the lawmen cruised up and down Lynch Street that night. But the next morning, the marching, praying, and chanting began again.

> "The girls were instructed to wear the school colors and all the boys were to wear black and white," James Meredith adds. "So they all were told not to go to school, but to come to the dining hall and meet at the earliest time it opened. Everybody was there and dressed out. This was early—I mean, like 6:00 in the morning—6:30 at the latest. That's when it all began. The demonstrations went on all day, one way or another. We shifted students from one place to another to avoid counter-influences."

But after the protest on campus had finished, one group of about sixty students walked single file down Lynch Street, heading east toward the city jail where the Tougaloo youths were held. The protesters carried American flags as they turned north off Lynch Street to avoid the city police. But just a couple of blocks from the campus, they looked down the road and saw lines of city police, county patrolmen, and deputy sheriffs waiting behind barricades. The officers warned the students to turn around. When they did not, the lawmen rushed the youths, swinging clubs, firing tear gas, and unleashing their snarling dogs upon the crowd. Choking and crying out, the students scattered.

Several black bystanders that afternoon observed that a price must be paid for opposing "the Mississippi way of life."

• •

Two years later, in 1963, the civil rights movement shifted into a new phase and Lynch Street was swept up in the quickened pace of events. Sit-ins had given way to boycotts and massive demonstrations to end segregation. The movement spread to more than a hundred cities in the South—cities like Birmingham, Alabama, where police used dogs and fire hoses to squelch dissent. Nationwide, vigilantes bombed thirty-five churches, homes and offices. Police arrested twenty thousand demonstrators. Ten activists were murdered.

In Jackson, the movement was directed by civil rights workers from the Masonic Temple on Lynch Street—a two-story office building of concrete and steel, home of several black businesses and organizations, including the Mississippi National Association for the Advancement of Colored People (NAACP).

The Masonic Temple had been built in the 1950s across the street from weed-choked Mount Olive Cemetery, where a black Reconstruction-era politician named Jim Hill was buried. Novelist Richard Wright, who had lived as a boy on Lynch Street, once attended a black school named for Hill. But that old school was gone now, and a more modern symbol of black aspirations was the Masonic Temple, or the "Black Capitol of Mississippi," as some called it. Here NAACP conventions, press conferences, and strategy sessions were held. In 1963 faculty and students from Tougaloo College used the building to run classes in nonviolent demonstration and to organize their boycott of white businesses. They aimed to force Mayor Allen Thompson to put an end to parks and rest rooms for "colored only." They wanted integrated theaters and restaurants, and they wanted black officers on the Jackson police force.

As the boycott of white businesses dragged on, merchants lost money and tensions mounted. Police and highway patrolmen arrested more than five hundred blacks picketing on Capitol Street, the white business district downtown. In a residential neighborhood northwest of downtown Jackson, NAACP Field Secretary Medgar Evers's home was firebombed. And each day in front of the Masonic Temple on Lynch Street police parked to keep an eye on activists. Those who left the building were often photographed and even followed while driving home.

On the night of June 12, 1963, after leaving a church rally, Medgar Evers drove into the darkened driveway of his ranch home. Clutching a handful of sweat shirts stenciled "Jim Crow Must Go," Evers walked toward the light glowing in his carport. A stranger crouched nearby in a honeysuckle thicket and peered through the scope of his high-powered rifle. Two blasts rang out and Evers fell, shot in the back. Hours later he was dead.

After word spread that Medgar Evers had been murdered that night, black Jackson was seething. Most blacks had been afraid to march for freedom, but now they were ready in spite of the danger. About two hundred protesters filed out of the Masonic Temple the next afternoon, singing freedom songs and walking east down the Lynch Street sidewalk. Hundreds of residents sat on their porches or stood on their front lawns. They watched as police in squad cars sped past the marchers to block them before they reached the business district a mile to the east.

In brown riot helmets, highway patrolmen joined the Jackson police, and their ranks stretched across Lynch Street. While flatbed garbage trucks pulled up along the curb, the demonstrators walked into Lynch Street, singing as they approached the line of officers. The blacks stopped. Suddenly the lawmen charged, clubbing the marchers and driving them toward the garbage trucks. Onlookers shouted "Freedom!" as the officers shoved the protesters onto the trucks. When full of the protesters, the garbage trucks lumbered down Lynch Street toward the state fairgrounds downtown. There the marchers were herded into livestock pens.

Few Jackson State students were among the protesters that June day on Lynch Street. Though just two blocks from the Masonic Temple, their campus might as well have been fifty miles away, for all the help they were allowed to give the Tougaloo activists. The cadre of militant veterans that James Meredith had once worked with were no longer active at Jackson State. And unlike Tougaloo, a private college, Jackson State was run by compliant black administrators who depended upon the all-white State Board of Higher Education to keep their school open.

> "The Jackson State students had no academic freedom, no classroom freedom, and certainly had no freedom as blacks to participate in the civil rights movement," Reverend Edwin King, a former Tougaloo chaplain, recalls. "The students would have been expelled. Ultimately it would have been due to state pressure, but actually it was due to the fears of the middle-class black leaders at Jackson State. They would rather purge 'dangerous' students before they did anything. The Tougaloo students felt sorry for the Jackson State students. In the early sixties, a majority of the Tougaloo students were active in the movement, to the point of being in demonstrations. I would say over 50 percent in the highest years—1963, 1964—along in there. Tougaloo was the most active campus in the nation, black or white. And Jackson State—one of the most inactive. Almost no political activity. Before the death of Medgar Evers there had been six months of leafleting, meeting after meeting after meeting for the Tougaloo students. Very careful work—whereas Jackson State would just erupt into demonstrations almost overnight over something, but not channeled. And it would die out almost as quickly as it erupted."

The morning after Medgar Evers was assassinated, President Reddix made sure that all classes at Jackson State were held as usual. His students were not to march down Lynch Street or picket the white stores downtown. Instead, the students found another way to protest Evers's slaying. A few noticed there were police cars parked along Lynch Street near the campus.

The black youths lobbed bottles at the cars, and the officers sent out a call for help. More squad cars rushed to the campus, but the students quickly dispersed, and the incident was over.

• •

A year later, in 1964, the level of racial tension escalated on Lynch Street, just as it had in the rest of the nation. This was the year the smoke of ghetto rebellions rose above Philadelphia, Rochester, and Jersey City. This was also the year that four national civil rights groups formed an alliance known as COFO, the Council of Federated Organizations, to single out Mississippi for massive voter registration drives. From the shotgun homes and storefronts along Lynch Street, the Congress of Racial Equality (CORE) and the Student Nonviolent Coordinating Committee (SNCC) had spent the previous two years organizing Freedom Rides, voter registration drives, and demonstrations in Mississippi. But their struggle to end Jim Crow in Mississippi had failed. Black activists across the South had achieved far better results, so in a last major bid to turn Mississippi around, CORE and SNCC locked arms with the NAACP and the Southern Christian Leadership Conference. Their program was called the Mississippi Summer Project, or "Freedom Summer." It would bring hundreds of northern white students to Mississippi to end segregation.

Planning for the summer project began in the winter of 1964 in a tiny cinder-block storefront on Lynch Street. Here David Dennis of CORE and Robert Moses of SNCC planned voter education programs and registration drives, as well as Freedom Schools for the young. From their Lynch Street headquarters, they could keep tabs on activists in dangerous towns like McComb, nicknamed the "Church-bombing Capital of Mississippi," and Philadelphia, where three project workers—two white and one black—would be buried that summer in an earthen dam after their arrest by local lawmen.

While COFO workers developed strategies for Freedom Summer, the state's lawmen were making preparations of their own. They had learned that hundreds of white students from the North would soon invade their state. To meet this challenge, the highway patrol's ranks doubled, and the Jackson Police Department went on a shopping spree. Mayor Allen Thompson saw to it that the police got new troop carriers, two half-ton searchlight trucks, and three trailer trucks to transport protesters. New tear-gas masks were ordered, along with two hundred new shotguns. An armored van was purchased, complete with bullet-proof glass, searchlights, and gunports for firing tear-gas launchers. The city's blacks named it for their mayor. They called it "Thompson's Tank."

The first opportunity to use this new hardware came in February of 1964. Newsmen from across the nation were in Jackson for the trial of Byron de la Beckwith, the fertilizer salesman whose fingerprints had been found on the gun used to kill Medgar Evers. The reporters were expecting to see how justice operated in a Mississippi courtroom. First, they would see how it worked in the street.

On the chilly evening of February 3, 1964, a popular student named Mamie Ballard stepped from the curb in front of Alexander Hall dormitory and was hit by a car. She fell to the Lynch Street pavement and broke her leg. Students surrounding her became angry when they saw the motorist was a white man, and that the police let him drive on. Shouting and marching back and forth across Lynch Street in front of the women's dormitory, the students blocked the traffic.

Soon bricks and bottles were flying at police officers and motorists on Lynch Street. But Charles Evers, leader of the state's NAACP since the death of his brother Medgar, arrived to calm the students. "None of us are afraid, we know that," he told them. "But this is no way to get what we want."

The students dispersed and left the street to attend a basketball game. The police withdrew, and it looked as though the trouble were over. But during the basketball game, COFO activists seized the opportunity to organize the students. The activists handed out leaflets urging the students to take to the street:

> If you are a person of action and are willing to do all that is necessary to protest what has happened, AFTER THE GAME TONIGHT mass on Lynch Street in the cross walk where Mamie was hit and REFUSE TO LET TRAFFIC PASS.

After the game, again white motorists were dodging bricks and bottles. And as before, students blocked the traffic in front of Alexander Hall dormitory. For the second time that evening, police arrived on Lynch Street to put down a demonstration. This time they brought their shotguns and new searchlight trucks and set up sawhorse barricades bearing the legend, "Building A Better Jackson." Nevertheless, students and cornerboys pelted the officers with rocks. Instead of responding with tear gas, the policemen raised their shotguns. First they fired into the air. Then they lowered their weapons.

> "To tell you the truth, I threw things," Gregory Haygood, a local high school youth at the time, recalls. "That night the cops had a big searchlight up on the corner of Dalton and Lynch near M-L-S Drugs, and they were shining it around. There was a dormitory being torn down nearby, so we took a lot of bricks and we decided we were going to put that light out, you know, just get a handful of bricks and put that searchlight out. I think there were about nineteen of us and we decided to line up and unload those bricks, everybody at the same time. And when we did let them go, you could hear the bricks hit. After that, we started running the other way. Then the police began opening fire on us. You could hear the shots coming through the trees—buckshot and things. By the time I got behind the library, I saw a motorcycle policeman with a shotgun. He had actually come up on campus. He hollered at me, and when I didn't stop, he dropped his shotgun on me. I was about twenty-five or thirty yards from him. When I went to turn the corner by the library, he fired. I didn't know it, but he had hit me, so I kept running and went over to Sampson Hall and stood over there. We were saying, 'Man, they've got too much firepower—everybody's going home.' I was leaning up against a car when I looked down at my pants and saw I had blood running down them. I was hit in the hip.' "

After reporters called local hospitals, they discovered that three youths had been wounded by buckshot fragments. Two of them were Jackson State students. Reading the local newspapers the next morning, Jacksonians learned that the official reason for all the shooting was "sniper fire," though not one officer had been wounded. In the next day's *Jackson Daily News,* an editorial commended the police and noted: "Mississippi law enforcement officers have a fine record of acting coolly and efficiently under fire."

• •

Three years later, in 1967, race relations in Jackson were even worse. In the rest of the nation they were not much better. Ghetto uprisings that summer resulted in two thousand injured, more than eighty dead and 664 million dollars in property damages. In Detroit alone, thirty-three blacks and ten whites were killed, and the property loss totaled about 85 million dollars. The movement for racial equality had shifted into a new phase, "black nationalism." Its leaders—bitter young men like Eldridge Cleaver, Bobby Seale, and H. Rap Brown—had no regard for church rallies, freedom songs and pledges of nonviolence. The militants argued that in the Deep South, these methods had brought upon them the fists, clubs, and guns of white police and vigilantes, but resulted in little substantive change. So the radicals rejected the passive resistance of Martin Luther King, Jr., and rid themselves of the white liberals in their ranks. In Jackson, for example, few white students worked with black activists on Lynch Street. "Black Power!"—the separatist cry of Stokely Carmichael in the Mississippi delta—was the slogan of the times.

But in 1967, another slogan was "Hell no, we won't go," coined by black militants. Across the nation, both black and white youths had begun to oppose the war in Vietnam. In Jackson, a black civil rights worker named John Otis Sumrall had proclaimed that he would not go to war. After refusing induction into the military, Sumrall told Jackson reporters that other blacks should do the same. After all, Mississippi's draft boards were segregated, and the war was just plain wrong.

In Jackson, another divisive issue was Lynch Street itself. Since the shootings there in 1964, Jackson State students complained that young white drivers roared down the street at night, screaming "nigger" and tossing bottles and rocks. Others said that white hooligans shot at pedestrians or into storefronts. College officials and Mayor Allen Thompson discussed building a traffic tunnel under the campus and a bridgewalk for students crossing Lynch Street. But this was just talk. Only a traffic light had been installed in front of Alexander Hall, a women's dorm.

The issue surfaced again on the night of May 10, 1967, when a Jackson State student driving a red convertible was chased onto the campus for speeding. The student parked quickly on Lynch Street and scurried into a men's dorm. To keep the police from entering the dorm, students poured from the building and blocked the traffic on Lynch Street. More squad cars rushed to the college, and barricades were set up at opposite ends of the campus on Lynch Street. Behind the barricades, police ducked a hail of rocks and bottles. The officers were forced to flee, and black youths set fire to the barricades. One block east of the campus, cornerboys looted M-L-S Drugstore.

At about 9:00 the next morning, it was sunny and warm when Mayor

Allen Thompson drove to Lynch Street in his Cadillac, hoping to talk sense to the Jackson State students. He wanted to tell them they were educated people who should know better, and they should clean up the litter they had left the night before in the middle of Lynch Street. Mayor Thompson got out of his car, took off his suitcoat, sunglasses, and gray fedora, and stepped past a pile of charred debris in the barricaded street. Guarded by armed officers, Mayor Thompson walked west up the middle of Lynch Street. He headed toward a crowd of about five hundred students in the street in front of Alexander Hall. The crowd approached Mayor Thompson, and they met in front of M-L-S Drugstore. Climbing up on the hood of a black and white squad car, Mayor Thompson tried to address the students. At first they seemed to listen, but then they booed the mayor and chanted: "Hell no! Hell no! Hell no!"

Frustrated, Mayor Thompson ordered a city official to get a work crew to clear the debris in the street. Thompson returned to his Cadillac and drove from Lynch Street.

At 5:00 P.M., police were ordered to remove the barricades on Lynch Street so that commuter traffic could pass the campus. But in daylight, students again lobbed rocks at white motorists and blocked the traffic. And again, the city police rushed to Lynch Street. This time, officers from District 1 of the Mississippi Highway Patrol joined them. The sawhorse barricades reappeared on Lynch Street, and the National Guard was alerted.

After dark, a crowd of about one hundred cornerboys and few, if any, Jackson State students gathered around a bonfire in the middle of Lynch Street near M-L-S Drugstore. They were less than a block from the heart of the college campus. Someone shouted they should rush the police barricades two blocks east down Lynch Street. The shrieking crowd streamed down the street toward the line of officers and unleashed a volley of rocks that sent the police scampering from their barricades. But a few patrolmen held their ground, and the black youths turned and ran back up the street to their bonfire.

As more highway patrolmen arrived at the barricades on Lynch Street, the police and patrol regrouped. Again the black youths went tearing down the street toward the officers' lines. When a highway patrolman was cut in the neck by a bottle, he fired his shotgun in the air. Then, as the youths were running back up the street toward their bonfire, it happened.

"I was standing immediately behind the line of highway patrolmen and policemen with their guns drawn," Wilson Minor, a former reporter for the *New Orleans Times-Picayune,* recalls. "They were spread out

> across Lynch Street, about two or three feet deep, you see, when the black kids ran down the street a little bit and started in hurling some rocks. And that's all. I mean, I didn't see them do anything other than throw some rocks toward policemen. And all of a sudden—baroom! The guns went off and the next thing I saw was this guy lying on what was a dirt sidewalk off Lynch Street. My friend Reverend Ken Dean said to me, 'I'm going in to see him.' And I said, 'Well, then I'm going with you.' As we were bending over the guy, the guns were just aimed towards us. I could see they had shot the man right in the back."

Crouched beside Minor was Reverend Kenneth Dean, a white Tennessean who had been standing under a storefront awning near the old COFO headquarters. He was seeking shelter from the hail of rocks thrown by the crowd.

> "This guy was lying face down and he had been shot in the back of the head and in the back," Reverend Dean remembers. "I turned him around and I saw he was my friend, Ben Brown. I called for help and a highway patrolman came up to me. I still have a newspaper picture of myself with Patrolman Lloyd Jones carrying Ben out. We got him to a National Guard ambulance, and I got into the back of it with Ben. He was choking on his tongue, so I put my finger in his mouth and pulled the tongue up and held it. I talked to him all the way to the University Hospital. He was breathing, but unconscious."

As Brown lay dying, armored vans, jeeps, and troops with bayoneted rifles were sweeping west up Lynch Street toward the Jackson State College campus. Mississippi's all-white National Guard had arrived. But highway patrolmen had entered the campus ahead of the troops, and again there was gunfire. Patrolmen shot two male students: one in the leg while he stood near Alexander Hall, and the other in the face while he sat in his second-story dormitory room.

In the morning, the offical version of the shootings appeared in the *Jackson Clarion-Ledger:* "POLICE AND GUARDS CLAM JSC RIOTERS." The injured were "Negro members of a screaming, rock-throwing riot mob." In the next day's *Ledger,* columnist Tom Ethridge summed up white opinion of the lawmen's conduct: "ADMIRATION is a word that best expresses our feelings."

Soon after the shootings, a leaflet circulated by a group called the Black People's Unity Movement revealed a deepening mood of black militancy:

America is the black man's battleground. Ben Brown, a 22-year-old, courageous, black soldier was shot in the back and left there in the street to die like a dog. His murderers are the same pigs we've been dying for in Vietnam. For them we will die no more.

• •

In April of 1968, after Martin Luther King, Jr., was assassinated, and again in May of 1969, students and cornerboys set fires, tossed rocks at motorists, and broke storefront windows in the Lynch Street neighborhood. Both of these "miniriots"—as students called them—were snuffed out by the city police without resorting to gunfire.

But in the spring of 1970, on May 4, students were again shot on an American campus. This time the youths were white, and the school was in Kent, Ohio. Frustrations over the Vietnam War had sparked the confrontation in which four students were killed and nine others wounded. The Kent State shootings touched off protests and rioting on hundreds of campuses across the nation.

In Mississippi, however, the *Jackson Clarion-Ledger* bragged that nothing like this would happen here. On the same day as the Kent slayings, an editorial reassured citizens of the Magnolia State that they need not worry about student unrest:

> Mississippi's relatively minor and infrequent campus disturbances are matters of concern, to be sure, but at least they can't hold a candle to the unrest, rowdyism and even anarchy prevalent in higher education elsewhere across America.

Nevertheless, peace officers would return in force to Jackson State College soon after the May '70 killings at Kent State. As in 1964 and 1967, the lawmen would quell a first round of rock-throwing without reaching for their firearms. But perturbed by a second outbreak, they would fire high into the air. Then they would lower their weapons.

This time the firepower would be so overwhelming that newsmen from across the United States would fly to Mississippi to see the results for themselves. They would not know about the shooting of Benjamin Brown in 1967, and they would not know of a man named John Roy Lynch. But they would agree that it was odd, yet fitting, that in Jackson they called this Lynch Street.

2

MAYDAY IN AMERIKA

The essential American soul is hard, isolate, stoic, and a killer. It has never melted.

—D. H. Lawrence

In a tree-shaded park in downtown Jackson, Mississippi, a student from Kent State University addressed a small crowd. While facing his listeners, Tom D'Floure fidgeted with the zipper on his gold jacket—a jacket the Ohio student did not need down here in the eighty-degree heat. At the microphone, he told the crowd about the killings on his campus just five days before, when National Guardsmen had turned their M-1 rifles on his fellow students, killing four of them.

"Those [students] shot weren't the ones throwing rocks," he said, shifting nervously from one foot to the other. "Allison Krause, whom I knew, was nonviolent. She was just there to watch. Another person killed was an ROTC student. It's kind of ironic that he'd get it."

While the student from Ohio spoke, the crowd of about 125 Mississippi youths sat on the fallen oak leaves in the park and listened.

"If you give a scared soldier a loaded rifle, someone just might get shot, and someone did," D'Floure added.

After he finished speaking, the crowd applauded and a black student with a beard and Afro hairdo rose to speak. He was thirty-five years old and a veteran. He was Henry Thompson, a student at Jackson State College.

"White people are reaping what they've sown!" Thompson told the crowd, his amplified voice echoing off the churches, stores, and office buildings that surrounded the park. "If they had left us in Africa and hadn't been so greedy to have us here to pick cotton, we wouldn't have a lot of this trouble today."

"Right on!" several in the crowd shouted.

"We hear people talk about democracy. Just talk to the Indians about it! How do you expect me to obey your laws, when you won't obey God's law? . . . Why talk about a war eight thousand miles away, when we've got one right here? Instead of Cambodia or the massacre at My Lai, we should start worrying about the problems at home!"

"Right on!" the protesters cheered, as the black student left the microphone.

The day was Saturday, May 9, 1970, the weekend after the Kent State slayings. The place was Smith Park, behind the Governor's Mansion in downtown Jackson. And among the protesters were civil rights lawyers, a half dozen self-described "hippies," and students from two four-year colleges in the capital—Jackson State, which was black, and Millsaps College, predominantly white. The speeches, the cries against the Establishment, and the police nearby, watching from their paddy wagons and photographing the protesters—it was much the same in Jackson that weekend as in hundreds of other college towns where there were cries of outrage over the Kent State slayings.

> "We were trying to bring out some of the injustices of the war that day," recalls Henry Thompson, who led the group of about a dozen Jackson State students attending the peace rally. "They were sending black soldiers over there to fight people we didn't know a damned thing about. I wanted to bring to people's attention that we were fighting people that never called us 'niggers' before. That was my point at the time. But back then the situation was going from bad to worse. The kids at Kent State had become second-class niggers, so they had to go. Anytime you go against the system, you become a nigger, regardless of your color."

In ultraconservative Mississippi, there were few militants to protest the Vietnam War. Still, they were a voluble minority ashamed of their state's ardent support for the war and angered by the all-white draft boards that sent black youths to the front lines. But these war resisters knew what most Americans did not know about Mississippi. They knew their state suffered only the most virulent strain of the same disease afflicting the rest of the nation: an intolerance that winked at killing nonwhites. To them, Mississippi was all-American.

• •

To a northerner visiting Mississippi in 1970, it seemed like a different world. In late spring you felt the subtropical sun burn your scalp and the smothering humidity that can curl the straightest hair. Up from the Gulf Coast, swift black stormclouds rolled suddenly over Jackson, tornado sirens wailed, and sheets of warm rain fell. Yellow waters from the local creeks would rise above the street curbs. But soon there was sunshine.

The first time you ate in a restaurant in Jackson, you were surprised when the waitress called you "darlin' " or "honey." As you scanned the menu, you wanted to try the catfish, the black-eyed peas, or the creamed grits. And when you paid the check after the meal, the cashier smiled and said, "Hurry back."

Jackson was very different from the cities of the North, where in 1970 the flower children sold pot and dropped acid and wore army surplus jackets and tattered jeans. Down here in the beauty-queen, Bible-belt culture of Mississippi, white girls wore stockings, heels, and modest miniskirts. They didn't know anybody who smoked grass, and on Sundays you saw them walking to church with their fathers and boyfriends in seersucker suits. The church pews were packed because in Baptist Mississippi, religion was in a flourishing way.

Amid the churches and office buildings in downtown Jackson were countless reminders of the "Mississippi way of life." It was hard to miss the massive white columns of the Greek Revival city hall, built with slave labor and used as an army hospital after Sherman drove the rebels from the capital. The city was called "Chimneyville" in those days when the bluebellies were supposed to have torched so many shops and warehouses that Jackson was just a forest of chimneys. Not all of the city burned, though. The dome of the Old Capitol still loomed above the Capitol Street business district. In 1970 it was a museum stuffed with the muskets, uniforms, and flags of the Confederacy and the mementos of Mississippi's favorite statesman, President Jefferson Davis. Behind the magnolias on the south lawn of the Old Capitol was the white spire of the revered Confederate Monument, a six-story-tall obelisk of limestone. It was dedicated to the crusaders of the Lost Cause. And near the foot of the Capitol Street hill was the Governor's Mansion, its great white-columned veranda shaded by oak trees.

> "You're reminded in this whole city of the past, about the glorious past of the South," recalls Charles Carr, a Jackson State student in 1970. "It's that irrational dedication that some folks had to keeping alive the Rebels-this and the Rebels-that. That's primarily what the Old Capitol museum is built on. You look at the Governor's Mansion; it was built to

remind you of the old plantation home. And frequently, right down State Street, the architecture of the city. There are the old, fantastic plantation homes. You couldn't help but see them. In the late sixties, blacks were often reminded that you should be more aware of who you were and where you were from, and how white people raped you of your heritage and your culture—yet you should be proud of what you had accomplished. But these folks, the powers that be in this city, in this state, in this country, always reminded you that there was once a time, a good ol' time, and we need to get back to those good ol' times, back to the Old South with its beautiful and glorious heritage."

But to focus on the antebellum mansions and the Spanish moss dangling from cedars—the peculiarities of life in the Deep South—was to miss much that linked Jackson to the rest of America. No longer was it a frontier capital of dueling lawmakers, slave traders, and dusty streets. In 1970 Jackson was a small but modern city of 155,000 with a zoo, a coliseum, a football stadium, and new interstate highways soon to connect the capital with Memphis, two hundred miles north, and New Orleans, two hundred miles south. Travelers could stay at a Travelodge or a Holiday Inn. Or if just passing through, they could gas up at a Mobil station and get a new set of tires at one of the Goodyear shops.

Like Middle Americans everywhere, white Jacksonians went to R-rated movies on Saturday nights. After church on Sundays they took rides in their long, chrome-plated cars that drank deep draughts of cheap gas and spent half an hour turning the corner. On many a bumper was the slogan of the times: "America—Love It or Leave It!" For many whites in Jackson, home was a suburban apartment complex with a reassuring name like Belvedere Manor, River Oaks, or Fairmont. For others it was a ranch home in a pine-shaded subdivision that promised security and a measure of prestige. But the burghers who lived in these homes worried and scratched to pay the mortgage and prayed to God their jobs were safe and that nobody black would move next door. Just like the rest of America.

• •

At home in front of their televison sets on the night of April 20, 1970, Mississippians listened to President Richard Nixon talk of peace. This was not the rabble-rousing, red-baiting Nixon of the 1950s. This was the "New

Nixon." In office less than sixteen months, he had urged Americans quarreling over the war to lower their voices, and he had promised them "peace with honor":

> Tonight I am pleased to report that progress in training and equipping South Vietnamese forces has substantially exceeded our expectations last June. . . . I'm glad to report that in the first three months of 1970 the number of Americans killed in action dropped to the lowest first-quarter level in five years.

Nixon pledged to bring home 150,000 more GI's and reduce the number of troops to 284,000, down from the peak of more than a half million in 1968. After the televised speech, Eric Sevareid, grey-haired, square-chinned sage of CBS, told viewers that it looked as though Nixon was defusing the antiwar movement. And so it seemed.

In recent months, Nixon had signed a bill establishing a draft lottery. Tens of thousands of young men who had drawn high numbers no longer had to fear the draft. In addition, Nixon was "Vietnamizing" the war, shifting its burden to Vietnamese troops. He decided not to resume the bombing raids over Hanoi that President Lyndon Johnson had cancelled before leaving office.

So it was tougher, early that spring, for students to get worked up about the war and the Establishment. To many it looked as though, strangely enough, "Tricky Dicky" might end the war after all. As a result, many students began shifting their energies behind a new political movement—the movement to save the environment. To the chagrin of many radicals, this new cause seemed to be weakening the antiwar effort. For example, on April 18, 1970, named "Earth Day," thousands of students joined in parades and teach-ins and planted trees and picked up roadside litter to do their part for the environment. That same week, the Vietnam Moratorium Committee announced that it was disbanding. Discouraged by the tranquilizing effects of Nixon's reforms, the committee complained that it could no longer mount massive antiwar protests across the nation.

Underlying this calm, however, was widespread discontent that sprang from the war in Asia and racial inequality at home, the two chief political issues of the 1960s. Radicals felt the Nixon administration had fallen short on both counts, and as a result, sporadic protests and acts of sabotage continued across the nation.

In March 1970, while preparing bombs to protest the imprisonment of Black Panthers in New York City, two members of the Weather Underground accidentally detonated a hundred pounds of dynamite that ripped through their townhouse, killing them. In Baton Rouge in April, thirty sticks of dynamite exploded at the state capitol, shattering windows, rending marble slabs, and smashing lawmakers' desks. The bombs were an apparent retaliation for the slaying of three blacks by local police. That same month in Seattle, police reported that a total of twenty bombs had rocked the city's black community in the last four months. Eleven others were discovered undetonated.

Students were in revolt on several campuses across the nation, and either the Vietnam War or civil rights was at issue in most of these rebellions. At Mississippi Valley State College in the tiny town of Itta Bena, civil rights was the issue. There on February 10, 1970, America's largest mass arrest of college students took place. Nearly nine hundred black protesters were loaded onto buses and carted off to the state penitentiary at Parchman. On April 14 at Harvard, the issue was the war. An antiwar protest set off the worst riot in the university's history. Students and other activists clashed with police for five hours, damaging one hundred thousand dollars of university property. Meanwhile, Yale was bracing for a student strike and three days of massive demonstrations to support the Black Panthers charged with murder in New Haven.

On the night of April 18 near Santa Barbara, California, police shot into a crowd of students from the state university. The students and local youths had been trying to burn a branch of the Bank of America, which was for them a symbol of corporate complicity in waging the Vietnam War. Four youths were wounded by birdshot. After violence broke out again the next night—and despite orders not to shoot—police fired again. A student peacemaker named Kevin Moran was shot and killed as he emerged from a bank window after extinguishing a Molotov cocktail. Police denied they had shot him.

A week and a half later, this time in the Midwest, seven youths were wounded by shotgun fire, one seriously, as Ohio National Guardsmen and Columbus police clashed with students. The protesters were calling for an increase in black enrollment at Ohio State University and the removal of ROTC from their campus. The guard and the police denied pulling their triggers. They blamed the gunfire on snipers. The next day in Columbus, thirteen more students were wounded by shotgun pellets after lawmen broke up a peaceful demonstration on campus. Again the officers denied firing. But this time faculty witnesses told reporters they had watched the lawmen shooting.

The most explosive developments in the spring of 1970, however, were not occurring in America. During the second week of April, a thousand

Vietnamese bodies were found floating in Cambodia's Mekong River, their hands tied behind their backs and bound in groups of ten. Civil war was raging in Cambodia, and North Vietnamese Communists hiding from Americans inside the Cambodian border were treated as rebels by Cambodian Premier Lon Nol. As Nol's new U.S.-supported regime lost ground to the Communists, the Pentagon urged President Nixon to attack the North Vietnamese in their "haven" just inside the Cambodian border. By late April, Nixon agreed that something drastic must be done to prop up the Nol government, even though Nol had declared that U.S. troops should never enter his neutral nation.

On the night of April 30, 1970, just ten days after telling the public that the war in Southeast Asia was winding down, Richard Nixon went on national television to say that the conflict would expand into Cambodia. So far nearly forty-two thousand young Americans had lost their lives in a decade of fighting. Nixon now asked the nation to support a wider war that would mean higher casualties. In a dark suit and thin tie, Nixon held a thick sheaf of papers as he sat nervously facing the TV camera.

> Tonight, American and South Vietnamese units will attack the headquarters for the entire Communist military operation in South Vietnam. This key control center has been occupied by the North Vietnamese and Vietcong for five years in blatant violation of Cambodia's neutrality.
>
> This is not an invasion of Cambodia.

Nixon seemed nervous. Beads of sweat formed above his lips as he spoke, and he wiped his mouth with a handkerchief. Four times he got up from his desk to point to a map of Southeast Asia and name places where American soldiers would soon be fighting—places with strange names like Fishhook and Parrot's Beak. Once, Nixon lost his place in his speech and groped in uncomfortable silence to find it.

> My fellow Americans, we live in an age of anarchy, both abroad and at home. We see mindless attacks on all the great institutions which have been created by free civilizations in the last five hundred years. Even here in the United States, great universities are being systematically destroyed.

Now it was Nixon's war. A new and wider war, an Indochina war.

• •

Virtually no one had expected so drastic a departure from Nixon's policy of deescalating the war. The reaction to his speech was loud and swift, and it showed that even the Establishment was outraged. In an editorial, the *Washington Post* declared that the nation was "in the hands of an administration as incapable as the last of distinguishing between hard decisions and what Mr. Nixon is pleased to call the easy political path." The *New York Times* accused Nixon of asking the people "to swallow the military hallucination of victory through escalation."

The United States Senate, too, was shocked by Nixon's speech. Republican George Aiken of Vermont, "dean of the Senate," warned that the move into Cambodia could cost the GOP all chance of winning control of Congress in the fall elections. Several senators, including Republican John Sherman Cooper of Kentucky and Democrat Frank Church of Idaho, stepped up their efforts to cut funds for the war. In an unprecedented action, members of the Senate Foreign Relations Committee voted unanimously to ask President Nixon to meet with them.

Nixon's Cambodia speech was like a torch dropped on the kindling of academe. On the night of the president's televised address, forty-two demonstrators were injured in a four-hour rock-throwing melee with police at Stanford University in California. A day later, Mayday, violent demonstrations erupted on other campuses, and university presidents began sending the stream of distress signals that for nearly a month would draw police and National Guardsmen onto the campuses. In Maryland, Governor Marvin Mandel sent state troopers and the National Guard to the state university in College Park. Student protesters had attacked the campus ROTC building, burning uniforms, dumping files, and overturning desks. At the University of Cincinnati, a thousand students marched from the campus to a downtown intersection and sat on the pavement for ninety minutes, snarling traffic.

There was an element of adolescent, springtime shenanigans in some of these protests that often obscured the political discontent that had sparked them. For example, on Mayday evening at Kent State University in Ohio, a motorcycle gang, local youths, and university students poured from the bars of downtown Kent. They danced in the streets, set fires, tossed beer mugs at cars, and looted storefronts.

Still, most campuses remained calm. Students held peaceful protests at Temple University, Villanova University, State University of New York at Binghamton, and the University of Arizona, to name only a few. At Cornell, sixty-eight professors called for Nixon's impeachment, and so did the National Student Association. At Yale, organizers of a peaceful, three-day rally for the Black Panthers ended it one day early, fearing that the crowd of ten thousand might riot should Nixon begin bombing North Vietnam. Concluding the Yale protest, Tom Hayden of Students for a Democratic Society announced a National Student Strike. He said students would close their campuses for three major demands: an end to the expansion of the Asian war; an end to the universities' complicity in military research and training; and the release of all political prisoners such as the Black Panthers. Once again, the antiwar and civil rights movements were linked by student dissidents. The black fist, symbol of Black Power, was to become the emblem of the National Student Strike, the first such strike in American history.

While campus protests spread across America, the level of violence rose on the other side of the globe. Just as the New Haven organizers had feared, American pilots began bombing North Vietnam. At first, the Nixon administration denied early reports of the bombings in Hanoi. But after the White House could no longer deny the bombing raids, they were dismissed as "protective reaction strikes."

Students did some attacking of their own on May 2. At Michigan State and Princeton, they assaulted campus military installations. In Ohio, a group of nonstudents with flares marched onto the campus of Kent State University. There they were joined by students who helped set the ROTC barracks afire. As firemen tried to douse the flames, the youths sliced their hoses with knives. The building burned to the ground.

By Sunday, May 3, student strikes had been organized at the University of California at Los Angeles, Boston College, Haverford College, Northeastern University, Colgate, Rutgers, Syracuse, Amherst, Berkeley, Duke, and other universities. Student government leaders from thirteen colleges had met at the University of Pennsylvania and endorsed the National Student Strike. At Kent State University, it was a night of tear gas and helicopter searchlights as students protested the National Guard's occupation of their campus. They ignored a curfew and sat down in the middle of an intersection near the university. The guardsmen gassed the crowd, and the students retaliated by throwing rocks. With bayonets bared, the troops advanced on the youths, scattering and chasing them back toward their dormitories, cutting at least a half dozen.

Monday, May 4, was a cool yet sunny day at Kent State University. On the commons lawn at noon a crowd of students jeered and threw rocks at the National Guard troops patrolling their campus. The protesters and the gas-masked guardsmen began playing a macabre game, lobbing tear-gas cannisters back and forth across the campus. A crowd of spectators cheered each time a student made it behind the guard's lines with a smoking cannister. While the campus Victory Bell tolled, seventy-six guardsmen in battle dress followed students up a hill. Once on the hilltop, the guardsmen turned in unison and trained their guns on the students scattered about the commons. For thirteen seconds there were loud, staccato bursts of M-1 fire. After sixty-one shots, four students lay dying in the parking lot below the hill, spread out a distance of 90 to 130 yards from the rifles. Along with nine other wounded students, two guardsmen were whisked to the hospital. They were in shock. Others told newsmen the barrage had been touched off by snipers.

• •

After the first reports of the Kent State killings had made the television news, a collective shriek of outrage burst from the nation's campuses. This time most of the cries came from moderate students—students not usually regarded as political. For the first time they began chanting against the war and barricading federal buildings to halt the processing of draft records. Before Kent State, antiwar protesting was usually the work of privileged, middle-class whites at the nation's best universities. But now the demonstrators were of every class and from every sort of school: women's colleges, junior colleges, Catholic colleges, and even black colleges, divinity schools, and military academies. For nearly a month after the shootings at Kent State, students marched on state capitols and military bases, staged guerilla theater plays, held candlelight vigils, and picketed classrooms to enforce the National Student Strike. They tolled bells, dug graves, lowered flags, and went on hunger strikes. They wore black armbands and carried white crosses, and on the walls of campus buildings they spray-painted the black fist and the phrases "Shut it down!" and "Free the Panthers!" Instead of attending classes and taking final exams, long-haired males got haircuts and female students shed their jeans and donned dresses to knock on doors and tell average folks why the war should end. Town meetings were held on many campuses so that members of the community, as well as puzzled faculty and administrators, could learn what all the demonstrating was about.

Though at more than 90 percent of the campuses the protests were peaceful, there was violence. College classrooms and administration buildings were set ablaze in every region of the nation. ROTC buildings were firebombed on campuses never regarded as bastions of radicalism—campuses like Colorado College and the University of Nevada in the West, and the University of Kentucky and the University of Alabama in the South—to name just a handful. At the nation's largest universities, students were smashing the windows of downtown stores, tossing rocks and bottles at peace officers, and lighting bonfires in the streets. Fistfights broke out when conservative students challenged the militants who disrupted classes or lowered flags.

As before at Santa Barbara, Columbus, and Kent, there was gunfire. At the University of Maryland on the night of the Kent State slayings, a student was wounded by buckshot in the legs and buttocks. State police on the scene claimed they had not fired. In Buffalo, twenty students suffered birdshot wounds after a confrontation with city police. The officers maintained they never opened fire. In Albuquerque, New Mexico, city and state police joined the National Guard to clear a building occupied for two days by students. Nine youths were bayoneted and a TV newsman filming the scene was stabbed three times, almost fatally.

On May 10 at the University of San Diego, there was another kind of violence. Twenty-three-year-old George Winne poured kerosene on his clothing and set himself afire. As he burned to death, he held a sign that proclaimed: "In the name of God, end the war."

The turmoil of May '70 was so fierce and sudden that many Americans feared a revolution was at hand. Journalists said the unrest reflected the nation's worst ideological split since the Civil War. Some form of demonstration took place on nearly 80 percent of America's campuses. The National Student Strike closed the doors of at least one in five. To Nixon's Silent Majority, all the chanting, marching, and rock-throwing on the campuses seemed the work of Communists.

But to many liberals, the May '70 revolt seemed the work of gallant antiwar crusaders. True, May '70 was partly the rebellion of militant youths fed up with "Nixon's" war and the racism of "Amerika." But it was much more complicated than that. May '70 was the rebellion of draft-age youths who feared dying in a pointless war. May '70 was the collective revulsion of students who saw U.S. troops on television killing other students at Kent State. May '70 became a media-made fad—"Berkeley Comes to South Oshkosh College"—and burning the campus ROTC building was in fashion. Few protesters were truly pacifists. Some wanted as much to raise hell as fight the system. Even nonstudents joined in the excitement of campus protest, and for a cynical minority of college students, May '70 was merely a chance to close the campus before final exams.

The fires of student revolt were stoked by America's conservative politicians. A week before the May '70 demonstrations began, California Governor Ronald Reagan, a candidate for reelection, had been asked about resolving campus unrest. Reagan remarked: "If it takes a bloodbath . . . let's get it over with." Ohio Governor James Rhodes, in a primary for the U.S. Senate, said the protesters at Kent State were "worse than the Brown Shirts and Communist element." In Washington, President Nixon called the demonstrators "bums," and Vice President Spiro Agnew called them "paranoids."

To many in blue-collar America, Nixon and Agnew were "telling it like it is." Middle America was fed up with student protests. At demonstrations near both the University of Maryland and the University of Michigan, motorists plowed into lines of protesters, injuring several students. In Seattle, bands of middle-aged vigilantes roved through the state university campus, clubbing demonstrators. At Rutgers, thirty adult spectators at an ROTC drill bounded from their bleacher seats and attacked students protesting peacefully nearby. Several youths were injured before police ended the melee with Mace and clubs.

In New York and other cities, thousands of hard-hatted construction workers held flag-waving counterdemonstrations. Flags sprouted from the antennas of the workers' pickup trucks, and "Love It or Leave It!" stickers appeared on the bumpers of their big-finned sedans. To the hardhats, the students were an alien tribe of drug-crazed, long-haired cowards, brainwashed by Communists and afraid to defend their own country. On Wall Street on May 8, hundreds of construction workers with flags charged police lines to get at students chanting "Peace Now!" The lawmen stepped aside, allowing workers to beat the students. More than sixty youths were injured. Longshoremen and office workers later joined the hardhats, and for days afterward, there were parades and patriotism in Manhattan.

Throughout May '70, black students were more cautious than whites. When the blacks saw troops and club-swinging vigilantes, most stayed out of the line of fire. Many blacks felt that white students were merely playing a game of revolution and had little sense of the consequences. Still, black students played an important role in May '70. At predominantly white schools such as Ohio State, Kent State, Buffalo State, and Yale, blacks protested against both racism and the war. Blacks held demonstrations on the nation's predominantly black campuses, as well. In Georgia, black students staged demonstrations at Albany State College and Payne College, in Alabama at Miles College, and in Pennsylvania at Lincoln University. But these demonstrations were generally peaceful. No one was killed.

While student rebellions were breaking out in the rest of the nation, Mississippi's colleges were generally quiet in the first week of May. After all, students at Mississippi's predominantly white colleges were better known for panty raids than protests. And the state's three black colleges were run by conservative presidents who were under the thumb of the all-white State Board of Higher Education.

Nevertheless, there was student protest in Mississippi. Hours before Nixon delivered his April 30 address on Cambodia, a group of black students gathered to burn the rebel flag, symbol of the University of Mississippi in Oxford, about 150 miles north of Jackson. A shoving match broke out when white students challenged the blacks for desecrating their flag. On May 7 in Jackson, three days after the Kent State slayings, a group of sixty Millsaps College students and teachers lowered the campus flag on the commons and prayed for the dead in Ohio. That same afternoon on the west side of town, Jackson State students met on the steps of Roberts Dining Hall, where eight years before James Meredith and other students had gathered to protest segregation in Mississippi. But this time the issue was not race, as indicated by the signs on campus walls and doors at Jackson State:

JSC Students
Be Concerned.
Meet in Front
of the Dining Hall
at 2 P.M. Today
To Discuss Cambodia.

As a crowd of five hundred assembled in front of the dining hall, the rock music that signaled the rally quieted. Seven student leaders mounted the dining hall steps to speak. They talked of the draft, the war over there in Vietnam, and the war over here against black people. Some complained of the disproportionate number of blacks killed in the war and of the white draft boards of Mississippi, which had helped make the bloodshed possible.

> "We had a loudspeaker or a bullhorn and we were saying this thing is getting out of hand. There are enough Vietnamese—why should we go over there?" recalls Warner Buxton, the Jackson State student government president in 1970. "The students weren't too pleased about the Cambodia situation. They thought it was outrageous and it was probably going to cause a lot more people to go into the service and it might cause the war to get bigger and more prolonged. They didn't like what

happened at Kent State, either, because they thought it was Nixon up to his old tricks, and somehow, either directly or indirectly, he had something to do with it—Nixon-Agnew. It was strictly intellectual. There was no great outpouring or anything like that. The students were appalled by Kent State, I'm sure, but I don't think they ever thought at the time that it would happen to them."

The rally ended, and though a few students grumbled that nothing would come of this polite little get-together, they left quietly. The moderate tone of the rally was reflected in the handbills that student leaders distributed to urge a one-day boycott of classes at Jackson State: "To those of you who are sympathetic to this cause, we ask for your support. However, any students who feel otherwise and who would like to continue classes, no hostile efforts will be made to prevent you from doing so."

A group of young whites also had joined in passing out antiwar leaflets on the dining hall steps at Jackson State. These handbills were headlined: "4 ARE DEAD." Jackson State students did not know what to make of these whites on their campus. Some thought they were Kent State students. Others thought they were radicals from the Students for a Democratic Society. Their long, fourteen-inch handbills announced a demonstration on Saturday afternoon, May 9, at the War Memorial Building in downtown Jackson. A Kent State student named Tom D'Floure was to speak, and the rally's organizers, the Jackson Peace Coordinating Committee, sought common cause with black people:

> The blacks, the students, the working man, and the small businessman are powerless against the financial empires of the military-industrial complex. We are struggling against high taxes, inflation, unemployment, racism, a senseless war, and a deteriorating environment. But the corporations keep raising prices and polluting our land, and the president has let the Pentagon invade yet another country.

On Saturday, May 9, only a dozen Jackson State students made the one-mile trip downtown for the antiwar rally. Never a hotbed of activism, Jackson State was regarded as an apathetic campus by civil rights activists. So organizers of the peace rally that Saturday could only be glad that more than a handful of Jackson State students had joined in the protest against the Kent State slayings.

"These students weren't into these kinds of political things," Henry Thompson, a former Jackson State activist, recalls. "They were just kids.

They didn't know the meaning of 'political.' They were into dating and sororities and fraternities and shit like that. They knew about Martin Luther King and marching and freedom songs and all that crap, but they didn't know very much about Vietnam. I was trying to get my point over. My message to them was: 'Hey, when ya gonna wise up?' I was very frustrated with the attitude of the students there. I wanted them to wise up to what the System was all about."

As the dozen Jackson State students joined more than a hundred Millsaps College students and other protesters at the War Memorial downtown, two highway patrolmen approached them. The officers told the protesters they were breaking a state law which banned demonstrations on state property. The patrolmen gave them a choice: leave or be arrested.

So the small integrated crowd filed down the Amite Street hill and walked two blocks to Smith Park, which was city property. There under the oak trees, and right behind the Governor's Mansion, they set up their microphone and speakers. And they tried to tell Mississippi what it did not want to hear.

3

THE MINIRIOT

The white South said that it knew "niggers," and I was what the white South called "nigger." Well, the white South had never known me—never known what I felt.

—Richard Wright

"Better tell them security guards out there they better get them niggers into them dormitories, or we fixin' to have some trouble out here!" a Jackson policeman yelled into his squad-car radio. He was parked near the Jackson State campus and peering down Lynch Street in the dark.

"Ten-four," the police radio dispatcher replied.

"These niggers are congregated behind that fence, and them security guards should put them back in their rooms," the policeman added. "They're throwin' them bottles and things over the fence out in the street."

It was 9:20 on the night of Wednesday, May 13, 1970, and it was muggy and about eighty degrees on Lynch Street. A policeman cruising by the Jackson State campus had just drawn a spray of bottles and rocks. He had stopped and gotten out of his car near Alexander Hall, a women's dormitory, and stared at a crowd of about a hundred students milling behind a chain-link fence. He went back to his car and drove away.

Jackson State students had tossed rocks at passing white motorists several times that week, but security guards and student leaders had managed to keep things from getting out of hand. On Wednesday night, however, the crowd outdoors along the campus was larger than usual— about three hundred students and a few cornerboys along Lynch Street. They stood or sat on the lawns in front of the women's dorm, the Student Union next door, and up on the knoll beside Stewart Hall, a men's dorm. They eyed each motorist driving the two-block stretch by the darkened campus. When a white motorist passed, a group of rock-slingers let loose with a barrage, denting a fender or smashing a windshield, sending the white driver tearing down Lynch Street and jumping traffic lights to get past the college.

Just nine days after the Kent State killings, the turmoil of May '70 was spreading to Jackson, Mississippi.

To the Jackson State students watching TV in their dorms that Wednesday night after dinner, America had seemed awash in violence. Every night that week, film of antiwar protests, ROTC firebombings, and rock- and bottle-throwing appeared on the network news shows. There was racial confrontation as well. Six blacks had been killed in a riot in Augusta, Georgia two days before. All had been shot in the back, TV newscasters reported. Georgia's honey-tongued Governor Lester Maddox warned: "I've given orders to the troopers that if they're fired upon, that don't ask anybody to quit shootin', but blow whatever these people are in off their foundations if necessary to restore the peace."

But the night of May 13 had begun quietly enough at Jackson State. Male students were standing on the lawn in front of Alexander Hall, talking with their girlfriends. Others were playing cards or shooting pool next door in the Student Union. In the commons park across the street from Alexander Hall, a few couples were sitting on benches under the oak trees. On the campus sidewalks and lawns along Lynch Street you could always find a crowd of students after dark—maybe three hundred on the hottest nights—just rapping and jiving, and the guys charming the ladies. Sometimes they sat on blankets on the grass and listened to WOKJ's rhythm and blues pulsing from a radio.

Not everyone was hanging around on Lynch Street. Some students were in the library, while others were nearby at Dansby Hall taking part in a music recital. Down the street at Just Science Hall, the brothers of Omega Psi Phi were holding a fraternity meeting. Other students were walking east down Lynch Street to the Penguin or the Red Carpet Lounge to drink some wine and listen to the soul music throbbing from a jukebox. It was less than a week before final exams, but many students complained it was too hot to study in the dorms.

The four thousand students attending Jackson State College had come from segregated public schools. About half the students were from tiny rural towns like Coldwater, Pelahatchie, Tchula, and Indianola. Their state's public school system was one of the worst in the nation. Their teachers were the lowest paid in America, and fewer than half of their schoolmates graduated from high school. In some Mississippi school districts, the students were excused from classes so they could chop cotton in the hot fields at harvest time. And ever since the U.S. Supreme Court ruled against segregated public schools in 1954, education was not even mandatory for the children of Mississippi.

For decades Jackson State had produced black teachers for this school system, but the college's more militant students now had doubts about teaching in it. And a few complained their college seemed just another plantation run by black overseers for the Man.

"The System" in America was the subject of many a rap session on Lynch Street that spring. Students complained about the draft, Cambodia, Nixon and Agnew, and Kent State. After the May 4 slayings in Ohio, the black students grumbled that Kent State and other campuses had closed, so why not Jackson State? On Wednesday night, May 13, a rumor spread that Jackson State's ROTC barracks would go up in flames after dark. Many students wondered if this would be the night of the annual spring miniriot.

> "That's really how it got started," recalls Warner Buxton, student leader and former CORE worker. "It wasn't all that political. It was hot. We'd been there all year. So the feeling was, 'Let's close this sucker down.' Jackson State has never been all that political. The unrest might have had political overtones due to the fact that the Vietnam War was going on and everything like that. But that's as political as it gets. If the students were going to get drafted, they didn't want to go. They had no bone to pick with Vietnam. They knew that Nixon was a shitass, Agnew was a shitass, and the governor, John Bell Williams, was a shitass. They knew that the political system was designed to keep black folk down. But that was a realization that most black people were born with."

Another source of discontent, at least among the college's seniors, was a bell recently discovered in a campus warehouse. This bell apparently had been used at the turn of the century to summon students to class, chapel, and other activities. A group of seniors voted to hang the old bell in the commons park, but the more militant seniors objected. On the dining hall steps, the dissidents passed out leaflets that proclaimed: "To Hell With The Bell!" They argued the bell reminded them all too well of Governor John Bell Williams, an unyielding segregationist who had campaigned from the back of a flatbed truck, ringing a bell to draw his courthouse crowds. Other seniors said the old bell reminded them of plantation slavery. In *The Voice of Blackness,* an underground newspaper on campus, they railed against the bell-hangers.

> WAKE UP BELLS AND CHAINS NIGGERS
>
> See how damn backward, stupid, ignorant, conservative, passive apathetic . . . etc., you are for having voted to mount a damn "concrete" insignificant object instead of aiding our black community.

> 14–15 SENIOR CLASS NEGROES PROVE THAT
> NEGROES ARE STILL ACTIVE AND POWERFUL
> BUT
>
> They also express a need to return to slaverymaster's plantation! To show just how much they love master's plantation they are mounting master's *Bell* which reminds them of how master disturbed them from those 3–4 hours of sleep which they thought they would never get.

With all these frustrations at Jackson State, small wonder that students revived the springtime ritual of throwing rocks at white drivers on Lynch Street. But they were not the only ones to toss rocks. To some, it looked as though a few cornerboys had started it all.

> "A whole lot of students were sitting out on the grass—you know how kids are at the college—just sitting out and talking," recalls Frank James, a student in 1970. "There wasn't too much going on. Some fellows came down the street off the corner. They wasn't students—just people off the corner. And it kind of got stirred up about, 'You gonna let the ROTC come in and take over the college?' And, 'The college is preparing you for war as soon as you leave school,' and all this. That really wasn't my thing that night. I left. They were talking about trouble."

At 9:42 P.M. on May 13, bottles and rocks were hitting cars passing the campus on Lynch Street. As reports of shattered windows and dented cars came over police radios, one officer in a squad car asked the radio dispatcher: "Havin' nigger trouble on Lynch Street?"

By 9:45 P.M., police were stopping cars near the east and west ends of the campus on Lynch Street. The traffic ebbed as roadblocks were set up by the city's "colored cars," those manned by black officers. Sixteen of the city's 280-man police force were black. Their job was to control the black community, and until recent months, they couldn't even shower with their white co-workers. So when the rock-tossing erupted on Lynch Street, it was only natural the colored cars were sent there first.

Meanwhile, Jackson State officials were calling off-duty security guards, hoping the black, eleven-man force could calm the students. But the rock-throwing and window-shattering continued as motorists entered Lynch Street from the side streets. Police had not sealed those closest to the campus—Dalton at the east end and Prentiss to the west. The officers feared getting so close to the students would only inflame them.

At about 10:20 P.M., a shiny blue 1965 Buick carried four unsuspecting whites down the Lynch Street gauntlet. In front of the Student Union, someone shouted, "They're white—get 'em!" Rocks rained on the car from both sides of the street. One large rock flew through an open window in the Buick and smashed through another window inside and dropped to the pavement. A chunk of concrete bigger than a flatiron crashed through yet another window, striking a woman on the back.

Soon a yellow 1970 Dodge sedan came to a stop at the red light in front of the Student Union. A group of black youths yelled and ran toward the car. One slapped the car while another tossed a brick that shattered the windshield. The driver flinched when a sliver of glass lodged in his eye. Turning, he saw that his passenger's mouth was bloodied and his front teeth were broken.

> "You have to vent your frustrations some way," muses Henry Thompson, an activist at Jackson State in 1970. "These kids took them out on anyone that passed the college. It was like the whites were doing them an injustice for so long, and then they go and ride by in those nice big cars. It was like rubbing salt into the wounds. It was easy to throw rocks at them."

White motorists were not the only ones to draw fire. When students spotted a sedan driven by a woman, they took aim and hit her car with a volley of rocks. She was black, yet light-skinned, and she did not speed off like the other motorists. She was so angry that she got out of her car and gave the students a scolding.

A 1963 Ford came along. Inside were two white youths and a black. They were co-workers on break from their part-time jobs downtown. Before they made it to the other end of the campus, a brick hurtled through the car's right rear window and cut the black youth's left eye. The wound looked serious to the young white driver, so he stomped on the accelerator and screeched off to the hospital.

At about 10:30 P.M., a college security guard named George Jones was driving his red pickup truck to the campus to join his fellow officers. As he passed Stewart Hall on Lynch Street, a rock burst through a window in the black officer's truck. A piece of glass lodged in his eye. Stunned, Jones watched as a crowd closed in on him. He reached for his revolver and fired three times above his head and sped off.

A group of about ten male youths spotted a campus security car parked on Lynch Street. It was empty. They lobbed chunks of concrete at it, shattering the back windows. They grabbed the bumpers and began rocking the car. Just as it was nearly tipped over, two security officers came running and shouting, firing their pistols above their heads. The youths scattered.

Some students did not want campus property destroyed, so they tried to get the vandals to cool it. One of these students was Warner Buxton, the recently elected president of student government. A heavy-set, brown-skinned man with a scraggly beard, Buxton had been a civil rights worker with CORE during the mid-1960s. As he stood on the darkened lawn in front of Alexander Hall, Buxton pleaded with the dorm residents to stay away from their windows. He asked them to stop throwing Coke bottles to male friends below, and to stop cheering on the bottle-throwers.

A security guard with a battery-powered bullhorn ordered the crowd in front of the dorm to leave. It was Sergeant M. R. Stringer of campus security. Stringer announced that a 10:30 P.M. curfew was now in effect, and all students should return to their dormitories. But few students moved, and the crowd began jeering Stringer. A young black man with a moustache borrowed Stringer's bullhorn. This man had just driven by in his Thunderbird, when students had surrounded his car and refused to let him pass. "Why do you want to tear up your campus?" he asked the crowd in front of Alexander Hall. "There is no sense in this stuff!" But the students booed and shouted the man down.

At about 10:30 P.M. in front of the Student Union next door to Alexander Hall, a group of about 150 students began chanting against the Vietnam War and ROTC training on campus. The crowd charged across Lynch Street, passing Just Science Hall and heading across the lawn toward the two ROTC buildings. These were white wooden buildings that looked like giant, two-story versions of the shotgun houses on Lynch Street.

"Get the ROTC building! Let's burn down 'Rotsy!' " the crowd shouted, after stopping in front of the first of the buildings, Barracks 1-A, where the ammunition was stored. Inside were a few ROTC students, security guards, and ROTC officers. They had been warned there might be trouble that night, so when they heard the howls of an approaching crowd, they went outdoors to order the students away. But the crowd threw stones and bottles, smashing windows and pelting an ROTC officer's car.

> "The kids were just rushing," recalls Vernon Weakley, who had watched from behind Just Hall, where his fraternity had been meeting. "It looked as if the kids had surrounded the ROTC building. Sergeant Stringer was talking to them, trying to make them get back. It kind of scared me, man, because by that time the security guards had drawn guns and everything. The kids were having a good time. They were screaming

and hollering, 'Burn it down! Burn it down!' That type of thing. They were rushing the building, as if trying to get in or tear it down or something like that. The security guards would pull their guns and make a run, and then the kids would go back aways. Now my estimate may be big, but I'd say there were two or three hunded of them. If that ROTC building was ever going to burn down, it was going to be that night, because, man, the kids were fired up."

But the students tired of trying to break into the building, and they scattered. Yet one small group lingered nearby. A security guard watched as these black youths talked of coming back to burn it all down.

At 11:00 P.M., TV newsman Bert Case of WJTV was driving east on Lynch Street toward Jackson State. A white native of Jackson, Case was considered one of the city's best journalists. He was a progressive Mississippian with long brown sideburns and a deep, full-throated broadcasting voice. He had heard there was trouble at the college, so after WJTV's 10:00 newscast, he packed his camera equipment into a white Plymouth news cruiser and headed for Lynch Street. At a roadblock three blocks west of the college, he was stopped by police. Case talked with Police Chief W. D. Rayfield, veteran of thirty-three years on the police force and its chief since 1952.

"I pulled up to him and said, 'Chief, what's going on?' " Case recalls. " 'They're throwing rocks and bottles up there at passing cars and the situation's getting pretty tense,' the chief said. And I said, 'Well, I'd like to go in there.' He said, 'You're crazy. I don't want you to go in there. It's not safe.' So I said, 'If I go in at my own risk, can I do it?' And he said, 'Oh yeah, if you want to go in at your own risk, I'll let you go in, but I strongly advise you against it. I think that's very dumb on your part.' I had a lot of confidence that nothing would happen to me, because in many civil rights demonstrations, quite frankly, I felt a lot safer being behind the black lines than being behind the police lines—in a lot of rural areas. So he let me on by, and there was a traffic light at Prentiss and Lynch near a dormitory, and it was green. But I had to stop at the next one. Then I heard them yelling at me, 'There's one, get him! Get him!' A group charged out into the street and started throwing bottles and bricks at the car—just a rain of missiles. When the light turned green, it all showered down. I put it on the floor pretty fast—the Plymouth had a V-8 engine in it. And as I pulled out from the light, a bottle broke through the back window of the car and smashed near the front seat. I got some glass—

little slivers of it sprayed all over me. I ran every red light from there on in. And at Rose and Lynch Streets on the other end, a policeman told me: 'That'll teach you to fool around with those niggers, Case.' "

Minutes after Case streaked by, black youths were lugging benches from the park across the street from Alexander Hall. They set fire to the benches and stoked up a roaring bonfire in the middle of Lynch Street near the dorm's east-wing doorway. Someone threw tires on top of the blaze, and acrid black smoke arose from the snapping flames.

Another group of black youths came rushing up the middle of Lynch Street moments later, pushing a wooden garbage wagon. They set it afire to make a second bonfire in Lynch Street, this time in front of the Student Union next door to Alexander Hall.

Then another trash wagon was hauled up Lynch Street. The black youths tipped the wagon over and into the flames of the first bonfire in front of Alexander Hall. Flames leaped into the air, startling policemen at the Rose and Lynch Street barricade, two blocks east of the campus. To the officers, it looked like a car ablaze.

Throughout the evening, several students tried to damp down the flames of student rage, but they were Uncle Toms in the eyes of the fire-setters and bottle-throwers, who were louder and angrier and carried the night.

"I remember asking some students what was the bottle-throwing all about," recalls Charles Carr, one of the peacemakers that night. " 'What are we accomplishing?' I asked them. 'Why were we tearing up our campus like this?' Well, people expressed some general frustration that this is the only way we can get the attention that we need. 'Attention about what?' I asked. 'What demands are being made?' That didn't go over too well among the crowd of folks I was standing near, because it was like everybody should be committed to whatever was happening at the moment. These were students—not cornerboys—and as usual, the crowd did not think with one mind. The news on the radio and TV wasn't good about the war and about the other things. There were some perceptions that perhaps young black men in particular were like sacrificial lambs. And as usual, there was some alcohol around. I argued with one man about why must we always internalize our violence. Why did we destroy where we were? Some believed—'This campus is not ours—this is the Man's.' Others believed that this was some sacred ground that we needed to nurture and build on—'Because it's going to help me and help you and help the kids after us get more than we've got right now.' But there was still that other side of the coin where—'This college is just something that they put over here to indoctrinate us to the facts that they want, and as long as it's here it represents another way of keeping us down.' These people were very much a minority, but a vocal minority."

Three youths determined to destroy the ROTC barracks sneaked in the dark toward the two white buildings. Two of the youths carried gasoline-filled bottles. They lit the wicks, threw, then ran. One bottle landed on a roof but rolled off, falling harmlessly to the gravel parking lot below. The other lay on the porch roof of Barracks 1-A and set it afire. Sergeant Stringer saw the flames and ran toward the barracks. He clambered up the outdoor stairway and onto the roof where he found a large Coca-Cola bottle and a burning wick in a puddle of gas. He took off his shirt and snuffed out the flames.

• •

A mile east of the campus, behind the white floodlit columns of the Governor's Mansion, John Bell Williams received a telephone call. Police headquarters was calling to notify the governor of trouble at Jackson State. As prescribed by law, Governor Williams signed a proclamation authorizing the Mississippi Highway Patrol to join the city police in restoring order on campus.

An ardent advocate of "Law and Order," Williams was an Old South Democrat who had spent much of his career fighting for the Mississippi way of life. Williams's political career began soon after he had lost his left arm in a plane crash in South America during World War II. The sympathy vote for the wounded Williams swept him into Congress. On the House floor in 1948, this young congressman from Mississippi attacked President Harry Truman and other "civil rightists" pressing for civil rights reform:

> Chief among these are radical Negro, Communist and off-color mongrel organizations which, conceived in hate, whelped in treason and deceit, and nurtured on the breast of Communism, are attempting to bring about in this great country moral disintegration and mongrelization through a forced amalgamation of the races.

John Bell Williams was a race-baiting demagogue in the grand Mississippi tradition of Governors Vardaman and Bilbo. And he was proud of it.

Son of a druggist in tiny Raymond, Mississippi, about ten miles west of Jackson, Williams used his talents as a stump orator to keep his seat in Congress and later to make his way into the Governor's Mansion. But he had never become one of the capital's Garden Club set, those people of quality who never used intemperate phrases, and certainly never said "nigger." Williams had come from earthier stock. He was not ashamed, for example, to tell racist jokes. He once asked a Vermont governor if he'd like to swap a jug full of Vermont maple syrup for a busload of Mississippi blacks.

Even in 1970, Governor Williams remained an unrepentant segregationist. He still opposed school desegregation in Mississippi, for instance, and to turn the tables on the federal government, he had vetoed Head Start funds for Mississippi's poor children, most of whom were black. Williams had called the program "segregated." Blacks were just not ready for integration, Williams believed. And whenever they struck back at him in frustration, he was quick to invoke Law and Order. So on that night of fire-setting at Jackson State, Governor Williams ordered the Mississippi National Guard to Jackson. But first he would send the highway patrol, since the guard would need most of the night to get to Jackson.

Meanwhile, two blocks from the Governor's Mansion downtown, officers at police headquarters had been preparing to move on Jackson State. Because of the rock-throwing on campus, city police on the 11:00 P.M. shift had reported to headquarters a little earlier than usual. By 11:15 P.M., the officers were already on their way to the campus in two city trucks and Thompson's Tank, an armored van. They stopped three blocks north of the college in a middle-income neighborhood on Prentiss Street. This was a tidy, tree-lined street of small ranch homes and bungalows—a residential section once all white, but now becoming increasingly black. The tree boughs looked silvery under the streetlights as the policemen got out of their trucks and onto Prentiss Street's blacktop.

In light blue shirts and navy blue pants, the city policemen awaited the highway patrol in the middle of the dark street. These policemen in blue represented the same department that had enforced a policy of "instant arrest" on all civil rights protesters during the 1960s. These officers also represented a department that made a Saturday night sport of beating blacks outside the bars on Lynch Street.

The man in charge of the police that night was Warren Magee, the only officer wearing the white blouse of a lieutenant. Magee was a thirty-nine-year-old shift supervisor, a member of the force for sixteen years. He sent his children to one of the segregated Citizens' Council schools in town, and he was respected by his men. Ordinarily, Lieutenant Magee would never have led the police to Jackson State that night. That was the job of Major C. R. Wilson, who was specially trained in crowd control. But Wilson happened to be out of town for a training session, so Magee took over.

At about 11:30 P.M., Magee noticed the first officers of the all-white Mississippi Highway Patrol arriving on Prentiss Street. It would take nearly twenty minutes for all the patrolmen to gather, since they had been spread out patrolling the highways.

> "The highway patrolmen were no good. No good," says Charles Evers, who in 1970 was mayor of Fayette, Mississippi and the state's most powerful black leader. "A bunch of redneck murderers, most of them. Nigger-haters, let me call them, and long-haired-hippie-haters. So that's what they were then. Most of them were ignorant, and most of them were avowed racists, and many of them were ex-Klansmen or present Klansmen who went from the sheet to the badge. They were the Segregationist Army."

One patrolman who pulled up along the Prentiss Street curb was Inspector Lloyd Jones, the unit's commander. Jones was a huge, hulking, crew-cut man who stood six-feet-three and weighed more than 250 pounds. He sometimes complained that he had had no rest in Mississippi since the early 1960s, when the Freedom Riders were bused into Jackson. Ever since then, Jones had appeared on the scene of nearly every major racial confrontation in Mississippi. He was in Oxford on September 30, 1962, for example, when white students and vigilantes started a riot to prevent James Meredith from desegregating Ole Miss. The highway patrol stepped aside that evening, allowing the rioters to have their way. Two men were killed and more than 160 federal marshals injured in that confrontation.

Nearly five years later in 1966, Jones was in Canton—thirty miles north of Jackson—when Martin Luther King, Jr., Stokely Carmichael, and thousands of other activists were marching from the Mississippi delta to the state capital to protest the recent shooting of James Meredith. After the Meredith marchers set up a huge tent to sleep on public grounds in Canton, Jones ordered they be tear-gassed. One warm May night in 1967, during campus unrest in Jackson, Jones stood in a skirmish line stretching from curb to curb across Lynch Street. He faced a crowd of jeering black youths who tossed stones at him and his fellow patrolmen. The officers opened fire. Jones fired three times. Later he testified he fired into the air. Jones helped pick up young Benjamin Brown, who lay dying on the sidewalk that night and carried him to an ambulance.

Since the earliest days of the civil rights movement, black Mississippians had a special name for this big, burly patrolman. They called him "Goon Jones."

> "He was a legend in his own time—a redneck hero," recalls Davis Smith, a former *Jackson Daily News* reporter. "He was known as 'tough on niggers.' Everybody knew Lloyd Jones 'wasn't goin' to take no shit from no niggers'—or anybody else—but especially 'niggers.' "

Jones shut the door of his squad car and walked down Prentiss Street to where Lieutenant Magee stood in the road with two dozen of his men. Jones had worked with Magee before; for instance, during the 1966 Meredith march on the state capitol. But on this night Magee was in charge of Jones's men, since by law the all-white patrol could only assist local police in emergencies. So Magee told Jones they were to secure Jackson State's ROTC buildings, which had been attacked.

By 11:45 P.M., Jones's men had lined up in Prentiss Street in two parallel lines right behind Thompson's Tank and in front of the Jackson police. In all, there were two dozen patrolmen in blue pants and gray shirts. They were armed with twelve-gauge shotguns.

Before the lawmen moved out, Mayor Russell Davis pulled up in his car. Mayor less than a year, Davis was worried about the fires and the rock-throwing at Jackson State. Since 10:00 P.M. he had been shuttling from barricade to barricade to keep an eye on the situation. By Mississippi's standards, Davis was a progressive mayor. A square-chinned, silver-haired man of forty-seven, Davis sought to transform Jackson from a segregated backwater into a flourishing city.

> "Russell Davis—he and I were friends," recalls Wilson Minor, former reporter for the *New Orleans Times-Picayune*. "I mean, I felt that I was partly responsible for getting Russell to run for mayor. We had a terrible mayor for a long time in Allen Thompson. And back in those days, Russell and I used to go bird hunting sometimes, so while we were tramping through the woods, I used to talk to him about how he was the only one who could beat Allen Thompson. Russell was then a state legislator who was able to win reelection every time by a big majority. Anyway, he finally decided to run for mayor, and that's when Thompson backed down and stepped out. Davis was a very blunt, dogmatic kind of guy. He let you know where he stood. A very honest guy. He was conservative,

I mean, but not on segregation. No. When he finally decided he was going to run for mayor, I took him to meet some black people—people who could help him politically, and he established good rapport with them, and he took it from there."

Though a former member of the segregationist Citizens' Council, Davis had found it easier than most Mississippians to break with the past. Maybe because he was not a native. During World War II he had come south from Maryland to work as an Air Force instructor. He married a Mississippi woman, so he stayed. Twenty-six years later, Davis was running Mississippi's largest city. He sought new industries and applied for once-hated federal funds to get Jackson back on its feet. And he worked at keeping the rift between the city's whites and blacks from widening. But all this could have been for naught if Jackson State exploded. So Mayor Davis conferred with Lieutenant Magee about the situation on campus before Magee and his men began marching toward Lynch Street.

"Inform Chief Pierce that we are here at Central and Prentiss," Magee said, speaking on his walkie-talkie to headquarters just before the men moved out. It was about ten minutes to midnight.

"Ten-four, I'll give it to him," the radio dispatcher answered.

"Inform Chief Pierce the highway patrol has twenty-five men," Magee said. "We have approximately twenty-five or twenty-seven."

"Chief Pierce advises to go ahead," the dispatcher said. "Be on your way, and work with Inspector Jones."

"Ten-four," Magee replied, and he radioed Thompson's Tank to move slowly forward and lead the marching officers down Prentiss Street. Mayor Davis followed in his car, creeping behind the two parallel lines of officers as they marched behind the tank and down the street, their clubs dangling at their sides.

The steel tank, looking white under the street lights, carried ten city police inside. Thompson's Tank was an armored van, twenty-three feet long, with two spotlights on its roof. Each of the eight men in the back of the tank sat beside a bullet-proof window and a gunport. They had Thompson submachine guns and shotguns that could lauch tear-gas cannisters. The tank stored extra ammunition.

"Oh, that tank was a hated symbol," Charles Carr, a former student, remembers. "It stood for impregnable racism. I don't know if that thing was purchased for any other reason than as a symbol that said, 'We will run you down.' I mean, what else could you use it for?"

Thompson's Tank had a bizarre history: built to deal with civil rights demonstrations after the Evers slaying in 1963; introduced to the black community at Jackson State in 1964, when the men inside smoked themselves out by misfiring a cannister; then loaned to Memphis to protect James Earl Ray after he gunned down Martin Luther King, Jr., in 1968. During tense times in Jackson, the tank was parked conspicuously on a street near police headquarters. That way everyone downtown could see this shining example of white might. Blacks said Thompson's Tank was parked so it pointed toward them, facing Lynch Street.

Walking beside the tank were Inspector "Goon" Jones and Lieutenant Magee. At five-feet-ten, Magee noticed he needed to take almost two full steps to equal one of Jones's giant strides. To Magee, Jones's legs seemed longer than ordinary men's.

The officers' three-block march down Prentiss Street took just ten minutes. The men passed an abandoned, weed-choked swimming pool on their right that had been closed for years to thwart integration. As they marched, the officers noticed the lights of the New Men's Dormitory up on their left. This was a boxlike, seven-story dorm of brick, and Sergeants Truitt Beasley and Charles Lee—Magee's squad leaders—watched the windows carefully. The two sergeants looked for snipers as they marched, each holding an AR-15 automatic rifle with power scope. Beasley and Lee composed the platoon's sniper squad.

As the lawmen passed the dorm and marched toward the traffic light at the corner of Prentiss and Lynch Street, a crowd of black students emerged from the shadows to their left. The black youths stood on the grassy banks of a field at the Prentiss and Lynch Street corner.

"Pigs! Pigs!" they shouted. "Hey you white sons-of-bitches!" A few threw pieces of concrete, but the officers ignored them and kept marching. Once the men had crossed Lynch Street, Mayor Davis turned right at the traffic light and drove west down the street, away from the campus.

Walking south with his men down a gravel driveway near the football stadium, Lieutenant Magee turned around. He could see the students back on the grassy banks. To Magee, they seem crazed creatures: jumping up and down, hollering and cussing. But Magee would not stop to deal with them. His orders were to protect the ROTC buildings, so he led the men down the driveway and told them and the tank to turn east and cross a lawn. They approached the white ROTC barracks on the darkened campus.

"Can I tell you what it was like? Well, I would rather have been any place except there," Levaughn Carter recalls. He had been one of two black policemen at the ROTC buildings that night. "They threw a few rocks and what-have-you. The only abuse we had taken was abusive language and slurs, you know, from those students, and maybe once in a while they'd come and throw a rock at us."

The lawmen and the tank stopped in front of the white ROTC barracks, and Police Lieutenant Magee told Sergeant Stringer of campus security that the buildings were now secure. The police and patrolmen lined up in front of the two ROTC buildings and faced Lynch Street. As the officers looked ahead across the lawn, they could see the lighted windows of Stewart Hall, a men's dorm on Lynch Street. In front of the dorm was a screaming crowd of black students. Though out of range more than a hundred yards away, a few black youths hurled stones, trying to reach the officers.

"In front of the boys' dorm at Lynch Street and Prentiss, we have about two hundred jeering and heckling," reported Police Lieutenant Magee over his walkie-talkie. "We are in front of the ROTC buildings at this time. The group in front of the dormitory is on the campus. They're up on the banks—they're not in the streets. They're just hollering and heckling. I'm going to talk to Sergeant Stringer to see if he can't use his men to clear them out."

As the officers stood facing Stewart Hall, two black youths from about twenty yards away taunted the lawmen.

"Man, look at all of these men with guns," one youth yelled. "They are going to mow us down."

"He got a machine gun, he's going to kill all of us," the other said, pointing to Sergeant Lee's AR-15.

"There was a pretty good bunch out there," recalls Levaughn Carter, a black policemen in 1970. "I couldn't estimate the crowd, but it was a good bunch. They weren't rushing us, but every once in a while they would throw a rock. They seemed to have had—after we got there—their attention focused on the police. They was harassing us, yelling abusive slurs. Just a few things were thrown. They didn't try to go to war on us. I heard a few explosives—now it could have been firecrackers—I don't know."

At 12:14 A.M. in front of Stewart Hall, the crowd of students and a handful of cornerboys began shouting, "We're going to town! We're going to town!" The crowd ran east down Lynch Street, heading toward Jackson's business district. Immediately Lieutenant Magee radioed headquarters: "Approximately 125 or 150 are moving back east on Lynch Street towards Dalton!"

"Chief Pierce said for you to spare some of your men." the radio dispatcher told Magee. "Those that are running east on Lynch Street—they want you to stop them at Rose and Lynch Street, and not let them get any farther. If you need any more cars, we'll try to get them for you."

"Ten-four," Magee replied. "Have one of the units there on Prentiss Street send me one of their trucks."

Magee knew from the radio traffic there was only one squad car at the corner of Rose and Lynch Street to turn the crowd back. Just two officers three blocks from the campus formed the only buffer between the crowd and downtown Jackson. On his walkie-talkie, Magee ordered the driver of Thompson's Tank to hurry to the Rose and Lynch barricade, about a half mile east of the ROTC buildings. But the tank would not budge. Battery trouble. So Magee had to wait for a transport truck to send his men to stop the crowd. White Jackson had always feared that black hordes would break loose from Lynch Street and sack the shops of white merchants on Capitol Street. This could have been that moment, yet there was nothing Magee could do about it.

But about three minutes later, the radio man in Thompson's Tank reported the driver finally had managed to get it started. Magee gave the go-ahead, and the tank lurched from the gravel lot in front of the ROTC barracks. A transport truck for Magee and the rest of his men arrived soon afterwards. The police piled in, and their truck, like Thompson's Tank moments before, moved in a circuitous route around the college to avoid the crowds on campus. About five minutes later, Magee and his men arrived at the barricade near the east end of Lynch Steet. They formed a skirmish line there in the street to keep students from downtown Jackson.

A half mile to the west on the Jackson State campus, Inspector Lloyd "Goon" Jones and his men remained in another skirmish line to protect the ROTC barracks.

• •

The crowd of students and a handful of cornerboys who had been rushing east up Lynch Street stopped in front of Alexander Hall's staple-shaped facade. There they listened to a cornerboy standing on a park bench and haranguing the crowd. He was trying to get fresh recruits for the charge downtown, but the students told him and the other cornerboys to go ahead, alone.

Another cornerboy yelled up at the women in Alexander Hall. He was trying to get them to come out and join the crowd. "We want to help you!" he bellowed to the silhouettes in the dorm-room windows above. "Come on down and help us!"

But the women in the dorm were afraid and remained in their rooms. When the cornerboys saw that no one was coming out, they pelted the dorm with rocks and broke windows. They shouted that if no one came outdoors, they were going in. A cornerboy who wore a headband threw what looked like a lead pipe. It smashed the glass door to the east wing.

In the street in front of the women's dorm, someone in the crowd tossed a cable up over the traffic light. Several youths tugged at the cable, trying to bring the light crashing to the pavement. But it would not give. So the cornerboys and the students pelted it with rocks, and the shattered lenses fell to the street. At about 12:35 A.M., a cornerboy raised his pistol into the air and fired.

• •

"The shooting's up here on Lynch Street," Lieutenant Magee reported on his walkie-talkie. "We heard it. It's this group on Lynch Street."

Magee was only a block east of Alexander Hall and looking west down the street at the crowd near the traffic light. Magee and about four other officers had just left the Rose and Lynch Street barricade to see whether the crowd on campus would make another rush downtown. As he stood near the shattered glass storefront of M-L-S Drugs, Magee could see a bonfire in the street in front of Alexander Hall. A crowd of about two hundred had been standing near the flames and the traffic light when the shot had rung out. The black youths scattered. But a few ran toward Magee's squad car, hollering and throwing rocks in his direction. The lieutenant got back into his car and hurried to the Rose and Lynch Street barricade.

Once he was back at the roadblock, Magee saw that his men had formed a skirmish line stretching across Lynch Street. They stood at port arms—their shotguns held diagonally in front of them, barrels up, their right hands grasping the stocks. Three years before, at this same intersection on Lynch Street, lawmen had opened fire on rock-throwers, and one black had been killed.

One person who feared more killing was Martel Cook, a Jackson State student who was also a WJTV cameraman for Bert Case, the newsman with the brick-battered news cruiser who stood nearby. Cook was a light-skinned man of twenty-nine with a square chin and close-cropped hair. A full-time student and full-time cameraman, Cook was playing both roles this evening. While trying to convince students to stop vandalizing their campus, he was also investigating their motives. Some students had refused to be interviewed, and Cook had been heckled when he urged a crowd at Alexander Hall to cool it.

A former Illinoisan who served as an Army M.P. in racially divided Selma, Alabama during the 1960s, Cook had seen the way southern lawmen sometimes handled black crowds. He feared that the Jackson State students and a few rabble-rousing cornerboys were giving police just the excuse they needed to shoot. So Cook sought out Mayor Russell Davis to convince him the campus unrest would subside, if only the police would leave the students alone. Cook found the mayor near the police skirmish line at Rose and Lynch Street.

> "The Jackson police were on Lynch Street in force, and I knew right then if they had gone on the campus there'd be bloodshed," Cook remembers. "I knew that Mayor Davis was on the scene and I found him and told him what I thought. There were a lot of kids on campus; but again, where a lot of people blamed the rock-throwing and disturbances on the campus kids, there were some kids that were not really affiliated with the college that were doing rock- and bottle-throwing at cars. I would say the trouble on campus was just moderately serious, so I told Mayor Davis I thought if he sent his police officers in, there would be unnecessary bloodshed. I told him the crowd up there was getting smaller, and if he left them alone, it would die out."

At 12:45 A.M., while Cook conferred with the mayor, Lieutenant Magee was back at M-L-S Drugs to reconnoiter the campus.

"I'm at Lynch and Dalton at this time," Magee reported to Chief Pierce on his walkie-talkie. "You've got a crowd of about 200 to 250 around a pretty good-sized fire in the middle of Lynch Street in front of the girls' dormitory. They're just millin' around, not doin' much whoopin' and hollerin'—movin' around a little bit. Somebody apparently addressin' them and everything. They have not started to tryin' to move yet, sir."

"Lieutenant Magee, can you hear me?" Chief Pierce asked on his radio at headquarters.

"Right, ten-four, Chief."

"Take the tank and move 'em out of the street," Pierce ordered.

"It's going to take a few minutes to get the men up here and move them out," Magee said. "But we will move them out."

• •

From behind the Rose and Lynch Street barricade—three blocks from Jackson State—television and newspaper reporters were trying to make sense of the night's chaotic events on campus. They strained to hear the static-scrambled messages on the squad-car radios. They photographed the shattered window in newsman Bert Case's white news cruiser. They watched as Mayor Davis, in a dark suit, sat in his car with the door open, dragging on a Picayune cigarette and talking over his car telephone with Chief Pierce.

To find out what started the campus turmoil, the best the reporters could do was buttonhole a few students leaving the campus and walking to the roadblock. One student told a reporter there had been an argument over a bell on campus. Another said: "It's a lot of things: the war, Cambodia, the draft, the governor, Mississippi. It's not just any one thing."

Meanwhile a second student was conferring with the mayor. He was Charles Carr, who, along with his friend Martel Cook, had been trying to calm his fellow students.

> "The mayor seemed as nervous as the rest of us were," Carr recalls. "He seemed not to know exactly what would be the appropriate level of response. I think the mayor had enough common sense to know that police are trained, in this state, to control. The only way they can demonstrate control is to go in and use force. And if the students were about to play out their hostilities for an evening, why add another layer on top of that? They hadn't rushed downtown. They hadn't in mass mobs beaten and attacked anybody or anything like that. I perceived some concern from Davis. I'm not sure his concern was to make sure nothing happened to harm the students, but I think that his concern was that this thing could spill over into the rest of the city and become something much larger. Now that night he didn't come across as totally authoritarian, strictly law and order— 'Now we goin' to put a stop to this, whatever it takes!' I was impressed that at least he was talking to some folks about what was going on and why it was happening."

Lieutenant Magee intended to take Thompson's Tank on a sweep up Lynch Street. Those were his orders. But at the roadblock on Lynch Street, Magee learned the tank had gone dead on him again. Moments later, Chief Pierce radioed Magee and told him to postpone his sweep through the campus for about thirty minutes. Maybe by then the students would go to bed by themselves.

Every half hour afterwards, Magee drove back to the drugstore corner to check the campus. He saw that the crowd in front of Alexander Hall was dwindling, and so was the fire in the middle of Lynch Street. Eventually Magee told his men back at the barricade that they could relax. They took seats on the curb. They drank water and ate the sandwiches brought by volunteers. One group of National Guard officers stopped by to look the situation over. The guardsmen said more troops would soon arrive in the Jackson armory.

With the night's events apparently played out, Corris Collins, a black TV newscaster for WLBT, began preparing a news report at the Lynch Street roadblock. Like the other reporters at the scene, Collins had tried to figure out why the students and the cornerboys were raising Cain. He did his best. In a plaid shirt, he held a notebook in one hand and a microphone in the other. The camera lights flashed on, and while Collins spoke, the streetlights behind him poked through the dark over the Jackson State campus.

> In the Lynch Street area, college students and nonstudents were throwing bricks and bottles at cars that contained white people. The persons involved were believed to be dissatisfied with American policy in Vietnam and Cambodia. It was also said persons were dissatisfied with the school situation in Mississippi. One member of the black community said that he believed the problem was over and there would be no more demonstrations. Others believe the situation is not yet settled. There were about fifty law enforcement officers on hand to contain the situation in small areas. Mayor Davis arrived at the height of the demonstration and later talked with two black persons from the immediate area. This is Corris Collins, Channel 3 News, on Lynch Street.

By 2:30 A.M. all was quiet on the campus and on Lynch Street. An hour later, the patrolmen departed from the ROTC barracks and returned to their squad cars. The Jackson police remained at their roadblocks till dawn. At daybreak, the police stacked the sawhorse barricades in city trucks and returned tense and weary to headquarters. Meanwhile a sanitation crew swept up the broken glass, concrete, and charred rubble from the pavement. As the students slept, the white commuters from the suburbs drove down Lynch Street, passing the Jackson State dormitories on the way to work downtown.

4

By the Magnolia Tree

The Belgians cut off my hands in the Congo
They lynch me still in Mississippi.

—Langston Hughes

At their breakfast tables on Thursday morning, May 14, Mississippians unfolded the *Jackson Clarion-Ledger* and read the official version of the night's miniriot at Jackson State. They had to look for the story, though. It was under a front-page article about racial unrest twelve hundred miles away in a Syracuse, New York high school.

> MOB ATTACKS
> AUTOS HERE
>
> The Mississippi Highway Patrol joined Jackson police shortly before Wednesday midnight on the Jackson State College campus, in an effort to quiet rampaging students who started stoning cars and buildings about 9:30 P.M.
>
> There were unofficial reports, also, that some National Guardsmen had been alerted for possible service at the college.
>
> Shortly before midnight, also, newsmen standing at roadblocks some four blocks from the college reported "something" burning in Lynch Street in front of the college. They speculated it might be an auto.
>
> There were also rumors that students were threatening to burn a Reserve Officer Training Corps building on the campus.
>
> Police quelled them after less than an hour, forcing the students back to the campus. No early arrests were reported.

The *Ledger* added that nobody was seriously injured and the melee had been started by the cornerboys, the "college dropouts or kickouts" hanging around the campus. Riddled with errors and glorifying the role of local lawmen, the *Ledger's* story was typical of newspaper reporting in Jackson.

There were two daily newspapers in the capital: the *Clarion-Ledger* and the *Jackson Daily News*. Both were sold statewide and both were owned by the Hederman family. The *Ledger* had the highest circulation of any morning newspaper in Mississippi, while the *Daily News* had the highest of the afternoon papers. For decades, the Hederman press had shaped the unyielding segregationist ideology of white Mississippians.

According to Hederman family lore, their publishing empire began in 1894 when two teenaged brothers, Robert and Thomas Hederman, left a farm in Hillsboro, Mississippi and journeyed west by ox-wagon and train to seek their fortunes in Jackson. They were going to work for "Cousin Hi," better known as Colonel Robert Henry, who owned the *Clarion-Ledger*. From him they learned the printing and newspaper trades, and through luck and pluck, the Hederman brothers heaped up enough capital over the years to buy the *Ledger* in 1920. A half century later, their offspring inherited their wealth and influence, and a new generation of Hedermans became a power in the economic and political affairs of Mississippi. Among them, brothers Zach, Henry, and Bob, and cousin Tom Hederman held positions on five state boards, presided over the Jackson Chamber of Commerce, and chaired the board of the Magnolia State Savings Bank. They owned some of the most valuable real estate in the capital, promoted the cause of the segregationist Citizens' Council, shaped the future of the elite First Baptist Church, and used their news columns to make or break candidates for state and local offices. The Hedermans owned the largest printing company in the state and held the lucrative state contracts to go with it. They also owned two weekly newspapers, another daily paper in Hattiesburg, and a 40-percent interest in WJTV television in Jackson. Because of these and other enterprises, the Hedermans remained the chief force in the "Capitol Street Gang," the corps of banking, real estate, and political figures who ran Jackson, and to a great extent, controlled the fortunes of Mississippi.

The Hedermans' most lasting influence sprang not from their many properties or political connections, but from their monopoly of ideas in Jackson's newspapers. For better or worse, a newspaper can direct the light in which a community sees itself, obscuring or highlighting its problems and aspirations. In Greenville, for example, the Hodding Carter family had used the *Delta Democrat-Times* to improve the city's race relations—a policy that benefited its economy as well. But by reassuring whites that they were superior and by denigrating blacks day after day in print, the Hederman press had turned Jackson into fertile ground for racial conflict.

Only white was beautiful in Jackson's daily newspapers. Glancing at the front pages week after week, readers were treated to an unending succession of creamy, bosomy, swimsuit-clad beauties—Miss Mississippi, Miss Mississippi College, Miss Ross Barnett Reservoir, Queen of the Deep Sea Fishing Rodeo and even Miss Ole Miss—all of whom demonstrated the enduring superiority of undefiled white womanhood. And white was always right in the Hederman press. Its headlines attacked black activists as "civil rightists" and white liberals as "race mixers." News stories from the police blotter almost always included the race of black suspects. As for the accomplishments of blacks, there weren't many as far as the Jackson papers were concerned. Even black obituaries and wedding announcements rarely appeared in the Hederman press. The *Daily News* relegated them to a special supplement in its "no-star" editions sold in black neighborhoods.

As patriarchs of the First Baptist Church, the Hedermans were known for their uncompromising opposition to Demon Brew. Prohibition was the law in Mississippi until 1967, and that was often attributed to the Hedermans' influence. But so many of their reporters were heavy drinkers that other journalists likened their newsrooms to alcoholic wards.

> "Everybody did whatever the hell they wanted to do—everybody who worked there," Davis Smith, a cub reporter for the *Daily News* in 1970, recalls. "And we had several who stayed drunk five days a week and came in on Tuesday to get their paychecks. It was a real loose operation. Now I was enthusiastic and I wanted to work, so they were just glad to see me—'Hey, the kid wants to work! So let him work' "

Not surprisingly, local reportage was scarce in the Hederman press. Editors filled the pages with ads, wire service stories, and press releases. But there was no shortage of editorial comment. *Daily News* Editor Jimmy Ward, for example, wrote a front-page column entitled "Covering the Crossroads." He liked to keep it funny. "Did you hear about the new NAACP doll?" he once wrote. "Yep, you wind it up and it screams 'police brutality.' "

The Hedermans' editorials were just as mean-spirited. On the day after the Kent State killings, a *Daily News* editorial explained: "As was expected, the thrust by allied forces to destroy the Communists' havens in Cambodia is bringing the usual squealing from soft-headed liberals and their rock-throwing pack of peaceniks."

The Hederman's flagship newspaper, the *Clarion-Ledger,* was even more scurrilous. For example, after thousands of activists joined in the March on Washington in August 1963, the *Ledger* published a picture of littered grounds and declared: "Washington Is Clean Again With Negro Trash

Removed." By the spring of 1970, the *Ledger* had not significantly changed. It still opposed full civil rights for black Mississippians, and on the other great issue of the day, the Vietnam War, the *Ledger* was unrelentingly hawkish. After Nixon's invasion of Cambodia, the *Ledger* published a survey of readers' opinions on the issue. The headline stretched across the front page: "Drive Into Cambodia Draws Overwhelming Backing." Just four days after the Kent State killings, *Ledger* columnist Tom Ethridge sided with the guardsmen who had opened fire. He rhetorically asked his readers: "Would YOU hold still for being hit by brickbats, bottles or whatnot, cursed and spat upon—then suddenly find yourself under fire from . . . hidden snipers?"

The Hederman press had its roots in a frontier settlement that had long approved of summary justice by lynch law. Way back in June of 1919, for instance, the *Clarion-Ledger* had announced a lynching: "Negro J.H. to Be Burned by the Crowd at Ellistown This Afternoon at 5 P.M."

A half century later, on the night of May 14, 1970, the spirit of old Judge Lynch would descend upon Jackson, Mississippi.

• •

On Thursday morning, May 14, there were few signs of Wednesday night's miniriot at Jackson State. Students passing Alexander Hall on the way to class noticed the black scorch mark on the Lynch Street pavement—the only evidence of the fire there on the night before. By afternoon, city workmen had repaired the traffic light in front of Alexander Hall, and the shattered glass door to the dorm's east wing had been replaced. The Jackson State campus was quiet and class attendance normal. To avoid a stir, college officials had cancelled the campus ROTC drill scheduled for 3:00 P.M.

For President John Peoples of Jackson State, Thursday was proving an exhausting day. When the miniriot had subsided at 1:30 in the morning, President Peoples had asked students to meet him in his home on Lynch Street. About twenty-five students and one cornerboy showed up. The black youths told Peoples there was no one cause of the unrest. Cambodia, the draft, and Kent State had all contributed, they said. After the students left Peoples's home, Major General Walter G. Johnson of the Mississippi National Guard stopped by. General Johnson told Peoples that six hundred troops had been mobilized and they would be stationed nearby at the guard's armory on Raymond Road.

Peoples was not put off by the presence of a military man in his home. Though many students resented the military, President Peoples respected it. He felt the armed forces had a lot to offer black youths. An ex-Marine drill instructor, Peoples belonged to a generation of black southerners who had found a measure of dignity in the armed forces—the sort of dignity they had seldom found in small segregated towns like Starkville, Mississippi, Peoples's hometown.

John Peoples was a brown-skinned, lanky man more than six feet tall. He was forty-four and had a streak of gray through the right side of his close-cropped hair. A Jackson State student himself back in 1947, Peoples had enrolled right after his stint in the Marine Corps. He was a model student and had studied hard to become a high school math teacher. He was elected student government president and tutored other veterans.

Jacob Reddix was the college president in those postwar days when Peoples brought student grievances to the administration's attention. Peoples fought for senior-class privileges and scholarships for veteran students, for instance. And before long, that earned him the label of "persistent radical" from the dean of students, who threatened to expel him. But Peoples went on to graduate from Jackson State in 1950, and like so many other educated Mississippians, both black and white, he left the Closed Society and headed north. He taught high school math in Gary, Indiana, and by 1961 had earned his Ph.D. in education at the University of Chicago.

Three years later, and after repeated attempts to hire Peoples, President Reddix managed to lure him back to Jackson State to become his assistant. Reddix had always known Peoples was no radical, and he saw in him a capable successor. In 1967, when Reddix decided to end his twenty-seven-year tenure as president, he tapped John Peoples to become the college's sixth president. After that, Jackson State had a new and more liberal leader. A man who would resist faculty criticism and end mandatory chapel for students. A man who would manage to find money for fellowships to upgrade the Jackson State faculty, which included only a handful of Ph.D.'s.

Peoples was a progressive administrator—as progressive as the all-white State Board of Higher Education could endure. Yet by the standards of the 1960s, he was no firebrand. For example, at a time when other colleges were yielding to student demands to remove ROTC programs, Peoples proudly announced he had drawn an ROTC division to Jackson State.

"I wasn't too keen on ROTC, and the kids weren't too keen on it, and *The Gadfly* wasn't too keen on it," recalls Henry Thompson, editor of the underground newspaper by that name at Jackson State. "Dr. Peoples called me into his office and asked if I would not mess it up. . . . He told me about how we needed more black officers and all this. I said, 'What do we need this war for? Why do we need officers? Let the Caucasians tend to that war.' He seemed to think there was something proud about Negroes' making officers' status."

Hoping to find out what caused the ROTC firebombing and to prevent another incident, Peoples met with student leaders at 3:00 P.M. Thursday, May 14. Sitting at a conference room table in the student union, he talked with the students for nearly two hours. Again, the students told Peoples there was no single issue behind the trouble. There were several issues: Kent State, Cambodia, and the lack of a promised bridgewalk over Lynch Street, they told him. They complained also about the strict curfew for women and the food in the dining hall. Peoples responded that he would look into these grievances, but he could make no promises. In turn, the student leaders pledged to keep things cool after nightfall.

Immediately after his meeting with the students, Peoples addressed the college faculty. He described the previous night's miniriot and the conciliatory mood of the students he had just left. At 5:00 P.M., after the faculty meeting adjourned, a two-page letter that Peoples had written to the students was circulating through the campus. The letter blamed a "faceless, mindless mob of students and nonstudents bent on doing violence." Peoples's letter added that six hundred National Guardsmen had been mobilized in Jackson. "My understanding is that the guardsmen will be reluctant to use force," Peoples warned, "but if it is necessary to use force to protect life and property, it will be used decisively."

Fearing another incident, Peoples called Police Chief Pierce to ask that Lynch Street be closed after dark. Pierce declined. As so often in the past, white Jackson refused to give up its right of way through black Jackson.

• •

Since leaving the Lynch Street roadblock in the wee hours Thursday morning, Mayor Russell Davis had had a long and tiring day. He had attended an early-morning prayer breakfast forty miles away in Vicksburg, but by 10:00 A.M., he had returned to Jackson and driven down Lynch Street to see if there was trouble. The campus was quiet, so Mayor Davis returned to city hall for a day's work, which included videotaping a television speech on the previous night's miniriot.

At 6:00 P.M., Davis sat in front of his television set at home to watch the news about Jackson State and to see how his taped speech had turned out. Davis was pleased as he watched one news story with a report on student leaders' views at Jackson State. The students were saying just what Davis had been saying: that there was no one explosive issue and that probably the whole thing would soon blow over. As his own silver-haired image appeared on the set, Davis listened:

> This thing last night, to the best information I have been able to gather, was spontaneous and involved only a very small percentage of the students at Jackson State, which I think certainly speaks well for the student body of that school. My information is that involved at the beginning were some outsiders who threw a rock—or someone threw a rock—and then it built up and it began to look pretty serious around 9:00 or 9:30. In the process of the night, tempers cooled down and people went home and went to bed. . . . This administration has and will continue to take the position of communication and working with all the people in this city. This is my position, this is my belief, that if we're going anywheres, we're going there together. And I just feel like this thing last night could have been real serious. It was not. Everyone involved did a good job. And I hope this is the end of it.

• •

It was hot and muggy on Lynch Street. At dusk, the long shiny cars of the suburbanites and the clattering hulks of young blacks were passing by the Jackson State campus. Gunblasts rang from the commons park. Someone with a pistol in Dansby Hall was firing blanks into a long metal barrel. He was practicing the cannonade for the 1812 Overture.

It was a busy night at Jackson State. In addition to the concert, the Interfaith Choir was meeting and there would be a gymnastics exhibition, followed by a big party for the varsity basketball team in the college gym. The pledges of Omega Psi Phi fraternity were walking about the campus in silence, just as they did every Thursday night during pledge period.

While it grew dark, some students left the campus for the bars on Lynch Street to share a quart of beer among friends. Meanwhile, other students drove out to the Ross Barnett Reservoir, the man-made lake about ten miles east of the campus. Many went there to eat sandwiches, drink, and swim with their friends on warm nights.

But at Alexander Hall, female students were at their desks in their rooms, studying for final exams and typing term papers. Across the street in the library, other students were doing last-minute research or whispering in carrels with their friends. In Jones Hall dormitory nearby, the football coaches were warning athletes to stay off Lynch Street after dark. If anyone was caught raising hell, that would end his hopes of going pro.

In the ROTC buildings on the other end of the campus, security police and military officers peered out the barracks windows. Though the campus had been quiet all day, rumor had it those barracks would burn.

> "There was tension on the campus," remembers Eddie Jean McDonald Carr, a former student. "A lot of things were contributing to it: the Cambodia invasion, and a lot of people said the war in general. A lot of guys that we had known had been drafted and didn't want to go, but they had to. Some came back. Some didn't. There was a lot of tension. It was kind of humid, a weary feeling."

At about 9:30 P.M., the crash of shattering glass and the roar of gunning engines broke the calm. Beside Stewart Hall, on the same darkened knoll where trouble had begun the previous night, a crowd of about 125 students cheered on a small corps of rock-throwers. A short, fat cornerboy in a white T-shirt appeared to be the ringleader. His companions called him "Tiny," and he stood on the knoll, eyeing the traffic below for white drivers. Whenever one approached, he signalled the band of cornerboys behind him to commence firing. Each time a barrage of rocks battered their target, the cornerboy in the T-shirt capered and clapped his hands, laughing as his victims sped away.

A block east on Lynch Street, a few students in front of Alexander Hall and a few more in front of the Student Union tossed a rock now and then. But the real action was down at Stewart Hall on the darkened knoll above the traffic.

By 10:10 P.M., a city policeman in a squad car spotted the crowd throwing rocks. Immediately he radioed headquarters: "Call that security guard out there at Jackson State, and see if they can't scatter them niggers!"

At about the same time, a black man with an Afro hairdo drove up in a tan Volkswagen, parking along the curb in front of Stewart Hall. He got out of his car and looked up at the crowd on the shadowy knoll. "Hey man, did you hear that Charles Evers got shot?" he yelled. "I hear that Charles Evers has just got killed—it was him or his wife—one of them got killed."

Several students shouted back that they didn't believe him. If Evers was dead, they yelled, then why wasn't it on the radio? Someone told the man to drive down to WOKJ, the black radio station three blocks away on Lynch Street. There he could check out the facts and come back. The man promised he would. He got back into his car and drove off.

Worried that Charles Evers might have been killed, several students ran into Stewart Hall to get their portable radios. To the Jackson State kids, Evers was a hero, a successful black politician who stood up to white folks. Evers was the state's most prominent black leader—a former head of the Mississippi NAACP and brother to slain civil rights leader Medgar Evers. As mayor of Fayette, a two-hour drive south of Jackson, Charles Evers was the state's first black to run a biracial town since Reconstruction.

Evers's daughter Sheila was a student at Jackson State, so the rumor of his assassination spread quickly across the campus. Though most students did not believe the story, tensions heightened. On the knoll near Stewart Hall, the cornerboy in the white T-shirt told a crowd of students to help him firebomb the ROTC buildings across the street. He showed them the Molotov cocktails prepared for the occasion, but the students refused to join him. Moments later, three cornerboys and at least one student left the knoll and crossed Lynch Street. They scurried toward the football field nearby where two bulldozers, a backhoe, and an old Chevrolet dump truck were parked. Workmen had left them there to finish a new sewer line on Lynch Street.

Soon the drone of heavy-equipment engines rose above the campus as the backhoe and the old dump truck jerked and groped about on the darkened lot. The cornerboy in the white T-shirt steered the double-wheeled dump truck onto Lynch Street, lurching and bucking all the way. Its engine sputtering, the dump truck stalled in the street right in front of Stewart Hall. Students approached the truck as the cornerboy tried to raise the truck bed. He wanted to spill its load of dirt onto the street so the students could jump aboard and ride downtown with him to stir things up. But the mechanism was jammed.

"We are trying to help you guys!" the cornerboy in the T-shirt shouted, urging the students to join him. "You guys come help us!"

No way, the crowd of students told him. Most were content to laugh and cheer the cornerboys from the knoll beside their dorm, but the students wanted no part of going downtown.

"That's what's wrong with black people today!" the cornerboy yelled to the students on the knoll. "They don't want to do nothin'."

Taking his frustrations out on the dump truck, the cornerboy hurled two Molotovs at it, but it did not ignite. He smashed the headlights and the windshield and still nothing happened. Then he opened the hood and pumped several shots from a white-handled revolver into the engine. Again no fire. While the crowd of students on the knoll cheered, the cornerboy in the T-shirt took a flaming smudge pot from the sewer excavation site nearby and threw it into the truck. Finally, the padding of a ripped seat caught fire, and the truck's cab burst into flames. The cornerboy crouched in the street beside the dump truck, and aiming for the gas tank, he fired his pistol. But there was no explosion. As the flames spread from the cab, students on the sidewalk scattered and clambered back up the grassy banks of the knoll alongside Stewart Hall.

"Move back—it might blow!" someone yelled.

• •

Assistant Police Chief M. B. Pierce was in his headquarters office, monitoring the radio calls of his men on Lynch Street. At 11:15 P.M. Chief Pierce heard there was a fire in the street and someone was driving a backhoe near Jackson State's football field.

"If they are running that backhoe, get a crew of men and go in there and scatter them damn—those Negroes," Pierce ordered on his walkie-talkie.

"That's ten-four, Chief," Lieutenant Warren Magee replied on his radio. Magee was still in the police station. "I am trying to get the men together now."

The 11:00 P.M. shift had just arrived, and as the men gathered in the roll-call room, they were handed shotguns and eight rounds of number-one buckshot. They climbed into paddy wagons and Thompson's Tank and headed for Jackson State.

Meanwhile Chief Pierce had called the highway patrol for help. Within minutes, patrol cruisers were careening through Jackson's darkened streets toward the campus.

At about 11:25 P.M., Lieutenant Magee and his men arrived at the police barricade a block north of the New Men's Dormitory on Prentiss Street. Magee heard on his radio there had been gunfire at the college and a truck was now burning in Lynch Street. Though Magee was tired from having slept so little since the night before, he was anxious to get to the campus and clear the street. Those were his orders. But until the patrol arrived, Magee and his men could only wait in the middle of Prentiss Street. Even the officers assigned to the tank stood in the street. Inside their tank the heat was stifling, and fumes leaked from one of the tear-gas cylinders.

Soon the slamming of doors signaled the arrival of the highway patrolmen. Inspector Lloyd "Goon" Jones had come with about thirty-five men. Already they outnumbered Magee's twenty-five policemen, but Jones said still more patrolmen were coming and he asked Magee to wait for them.

"We don't have time—they're burning a truck," Magee said, looking up at Jones. The lieutenant told Jones their orders were to clear Lynch Street immediately.

The men assigned to Thompson's Tank jumped back into the armored van, while the patrol and the other policemen lined up behind it. The Jackson police were wearing blue riot helmets, most with leather chin straps and plastic face shields. The patrolmen wore their "steel pots," military helmets painted blue with M-H-P stamped in gold letters above the brim. Two of Jones's men carried Smith and Wesson nine-millimeter machine guns. They could fire seven hundred rounds per minute. Jones wore his two pistols and carried a twelve-gauge shotgun.

"We're fixin' to move out," Magee radioed headquarters. It was nearly 11:35 P.M.

The lieutenant signaled the tank to follow him as he walked south on Prentiss Street toward the Jackson State campus. Only a block up ahead were a traffic light and the drifting smoke from the burning truck near the Lynch Street corner. While Thompson's Tank and the rows of blue helmets passed the New Men's Dormitory, students on the front steps and in the windows of the seven-story dorm yelled and cursed the lawmen. To the officers, the dorm seemed a shadowy canyon of whooping, riot-crazed blacks.

At the corner, the lawmen turned east and marched up the middle of Lynch Street. Just ahead in front of Stewart Hall was the burning truck. The black shapes before the flames vanished, and Thompson's Tank halted behind the fire.

Magee ordered both the police and patrol officers to form a skirmish line along the sidewalk curb in front of the men's dorm. With one foot on the curb and one in the street, the officers faced the dorm—Jackson police to the west side of the skirmish line, and the patrol to the east. Directly above the officers were five stories of students yelling from their windows.

"Pigs!"

"Motherfuckers!"

Right behind the officers, the dump truck was a mass of flames. The men feared it would explode. At the west end of the skirmish line, where the Jackson police stood, a crowd of students was up on the grassy banks and throwing rocks at the officers. At the opposite end of the skirmish line, where the patrolmen stood, another crowd was jeering the officers from an alleyway alongside Stewart Hall. More students were shouting from the darkened knoll above the alleyway. Lieutenant Magee was pacing back and forth on the dimly lit sidewalk in front of the policemen, nervously eyeing the crowd and his men.

"Notify Chief Pierce that we are in front of the boys' dormitory—streets fairly clear," Magee reported on his walkie-talkie. "We've got about two hundred over here on the campus just to our left. The truck's burning good. Think we need a fire truck in here? Should we commit one right now?"

"Just a minute—Chief Pierce is talking on the phone to Mayor Davis," the radio dispatcher replied.

"They're chunking us out here—they're throwing rocks at us," Magee reported.

"I'll call the fire department and have them send a truck," Pierce replied, now back at his radio. "Where do you want them to meet you—at the corner of Prentiss and Lynch?"

"Ten-four, Chief," Magee said. "The fire is just about one hundred yards east of the Prentiss Street corner. We have a perimeter set up here, but we are being rocked. Should we go ahead and gas them in these dormitories, or just hold off?"

"Where do you want the fire trucks to meet you?" Pierce asked.

Magee repeated his location, and told Pierce: "Chief, they are all on the steps of these two dormitories. They are rocking us—loud profanity—but they are on the steps of the dormitory. They are not out in the campus area."

"Where is the National Guard?" Pierce asked.

"They haven't come in yet."

"I'll call the fire department and have that fire truck meet you at Prentiss and Lynch," Pierce said.

"That's ten-four," Magee replied. "They will see us here when they come in. Have you committed the guard?"

"There's two platoons, I understand, coming in to secure the ROTC building."

Meanwhile Inspector Jones radioed the patrol's Jackson headquarters to report his location. He looked about, noticing the white ROTC barracks on the lawn across the street from Stewart Hall. His men had stood guard there for nearly three hours the night before.

"Uh, we're right here in front of the—uh, I don't know what the name of this buildin' is," Jones said on his walkie-talkie, referring to Stewart Hall. "It's in the street right in front of the ROTC buildings. They's a dump truck sittin' out in the middle of the road burnin'. All these niggers around in these buildings—we 'bout forty or fifty yards from them here—not that far from some of 'em. So far, uh, one of 'em just throwed a rock. So far it's pretty quiet. They're just hollerin' and cuttin' up."

"We'll be there directly to y'all," radioed a patrol officer at a roadblock near the campus. "Can you hold that long?" he asked Jones.

"We got this good," Jones reasurred him.

"Be there at the big dump truck there?"

"We're right here in front of the ROTC buildings in the street where the truck's burnin' near the last light," Jones said.

"We'll be there in just a minute."

"Okay, everything's all right," Jones said. "Just watch it when you come down the street by that dormitory."

Moments later, Lieutenant Magee heard two shots that he thought came from the dormitory windows above.

"We're being fired upon up here!" he shouted into his walkie-talkie.

As the tank's searchlight panned the walls of Stewart Hall, Sergeants Lee and Beasley stood holding their power-scoped AR-15's, scanning the dorm's windows for a sniper. They saw none.

• •

He was a white man in a dark suitcoat and tie. He was more than six feet tall and seemed to weigh about three hundred pounds. He just walked right down the middle of Lynch Street, right by the black students in front of Alexander Hall, never taking one hand from his pants pocket, but pushing back his mussed hair with the other.

About sixty students in front of the dorm stared in wonder at this dark-suited fat man. Imagine, a white man walking right through the campus in the middle of all this.

"Whitey! Let's get him!" someone shouted.

"Leave him alone—he's all right!" someone else yelled.

A few bottles broke on the pavement around the fat man's feet and small stones struck him. But no one ran after him, so he ambled off toward the fire burning in Lynch Street a block away.

Some students thought the dark-suited man was a decoy and that harming him would draw troops into the center of the campus.

Whoever that big man was, he looked mighty calm, considering.

•

The letters on the radio station's huge white sign were black and seven feet tall and spelled W-O-K-J. It was a soul music station, and the light from its sign revealed a group of reporters mingling with police and National Guardsmen in the middle of Lynch Street. Just three blocks to the east were the winking dorm lights of Jackson State.

Facing the campus, about sixty guardsmen in green battle dress wondered when finally they would be ordered to march there.

Mayor Russell Davis also was wondering, and he wanted the troops there now. Davis was tired and losing patience. At about 11:15 P.M., Chief Pierce had called the mayor at home, awakening him to report gunfire at Jackson State. When the mayor asked Pierce whether the guard had been sent in, Pierce said no, but that the patrol and police had been.

Davis was perturbed. He dressed hurriedly and sped off to Lynch Street. Arriving at the roadblock in front of WOKJ, he noticed the guardsmen still standing and waiting in the street. He radioed Chief Pierce for an explanation.

"Mayor Davis to Chief Pierce, can you read me?"

"Go ahead, Mayor," Pierce said.

"Chief, I am with the general of the guard here at Lynch and Valley Street. He has no orders to move into the campus—he's just standing by!"

Something suddenly went wrong with the mayor's radio. He could not hear Pierce's reply. Frustrated, Davis ordered the police dispatcher to get Chief Pierce to dial the mayor's car phone. "Get Chief Pierce to call me on this telephone, will you!" Davis snapped.

Standing nearby, WJTV newsman Bert Case approached Mayor Davis and asked if the guard was going onto the campus.

"Yessir," Davis replied.

Case, reporter Jack Hobbs of WJTV, and James "Hank" Downey of the Associated Press had been standing in front of WOKJ for several minutes. They had listened to squad-car radios and watched the guard jeeps and troop carriers arrive.

Hobbs, who worked with Case, was carrying a shoulder-mount TV camera. Hobbs was a short, wiry newsman in a white jacket and dark-rimmed glasses. He was a thirty-one-year-old Chicago native, and he was looking for his friend and cameraman, Martel Cook. Earlier, Hobbs and Case had given Cook their portable light and a small camera, reasoning that since Cook was both black and a Jackson State student, he had the best chance of getting good film. But while the guardsmen were preparing to move out, Hobbs needed a light to film them. He threw the switch on his shoulder-mount TV camera anyway, and he filmed in the dark.

The white AP reporter with Hobbs and Case was their friend "Hank" Downey, a six-foot-six, twenty-five-year-old Mississippian from Hattiesburg. Downey was carrying a special walkie-talkie to radio bulletins to the AP bureau in New Orleans. On the previous night, Downey had thought he would have quite a story to call in. While at the Rose and Lynch Street barricade that night, he had seen the Jackson police lined up and ready to march onto the campus. But a confrontation had been averted Wednesday night—narrowly, Downey thought. And that was what he had written in the story he had filed in the morning. Now on Lynch Street for the second night in a row, Downey noted the guardsmen fixing their bayonets to their M-1's. He listened as an officer gave strict orders about firearms to his men.

> "This was before the guard moved into position," Downey recalls. "They were still in front of the radio station. They were very clearly instructed that they would not load their weapons until they were so instructed. Further, they would not fire their weapons until they were so instructed."

Speaking into the microphone of a portable tape recorder, Bert Case noted that it was four minutes to midnight when the guardsmen in green began marching down Lynch Street toward Jackson State. Reporters Case, Hobbs, and Downey followed.

• •

Having heard a rumor that police were seizing cameras, WJTV cameraman Martel Cook had decided to play it safe. He had left his light and camera with friends living in the Lynch Street neighborhood. Cook, both a newsman and a Jackson State student, had been walking back and forth between the neighborhood and the campus all night. Cook hoped to help keep things cool, just as he had the night before.

Walking west down Lynch Street toward the campus, Cook passed a small fire that cornerboys had set in front of the M-L-S Drugstore. When he approached Alexander Hall, a crowd of about a hundred students stood in front of the west-wing doorway. That was nothing unusual. It was almost midnight, the curfew for women, and male students had just walked their girlfriends back to the dorm. The males often stayed there for awhile after curfew, just talking with friends before turning in for the night.

Passing the women's dorm, Cook noticed another fire, this one in the middle of Lynch Street in front of Stewart Hall. With their backs to the flames, a line of blue-helmeted officers faced the men's dorm. Cook stopped on the opposite side of Lynch Street to watch as a team of firemen hosed down the burning dump truck. Suddenly gunblasts echoed from the walls of Stewart Hall. Cook noticed three or four officers with shotguns who were running in the alleyway alongside the dorm.

Cook turned around and hurried east, back up Lynch Street toward Alexander Hall.

• •

In front of Stewart Hall, Lieutenant Magee looked east up Lynch Street toward Alexander Hall. It was about midnight.

"Tell Chief Pierce we've got them back in the dormitories on this end," Magee reported on his walkie-talkie. "We still got some out in the street up here ahead of us. We've got the fire out."

Magee began assembling his officers for a sweep up Lynch Street. He had a report that a second fire was burning two blocks east, past the women's dorm. But since the street rose then dipped up ahead, he could not see it. Carrying a bullhorn and stepping in front of Thompson's Tank, Magee signaled his men to follow. As the tank rolled forward, the blue-helmeted men marched in riot step, their rifles held diagonally before them at port arms.

• •

"Here comes the National Guard!" someone shouted.

"The men in green are coming!"

In the crowd of students near Alexander Hall's west-wing doorway, some thought the approaching troops were National Guardsmen—the troops that the radio and TV stations had been referring to all day, the troops that Dr. Peoples had warned of in his letter this afternoon. The students could see an armored van in front of the approaching men. It looked white and big. On top was a rotating spotlight that knifed through the dark. But the officer in front of the van was wearing a white shirt—not green. His helmet was blue. Behind this officer and the van were other men in blue helmets and slacks. These were not National Guardsmen.

As the blue lines marched nearer, a few female students darted into their dorm's west-wing doorway. Other students began to leave.

"You niggers afraid?" a male voice bellowed. "Don't go in!"

"Keep cool! If we just stay here, they won't do anything to us!"

"Don't run—we ain't done nothin'!"

Upstairs in the dorm rooms were nearly a thousand young women, many in their pajamas and nightgowns, reading, typing, playing their radios, and fixing their hair. Some students were asleep already, some were taking showers. Others were in the dorm's telephone booths, calling home. For those unaware of the fracas a block down the street at Stewart Hall, it was just another night in Alexander Hall.

It was like that for Climmie Johnson, a freshman who was wearing a white dressing gown and sitting in the second-floor TV lounge. While other students watched television, she was reading a copy of President Peoples's letter, the one that urged students to remain calm and stay out of trouble that night.

Other dorm residents were taking a more active interest in the uproar outside. Gloria Mayhorn was one. A special education major, she was taking a break from typing a term paper when a friend burst into her room and said: "Girl, they're at it again! They're burning a truck!" In a blue sunsuit, her hair in an Afro, Mayhorn and two friends scurried to a room in the dorm's west wing. There she peered out the window toward a fire down the street in front of Stewart Hall. For a better view, she walked down the hallway and into the west-wing stairwell that faced Lynch Street.

In the stairwell doorway below, a campus security guard was coaxing the few women outside to get indoors.

Among the crowd of about 150 students near the doorway was Vernon Weakley, a sophomore. He was talking with friends and standing by the chain-link fence along the Lynch Street curb. When Thompson's Tank and the lines of blue helmets came to a stop in the street in front of him, Weakley stayed at the fence. The guns of the lawmen were just a few feet away. Behind Weakley the crowd began screaming as the officers lined up. Weakley watched a policeman in a white shirt with a megaphone. As this officer stepped in front of the other lawmen, the shrieks and curses grew louder:

"You white pigs!"

"Hey, you motherfuckers!"

"White sons-of-bitches!"

"Pigs go home! Pigs off the campus!"

• •

Near a four-foot-high brick retaining wall at the corner of Prentiss and Lynch streets, Bert Case and Jack Hobbs paused a moment. Associated Press reporter Hank Downey was nearby, and National Guardsmen had halted behind the reporters in Lynch Street. About a block up ahead in the middle of the road, Hobbs and Case could see lines of officers. Just who these officers were, the reporters did not know.

"This is a good place to stay—let's just stay right here," Case said to Hobbs, indicating the brick wall. Case was nervous. He was thinking of the rock that had crashed through his car window on the previous night. He thought also of the report of gunfire he had heard earlier on a police radio.

"You white sons-of-bitches!"

"You bastards—get out of here!"

The shouts were coming from the New Men's Dorm nearby.

"Well, I'm going where the action is," said Hobbs, who had a reputation as a daredevil. "I'll meet you—I'll pick you up on my way back."

"You're right," Case said, reluctantly joining Hobbs, who was still shouldering the TV camera.

Hobbs, Case, and Downey walked east up Lynch Street toward the uniformed men in front of Alexander Hall. The reporters felt they were entering a no-man's land where anything could happen to them. The farther they walked, the farther behind was the protection of the National Guard. And still, the lawmen up ahead in Lynch Street seemed very far away. Because he was wearing a white jacket and balancing the TV camera on his shoulders, Hobbs feared that he made an easy target.

As the three reporters arrived at Alexander Hall, they found lines of police and patrolmen facing a crowd of more than a hundred shouting students. The black youths were in front of the women's dorm on a knoll. Only a chain-link fence separated them from Lynch Street. Just behind the crowd rose the dorm's towerlike, five-story west stairwell. Inside, female students were peeking out the lighted windows. Outside, the spotlight from Thompson's Tank was scanning the dormitory windows and the jeering crowd below. The tank was parked in the middle of Lynch Street, where officers with shotguns surrounded it.

"Pigs!"

"Motherfuckers!"

"White sons-of-bitches!"

The noise was so loud that Case and Hobbs had to shout to each other in the middle of Lynch Street. Case yelled that Hobbs should duck behind the tank with him. There it was safe. But Hobbs, the camera on his shoulders, insisted on moving closer for a better view of the crowd. Reluctantly, Case agreed to follow. They walked toward the front of the tank and Case aimed the microphone of his tape recorder at the screeching crowd. Then slipping back to the rear bumper of the tank, Case and Hobbs stood near a manhole in the middle of Lynch Street. They were surrounded by officers with shotguns. Hobbs wished again that cameraman Martel Cook were here to give them some light. But Hobbs decided to film anyway. Standing with legs apart to brace the heavy camera, Hobbs aimed the whirring machine at Alexander Hall.

"Are you shooting?" Case shouted to Hobbs.

"Yah!"

Then Case saw a green bottle hurtling toward him through the air.

• •

Among the students shouting behind the chain-link fence, Vernon Weakley watched as an officer in a white shirt approached the telephone pole near the fence. Using a bullhorn, the officer tried to address the students. But a bottle arched through the air and dropped to the Lynch Street pavement. It burst like a gunshot among the officers.

"They're gonna shoot!" a student screamed.

Weakley heard an explosion. Then another. In the roar of gunfire, students ran and fell to the ground or dived into the dorm's shrubbery. Bullets thumped into the grass around them. Shrieking students jammed the west-wing doorway, and a squirming pile of bodies four feet high formed outside the door. As bullets ricocheted off the dormitory walls, the quivering pile of students was showered with chips of brick and concrete. Glass fell from the windows above. Power lines from the telephone pole burst and fell in a hail of sparks.

The officers in the street crouched, knelt or stood, firing from hip and from shoulder, emptying their guns into the crowd, the dorm windows above, and the darkness about them.

> "One thing I probably never will forget: the fear in their eyes," Vernon Weakley recalls. "When that bottle hit, they just started shooting, man. They just started shooting. At that particular point—I wasn't hit at first—I was kind of shocked. I think everybody with me already took off. When I turned around to run, I got hit—got knocked down. And I lay flat on my back and all I can recall saying was, 'Oh God—God, I'm goin' to be shot. I'm goin' to be shot.' I had already been shot, but I didn't know it at first. And then I knew my leg was burned."

In a pair of rubber beach tongs, Gloria Mayhorn padded down the stairs of the west-wing stairwell in Alexander Hall. At the glass door, she looked outside at the crowd of students facing the lines of officers. She noticed one officer with a bullhorn.

There was a flash of gunfire, and somehow she was knocked down and landed on top of bodies.

> " 'They're shooting rice,' I was thinking, but they were pellets hitting my body. They were stinging—they just had me covered," she recalls. "Then I felt a big prick—it felt like a bee sting—and I felt blood running down my arm. I looked and there was a perfect hole on one side, and the other side was blasted out. 'I'd better get out of here,' I said to myself. I started scrimmaging my way out of there and I slipped—I guess on blood. I lost my beach tongs. I was on my hands and knees at the first step in the stairwell, and then when I raised up to continue, I felt what I thought was a shot hit my head, and another singed my back. Something hit me on the right side of the back of my head. Blood was pouring like from a faucet, and I thought if I ran, it would flow faster. I looked as if I had measles from all the pellet marks. I had glass cuts in my face and shoulders. Glass was in my hair."

In the dorm's second-floor TV lounge, Climmie Johnson stopped reading when she noticed that about a dozen students rushed from the room.

She got up to see what the ruckus was about and walked to the lounge windows.

> "I couldn't see what was happening, so I thought, 'Oh, nothing's going to happen. I'm going to take off my clothes and go to bed,' " she recalls. "And about the time I made just a little turn, something popped me on the head, and I thought it was a brick. And this is just what I said—I said, 'Damn, somebody hit me with a brick!' So I got down and I felt hot and something warm was running down my face. I looked and it was blood, you know, and so it was bullets, shots still hitting up against the wall. I was in there all by myself and these little pellets were hitting all against the wall and little pieces of brick were falling everywhere. I decided I better get out of there, so I got down on my knees to crawl out."

In the hallway outside the TV lounge, Climmie Johnson was shouting, "Somebody help me! Somebody please help me!" Students were running and screaming through the hallway. When a couple stopped to look at her bloodied face, they fainted.

• •

"We need some ambulances," radioed Sergeant Truitt Beasley. He was one of two marksmen on the police antisniper team.

"Where do you need them?" asked the dispatcher, who could hear screams coming through on Beasley's radio.

"The girls' dormitory on Lynch Street."

"Ten-four," the dispatcher said. "How many do you need?"

"You better send all that you can get," Beasley answered.

Unaware that Beasley had just called for help, Lieutenant Magee radioed headquarters: "You'd better get some ambulances up here to the girls' dormitory on Lynch Street."

"We've got them all in route that they've got," the dispatcher said.

"You'd better get an ambulance in here!" Magee repeated.

Lawmen stooped in the street, picked up their shells and stuffed their pockets. Inspector Lloyd "Goon" Jones was checking the dark, motionless forms on the lawn in front of Alexander Hall. City police joined in the search for the wounded, pointing them out to male students. The black youths picked up their wounded friends and laid them on the lawn near the sidewalk so ambulances could reach them more quickly. As he lay on the ground, Vernon Weakley watched the officers looking for bodies.

> "It seemed like they were directing traffic or something, telling folks: 'There's some over here—go check them out over there.' That type of thing, telling them to check people out to see if they were dead or whatever. Do this—do that. 'You niggers over there, go check behind those bushes. There's a nigger over in them bushes—check him out.' "

By a small magnolia tree in front of Alexander Hall, Inspector Jones found a young man's body. The face was bloodied and he seemed not to breathe. Near the dining hall across the street, Jones found another body in a pool of blood. Again it was a young man.

At 12:11 A.M., Jones radioed patrol headquarters to report the shootings: "All right, we've 'bout had it at one of these buildings. We've got several injured. None of the police are injured, but several of the students are injured. We come up to one of these buildings, tryin' to get 'em on the inside, and they threw rocks and bricks and bottles at us here and somebody opened firin'. We got some injured here. . . . We gonna try to get 'em outta here. . . . The best I can tell ya, ya got two dead and about five wounded."

"Advise who the subjects are that are ten-seven," the patrol dispatcher said. In radio code, ten-seven means "out of service."

"They're nigger students," Jones replied.

In the middle of Lynch Street, police and patrolmen were mingling with newsmen Case, Hobbs, and Downey. Even the officers assigned to Thompson's Tank were out on the street and talking. Inspector Jones questioned Case and Hobbs, and at 12:26 A.M., Jones radioed patrol headquarters again, this time to explain why his men had opened fire. Jones reported they had been caught in a crossfire from snipers in two women's dormitories.

"Okay, this man that totes the camera for Bert Case—he saw the first shot come out of the dormitory and come out past him," Jones reported. "We got his name. . . . His name is Jack Hobbs. He carried the camera. We got bombarded from both sides with bricks and bottles and then a shot come out of a girls' dormitory. Almost got this bottle. And that's when everybody opened up. . . . From the south side of the street there was some sniper fire comin' out of another girls' dormitory."

"A total of six injured there?" the patrol dispatcher asked Jones.

"No, we got two more males, they say," Jones replied. "Just a minute. I hear somethin'. . . . I think there are about three more nigger males there: one of 'em shot in the arm, one in the leg and one of 'em somewheres else. They ain't hurt all that bad. . . . There were two nigger gals—two more nigger gals from over there shot in the arm, I believe. One of 'em is over there in the east end. Well, that's a total of ten then: two nigger females, three males we just discovered. That's a total of ten injured. Ten-four."

Police and patrolmen told college security guards to search Alexander Hall for a sniper. The guards, stepping over a blood puddle in the west-wing doorway, headed up the bullet-riddled stairwell. In the halls upstairs they found blood-spattered floors. Women emerged from under their beds, screaming and crying. The guards looked, but found no sniper. Instead, they saw students using towels to wash blood from their friends' arms and legs. An announcement came over the dorm's loudspeakers: all men were to leave the dorm and bring the wounded downstairs to the lobby. Ambulances would be waiting.

In the glass-strewn lobby, windows had been shot out and blood streaked the floor. Women were screaming as the wounded were carried outside on stretchers.

In front of the dorm on Lynch Street, male students cursed the arriving ambulance attendants, who were white. The students grabbed their stretchers and said that no whites would carry their wounded. They warned one driver he had just better hurry to the hospital.

At 12:50 A.M., a team of National Guard medics and a doctor arrived at the dormitory. A hysterical student had swallowed her tongue and was choking to death. The doctor quickly inserted a tube down her throat, enabling her to breathe. He saved her life.

At about 1:00 A.M., National Guard troops with bayoneted M-1 rifles marched to Alexander Hall. They relieved the city police and patrolmen, who walked back down Lynch Street toward Stewart Hall. The Jackson police stood at the Prentiss and Lynch Street corner, while Inspector Jones and his men returned to their squad cars. At 1:06 A.M., Jones made his final report to patrol headquarters: "Okay, we sent our men back to the cars. Magee is stationed with plenty of police at the one end. The guard's gonna pull back on both ends of the street. They're still some nigger males in the nigger female dormitory. And they've asked them to leave so they can go back to their dormitories."

"Ten-four."

Lieutenant Magee returned to police headquarters with his men. He immediately ordered Sergeants Lee and Beasley to gather the men in the roll-call room. Magee wanted to know whether any police officer had opened fire on the women's dorm. Lee and Beasley confronted each man sitting in the room by asking for all eight rounds of ammunition that had been issued at roll call. Every policeman returned eight rounds, indicating he had not fired.

• •

Four miles north of the Jackson State campus, the emergency room lobby of the University Medical Center was crowded and noisy. It was packed with reporters, doctors, nurses, and policemen, as well as wounded students and their friends. The injured held bandages to their wounds as they sat in chairs or lay on gurneys while awaiting treatment. Ambulance attendants had passed through with two males on stretchers. They were dead. Two more were in critical condition. Ten other black youths awaited treatment, including four female students suffering from hysteria. One of them was four months pregnant.

All the known wounded were at the Medical Center, since one ambulance driver had been turned away from the Baptist Hospital, which was a mile closer to the campus. The hospital had declined to admit the black youths, stating there was no room tonight.

When WJTV reporters Jack Hobbs and Bert Case entered the University Medical Center's lobby, Hobbs carried the TV camera on his shoulders. Though ordered by officials to turn off the camera, Hobbs continued to film the wounded students, leaving his switch on, but removing his eye from the viewfinder so as not to appear to be filming. Nearby, Gloria Mayhorn lay on a gurney, her head bandaged. She watched the newsman with the camera.

> "I was lying in the lobby of the emergency room when a door opened and a man holding a camera came in," she recalls. "I realized the filming might have been live, so I covered my face. But he [the reporter] got me anyway. It was a long time before the doctors got to me. I think they even forgot me. It seemed like an hour or so. My head stopped bleeding, but my arm still bled. The doctors were kind of nasty at first. I didn't get treated until some newsman said, 'Somebody help this girl.' They completely ignored me until the cameraman started asking me questions."

Other students complained they were not being treated. But what made them even angrier was the attitude of the hospital staff. Leroy Kenter, a sophomore, lay with a leg bone protruding from his flesh. Kenter resented the white man attending to the wound.

"This guy says, 'I'll bet you won't be out there messing around no more, would you?' " Kenter remembers. "Then I told him, 'I weren't out there messing around, man'—just like that. That's when the nurse come in and I was telling her that I was hurt. And she says, 'Well, you won't be hurting long.' That's when she gave me a shot, and that was it. I blacked out."

Stella Spinks had been waiting in the emergency room lobby for nearly an hour. Hot ricocheting buckshot fragments had burned through her clothes and into the flesh of her legs, arms, and back.

"When I was finally waited on, there was blood [already] all over the examining table," Spinks remembers. "It was covered with the kind of paper they put on them, so I asked the guy there, 'Can't you take the paper with the blood on it off the table?' He said, 'Well, get up there!' Finally he took it off, but he did it as if he didn't want to. A person in a white smock who was treating me—I don't know if he was an orderly, an intern or a doctor—I think he was an intern—started asking me questions about the shooting. I told him what happened and another doctor—maybe an intern—said: 'Well, that's your opinion!' "

Meanwhile newsmen questioned a Medical Center spokeswoman. She declined to make a statement, but the reporters persisted. Standing among the reporters was Reverend Ken Dean, a white minister and activist who listened as the spokeswoman talked to the reporters.

"She said she didn't understand why there was such a fuss," Reverend Dean recalls. "So a reporter said, 'It's our information that several students were killed or wounded up at Jackson State.' She said, 'That's not our information, and it's not uncommon for students to come into our emergency room from Jackson State. We've got three women students who are in near-hysterical or some emotional state and our suspicion is they're either pregnant or miscarrying. But we have that sort of thing from up there all the time. And I do think we have one student from over there suffering from a flesh wound in the leg. I don't know how it came about.'

"The import of her statement was, 'Business as usual—what y'all doin' over here?' It was a 'No—never!' A typical Old-South denial of the seriousness of the situation by bringing up sexual mores."

• •

Back at Jackson State, nearly all students who lived on campus had gathered on the dimly lit lawn in front of Alexander Hall. They were told that President Peoples would address them.

Many moved through the weeping crowd, searching for friends to make sure they were all right. Others were shouting there should be a march downtown to show they would never submit to the white pigs. But the students who opposed the march yelled that the National Guard had sealed both ends of Lynch Street. A move off the campus would mean only more bloodshed.

In the glow of the dorm lights, a male student addressed the sobbing crowd on the lawn. He was Gene Young, a former civil rights worker called "Jughead." He was known for his imitations of Martin Luther King, Jr. and his "I Have a Dream" speech, which he knew verbatim. Some students had asked him to perform it now, to soothe the crowd. So he tried.

> I have a dream that one day even the State of Mississippi, a state sweltering with the heat of injustice, sweltering with the heat of oppression, will be transformed into an oasis of freedom and justice.

But the crying continued, and when President Peoples arrived in the yard, he was startled. He smelled gunpowder and blood. The sight of all the broken windows and the crying students sickened him. And all the talk of a march downtown scared him. Peoples turned to a student for suggestions.

"Jughead, help me," Peoples said. "How can I calm them down?"

"Doc, why don't you pray?"

So they brought President Peoples a table from the dorm and he lifted his tall, thin frame upon it. The students knelt and bowed their heads as he said a prayer. "There's been a slaughter tonight," he told them, and he asked the students to go back to their dorms so there would be no more killing. But their grumbles told him there was no way the students would leave.

"We ain't goin' in, Doc," Jughead yelled. "Every sister, get with a brother—all of you—come out from the dorm and bring some blankets!"

After Peoples left to call local hospitals, the students sat on the lawn under the dark sky. They prayed and sang freedom songs—the same songs they had learned as youngsters in the civil rights marches and church rallies of the early 1960s.

> Ain' gonna let nobody turn me 'round,
> Turn me 'round, turn me 'round.
> Ain' gonna let nobody turn me 'round,
> I'm gonna keep on walkin', keep on talkin'
> And marchin' up to Freedom Land.

They stayed there all night on the lawn, sobbing and singing, just waiting for the sun to rise.

5

JACKTWO

The government's work is always conspicuous for excellence, solidity, thoroughness, neatness. The government does its work well in the first place, and then takes care of it.

—**Mark Twain**

At dawn on Friday, May 15, the students dozing on blankets in front of Alexander Hall began to stir. Rubbing their eyes and folding their grass-stained blankets, they arose for their first daylight glimpse at the destruction on their campus.

It was a damp and misty dawn, sixty degrees, as the black students stood on the lawn and stared at the dormitory walls. It was true. It had really happened. It was not just a nightmare.

The students saw their dorm's brick walls were stippled by buckshot. The windows were shattered in the first-floor lobby. As they walked toward the Lynch Street sidewalk, they passed a bloodstain in the grass beside a small magnolia tree. From the sidewalk, they stared at the towerlike, five-story stairwell of the west wing. It looked like the target of an infantry assault. Two six-foot-tall windows—one on the second and one on the fourth floor—had been blown out by gunblasts. The drapes, shredded by gunfire, flapped in the morning breeze. The steel panels under the windows had been hit so many times they looked like blue-green Swiss cheese. Bullet holes in the dorm's concrete walls were bigger than silver dollars.

> "It wasn't till that morning in the sunlight that I looked at that building," recalls Stella Spinks, one of the wounded students. "The dorm was all shot up. I didn't think it could be that bad. Then I realized they came here to kill all of us. It was God's blessing that more us weren't hurt, because they came to kill."

On the morning after the shootings, two students peer from a shattered window in the west stairwell of Alexander Hall. Lawmen said a sniper had fired from the stairwell. (Associated Press)

Students moved about the campus, inspecting the damage. Someone found bullet holes in a window at Ayer Hall, the women's dorm next door to the dining hall. Two blocks down Lynch Street at Stewart Hall, there were more bullet holes in windows. The highway patrol had fired into a room on the fourth floor. Students photographed the holes in this and other campus buildings, and they gathered the bullet shells and wads of spent buckshot that officers had left along the Lynch Street curb. The students wanted the evidence because they expected a coverup. They had seen lawmen stuffing their pockets with their used shells the night before.

Later in the morning, President Peoples met with the students to discuss the killings. School was closing, President Peoples told them. Everyone must go home. There would be no final exams. But Peoples said these shootings would not go unavenged.

• •

In the city council chambers of Jackson City Hall, Mayor Russell Davis stood at a lectern to speak to reporters. Behind the mayor on the wall was a portrait of Andrew Jackson, Indian-slayer and seventh president of the United States—the namesake of this city.

Mayor Davis's silver hair was mussed, and he looked shaken and on the edge of tears. He wore a gray suit and spoke in a nasal, quavering voice. "We are trying to assemble the full story about what occurred at Jackson State College early this morning," Davis said, facing the reporters and TV cameras before him. "The facts, regardless of what they show, will record a dark day in the history of this city."

What happened at Jackson State was a tragedy he had never believed possible, Davis said. "It has occurred in spite of my most sincere belief that it would never happen in our city. It has occurred despite an honest effort to prevent its happening. I was wrong in thinking that it couldn't happen." Referring to the recent killings at Kent State, Davis added: "Events of recent weeks in our nation, including this one Friday morning, should point out that whenever people resort to the streets for whatever cause, and armed men are sent into the area to restore order, that disaster such as we have suffered is likely to explode."

Davis concluded: "This is the darkest day of my life."

In times like these, Mississippians had learned to expect racebaiting and demagoguery from their leaders. But that is not what Mayor Russell Davis had given them. However, Governor John Bell Williams's rhetoric was more in line with the public's expectations. Williams released a statement that he "regretted" the campus slayings, but he warned that "such force as may be necessary" would be used against "the Pied Pipers of hatred and insurrection" if there were any more trouble.

Meanwhile, the Hederman press was busy developing its version of the campus slayings. Relying chiefly on police sources, it played down the shootings by the lawmen and emphasized the misconduct of students. In fact, Friday morning's *Clarion-Ledger* never even mentioned that students may have been shot:

> VAST FORCE MOVED
> INTO J-STATE AREA
>
> Ambulances Rolling
> As Shots Reported
>
> Shots rang out on the Jackson State College campus shortly after Thursday midnight, and a police department spokesman said ambulances were on their way to the scene. A resident said there was "a whale of a lot" of shooting at the college, where rioting broke out earlier.
>
> It was the second night in a row for campus disorder, and officers openly feared it would get worse before morning.
>
> Students were reported to have taken over heavy construction equipment inside a barricaded zone, amid reports they might try to burn or otherwise destroy a Reserve Officer Training Corps building on the campus.
>
> National Guardsmen were standing by on the perimeter of the 30-block barricaded area, and highway patrolmen were assisting in attempts to quell the disorder.
>
> A radio newsman who toured the area just before it was closed off said "all hell has busted loose."

The *Ledger* speculated that "girl students" had played a role in both nights of unrest at the college. Though it was hard to justify firing hundreds of rounds into a women's dormitory, the *Clarion-Ledger* had done its best.

By late morning, the presses were rolling off the first copies of the *Jackson Daily News,* which set the central theme for the local reports to follow: sniper fire.

> DORM WINDOW SNIPER
> BLAMED IN SHOOTING
>
> Two Dead, 8 Hurt
> In Police Fusillade

> Sniper fire from a fourth-floor window of a girls' dormitory at Jackson State College here resulted in the shooting deaths of the male students when law enforcement officers returned fire at the building and a crowd of demonstrators who were gathered in front of it early today, police said.
>
> Eight other students were wounded by the volley of automatic rifle fire and a non-student is in critical condition at University Hospital.
>
> Two city policemen and a highway patrolman were injured by flying bricks, but none of the approximately 100 officers who moved in to subdue the violence received bullet wounds.

The *Daily News* story included the fact that the two dead students were Phillip L. Gibbs, 21, of Ripley, Mississippi and James Earl Green, "age and hometown unknown."

• •

At Alexander Hall just before noon, female students were lugging trunks and suitcases to their parents' cars parked on Lynch Street. Though the college was to close at 5:00 P.M., a crowd of male students was milling about at the women's dorm to talk to newspaper, television, and wire service reporters. President Peoples had warned the students not to talk to the press, but the students talked anyway. They hoped to get a federal investigation of the shootings by publicizing their side of the story.

As the students led the newsmen into Alexander Hall's blood-stained stairwell, the reporters noted the stairwell lamps had been shot out and gunfire had pierced a heavy steel handrail. There were bullet holes in the stairwell's walls and ceilings and in the wooden doors leading to the dorm's hallways.

The students told the reporters the trouble had begun when lines of city police and highway patrolmen had stopped in front of Alexander Hall. An officer in a white shirt and carrying a megaphone had said: "Ladies and gentlemen." He then lowered his right hand to signal the firing, the students claimed. They guessed the gunblasts went on for five or ten minutes. After the shooting stopped, the officers just picked up their empty shells and ignored the wounded. The officers kept calling them "niggers." It was all "pre-planned," the students told the reporters. It was all "pre-planned."

The black students were eager to tell their story to journalists, but not to all of them. Once they had learned that reporter Davis Smith worked for

The view from a west stairwell window in Alexander Hall where students had ducked bullets on the night of the shootings. (Associated Press)

the *Jackson Daily News,* they pinned him against the wall outside the Student Union. Indoors in the lobby, an angry crowd of students surrounded newsman Jack Hobbs of WJTV. Hobbs had the misfortune to be there when a TV set blared out an inaccurate report that he had seen a campus sniper. But Hobbs was freed from the students by Charles Evers, who had not been assassinated as rumored on the previous night.

> "One student just kind of turned and said, 'That's him! That's the guy who said there was a sniper!' " Hobbs recalls. "And all of a sudden I was sort of in a sea of black students. Very hostile. They jostled me around, got up in my face—very antagonistic. One grabbed me from behind and punched me. The more they talked, the more they worked themselves up. Then Charles Evers materialized—big ol' Charlie, and that big ol' body got between me and all this mess and said: 'Hey, Jack's okay. You let him go!' "

• •

It was just before noon at Millsaps College, a predominantly white campus two miles north of Jackson State. About 150 students gathered on the commons lawn under an oak tree to protest the slayings at Jackson State the night before. The Millsaps students, most of them white, wore black armbands and talked of going downtown to picket the Governor's Mansion. Only the week before, just sixty students and professors had gathered to lower the campus flag to protest the Kent State shootings. Now that the killing had spread to their own college town, the number of Millsaps protesters more than doubled.

But some professors feared for their students' safety, so about a dozen joined the students' quiet, mile-long march on State Street to the Governor's Mansion downtown.

> "At that time, the dress was rather sleazy: girls usually wore faded blue jeans, their hair uncurled," recalls Charles Sallis, a Millsaps history professor and native Mississippian. "Well, that morning I was shocked. The girls had on dresses and high heels, and remember this, it was a long way downtown. High heels, skirts, make-up. They looked terrific. And if there's something that really bugs a white Mississippi male, it's to see a white Mississippi female involved in some liberal cause like that. See, the girls understood that, and they were going to look their prettiest. So we marched downtown, and I never will forget, I was at the end of the line, and there was this guy who drove by in a car that had a Madison County tag. You could tell he was just absolutely upset. He drove by our line one time, and he came back again. You could just see him seething inside, he was shaking his head so. All he could do as he passed right in front of me was to give the students the finger. It's all he could do. I'm sure that he was so outraged that these pretty Mississippi white girls were protesting the killing of black people."

Two students led the Millsaps march. Each carried a wooden cross: one labelled "Phillip Gibbs," the other "James E. Green." As they marched quietly up the hilly street on the sidewalk, they passed the Baptist Hospital that had turned away wounded black students the night before. They passed the First Baptist and First Presbyterian churches, which were like most white churches in Jackson—segregated. A policeman on a motorcycle pulled up alongside the students, but they marched on as he followed. At the corner near the Old Capitol, the Millsaps students turned west and marched down the Capitol Street hill toward the Governor's Mansion. Near the mansion, a group of black students from Tougaloo College joined the march as plainclothesmen with cameras snapped their pictures. With clubs and shotguns, fifty highway patrolmen stood in the shade in front of the mansion. They stared at the students filing quietly by.

Later that day, several of Millsaps's benefactors threatened to cancel contributions to the college. They were angry about the protest at the Governor's Mansion. Nevertheless, the white students at Millsaps had opened the door to the Closed Society a little wider.

• •

At 4:00 P.M., a half hour after the Millsaps march had ended, Jackson State students and leaders of Mississippi's NAACP held a press conference at the Masonic Temple on Lynch Street. The purpose was to call for an impartial investigation and to dispute reports of campus snipers.

On a motorcycle, a Jackson policeman follows Millsaps College students as they march down the Capitol Street hill toward the Governor's Mansion on the morning after the killings. (*The Kudzu*)

Sitting at the table facing the TV cameras and reporters were three black men: Mayor Charles Evers of Fayette, a Jackson State student named Gregory Antoine, and NAACP Field Secretary Alex Waites. A gray-haired, light-skinned man, Waites was the first to speak. In a firm and angry voice, he made a brief opening statement to the reporters: "The actions of the highway patrol, and other officers if so involved, constitutes murder," Waites said. "The bullet holes in the girls' dormitory show a deliberate pattern to the violence. All floors of the building were fired upon, with a concentration upon a ground-floor doorway where fleeing students were trying to enter. Students were shot both inside and outside the building. We cannot find justification for the shooting of fleeing students, regardless of the supposed provocation."

Waites said the fusillade showed "the highway patrol's hatred against black people." There was no evidence that anyone had seen a sniper, he said, noting that officers had used no tear gas. Waites said he had no faith in an investigation controlled by "the white power structure" and called for a special biracial investigating committee.

"Do you have any questions?" Waites asked the reporters.

"Where were you?" one reporter asked, nodding toward Gregory Antoine, the black student in a short-sleeved shirt who sat between Waites and Evers.

"Where was I? Amongst the patrolmen," Antoine answered.

A pre-med student, Antoine had been doing research at Just Science Hall on the previous night when the campus violence had erupted. Hearing a commotion, Antoine had stepped outside the building and watched a cornerboy firing a pistol at a dump truck. The truck was in Lynch Street in front of Stewart Hall dormitory. Soon police and patrolmen were marching up the street and standing in a line between the blaze and the dorm. Students were jeering the officers, so Antoine crossed the street to help quiet the noisy crowd. With a bullhorn from a policeman, Antoine pleaded with the students to get away from the dorm's windows and stop hollering. The students called him an "Uncle Tom."

"A dust pan was thrown out one of the dorm windows," Antoine told the reporters, continuing his story. "And some officer said, 'Get ready!' Somebody threw a jug out a window, and then they fired a shot as they creeped up into the alley beside the dorm."

"Who was that?" a reporter asked.

"It was the Mississippi highway patrolmen, three of them creeping up beside Stewart Hall, the men's dormitory," Antoine replied. "And someone said to somebody—I don't know who it was—'If they stick their heads out of the windows, shoot 'em.' "

Antoine told the reporters he had walked alongside the lawmen as they had marched up Lynch Street to Alexander Hall. Antoine said he had heard no sniper shots before the officers' barrage at the women's dorm.

"Somebody is saying they heard gunshots there first? Well, I didn't hear anything, and I hear excellently," Antoine said. "And next thing I knew, the sky was lit up. They just opened fire. They busted down some of the telephone wires and they shot out one of the streetlights, and they continued firing, just kept opening up, round after round. Kids were screaming and some of them were falling down. After they stopped firing, first thing they did—while one girl was hollering for help—first thing they did was to reach down and pick up their shells that fell out of their guns and put them in their pockets."

Antoine told of "this big, fat patrolman," the leader who radioed for ambulances by saying, "We got some niggers dyin'." While this big patrolman searched the campus for the wounded, he kept calling them "niggers," Antoine said.

"Did they all fire at once?" a reporter asked.

"It was all at once, simultaneously," Antoine replied.

"All the highway patrolmen were firing?"

"The highway patrol and the Jackson Police Department opened fire all at once," Antoine said.

"Jackson police?"

Antoine nodded and said: "Jackson policemen."

Now it was Charles Evers's turn to speak to the reporters.

"Police shot my folks down—it was simple as that," Evers said. "We don't have to explain nothin'. It is obvious that they shot the building up. It is obvious that there are two dead blacks. And it is obvious there ain't nothin' been done about those that have been killed here in the past."

Evers said that if Jackson State had been a white campus, not a single bullet would have been fired. "In Mississippi, not a single one," he said. "Therefore, we say we have racism and hatred here. And we're sick and tired of it. If the mayor and the governor can't control their own policemen, they ought to be tried for malfeasance. They can't run their offices."

Evers singled out Patrol Inspector Lloyd "Goon" Jones. "In particular, I want Jones to be arrested and held for either murder or conspiring to murder. For he is the man—I keep saying this—who is always on the scene. He's the one who called us 'niggers.' "

In New York City at 6:29 P.M., Eastern time, Walter Cronkite sat at his desk facing a CBS television camera. He was shuffling his Friday night news script. The news was not good: more campus killings, more student demonstrations and military bases cancelling Armed Forces Day programs across the nation. Earlier in the day, former Chief Justice Earl Warren had told the NAACP the nation was going through its worst crisis "within the memory of living Americans." As millions of viewers tuned in to the *CBS Evening News,* they saw a map of the Deep South behind Cronkite. Written across Mississippi were the words "Jackson State."

Cronkite began with this story: "Good evening. The turmoil on the nation's campuses has brought death to two more young people. They died and nine companions were wounded in a burst of police gunfire last night at Jackson State College in Mississippi. Police said that snipers fired first, but students at the predominantly black college deny it. Dell Vaughn reports with film by station WJTV."

The network cut to a scene of almost total darkness: the underexposed film that newsman Jack Hobbs had shot on the previous night at Alexander Hall. Viewers could hear a shouting crowd and make out what looked like a spotlight on the wall of a building. Those who recognized the dorm could see the lighted doorway to its west stairwell. Suddenly there was the roar of weapons and white streaks of gunfire crossed the darkened screen. The barrage thundered on for nearly a half minute. Then the voice of CBS correspondent Dell Vaughn intoned:

> There was no clear explanation for the shootings or the two nights of rock-throwing that preceded them. Students say only they were confused and tension had built up over the draft, the war and violence on other campuses.

Film clips of a National Guard tank lumbering onto the campus, a sign exhorting students to protest the Cambodia invasion, hair curlers lying in a puddle of blood, and black students with luggage leaving campus for home—these images told the story of Jackson State in Mississippi.

> The college is closed, and some students are leaving. President John Peoples promised without explanation the deaths would be avenged. Dell Vaughn, CBS News, Jackson.

As the people of Jackson watched their TV sets, journalists from the nation's major news organizations were heading for Mississippi to cover the campus killings. This time the killings of blacks in Mississippi would not be judged as just another local misunderstanding. Jackson had given the South its own Kent State, and it was becoming one of the major news stories of this turbulent year.

• •

"I ain't gonna sign nothin'!" a Jackson policeman told about a dozen fellow officers huddling in the hallway of Jackson City Hall.

Standing nearby and watching the police was a group of reporters, including one from the *New York Times* and one from the *Washington Post*. To the journalists, the policemen seemed angry and defensive.

It was about 8:00 A.M. on Saturday, May 16, 1970. The officers, just off the night shift, had been ordered to report to city hall. They were there to face questioning about what had happened two nights before at Jackson State. Five of the police, however, said they would not talk.

The friction between the police and city hall arose after Mayor Davis had appointed a biracial committee only hours before to investigate the shootings. Among the committee members Davis had chosen were two black civil rights attorneys. This biracial investigating committee was unprecedented in Jackson, and city police were anything but pleased. Disgruntled officers told the mayor his biracial investigation was just an attempt to do them in before a grand jury could convene. But Davis reassured the officers, explaining the committee had no legal powers and that probably they would not have to take an oath. Several officers agreed to testify.

At 9:00 A.M., the mayor's biracial committee met in the second-floor conference room in city hall. It was a bright but barren room at the top of the winding staircase above the mayor's office. The wide windows looked out on the magnolia trees in bloom on the lawn outdoors.

The five attorneys on the committee sat at a long conference table to face each witness. Three of the attorneys were white: John Kuykendall, the white-haired co-chairman; William Pyle, a young, heavy-set man; and Francis Bowling, an established, middle-aged attorney. The young black attorneys were Fred Banks and co-chairman Reuben Anderson.

The mayor's biracial committee was charged with interviewing major witnesses behind closed doors and issuing a report to Mayor Davis within just ten days. That meant hard work under deadline pressure, as well as brief but careful questioning of only the most crucial witnesses. None would be highway patrolmen. They had refused to cooperate with either the city's or the FBI's investigation. Their refusal had the support of Governor John Bell Williams.

To complete the city's investigation, the mayor's committee wanted answers to two key questions: had there been campus snipers, and had city police opened fire at Jackson State? The committee decided to question the police first. They began with the officer in command at Jackson State.

• •

Police Lieutenant Warren Magee, the man in charge of both the patrol and the police at Jackson State, entered the sun-filled room and took a seat facing the conference table. Magee told the committee that on Thursday night the officers had been drawn to the campus by reports of a burning dump truck on Lynch Street. The officers had formed a skirmish line between the blazing truck and Stewart Hall, a men's dorm.

"Were any of your men hit?" Magee was asked.

"Yes sir," he replied, his voice taped by a recorder on the conference table.

"With what objects?"

"Rocks, stones," Magee said, adding that twice while at Stewart Hall he had heard gunshots. But Magee had been standing with the policemen at the west end of the skirmish line. From that position, Magee had not been able to see into the alleyway beside Stewart Hall, where the patrol had fired into the men's dormitory.

"I reported to headquarters that we were receiving fire, we were being snipered at," Magee testified. "I reported that we were being stoned, being cursed."

Magee said a college security guard had lent him a battery-powered bullhorn that he had used to order the students back into their dormitories. A male student, Gregory Antoine, also had used this bullhorn to help disperse the students.

"What did they do?"

"They began to move back," Magee said.

Magee had called for firemen, who promptly put out the fire in the dump truck. The National Guard then moved into position at Stewart Hall, Magee said, so the police and patrol marched east up Lynch Street behind Thompson's Tank. A crowd of shouting students had gathered about two blocks up ahead in front of a women's dormitory.

To indicate his position at the dorm, Magee drew a staple-shaped diagram of Alexander Hall (see figure 1). He pointed out that the tank had halted in front of the crowd at the dorm's west wing. He labelled the west-wing doorway "A," the tank "D," the ranks of the patrol "HP," and the lines of city police "JP." Magee marked as "M" the spot near the curb and the telephone pole where he stood facing the jeering crowd. He said rocks were lobbed into the street.

"Several" of his men were hit, Magee testified, "and, uh, I was hit in the area of—well, several of them hit my helmet and I could hear them hitting all around. I was fortunate I didn't get injured. . . . I was in the act of asking these people to move with the bullhorn, and the next thing I knew was the volley of fire."

"Technically, who did the firing?" Magee was asked.

"The firing came from our rear, sir."

"Did any of your men do any firing?"

"I did not see any of my men firing," Magee said.

The committee asked Lieutenant Magee, the officer closest to the crowd of students, if he had heard shots from anywhere other than right behind him, where his men had stood. Magee said no, but maybe that was due to his helmet and the echo from the bullhorn. Magee told the committee he

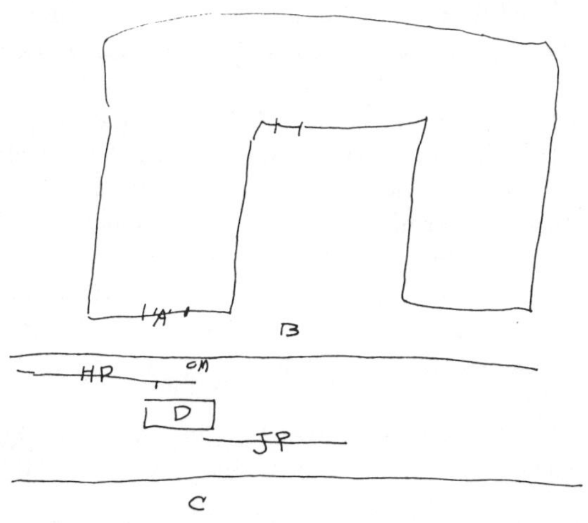

Figure 1. Facsimile of Police Lieutenant Warren Magee's sketch of the shooting scene.

had been stunned by the gunblasts behind him: "As I say, the first thing I heard was the explosion of the volleys of fire from my—well around me—coming over my head, was what I heard. I immediately was just like anybody else. I flinched, I ducked back and realized what was happening. I could see the glass come. I could see the people falling, and when I did realize what was happening, I immediately turned with the megaphone and began to order a cease fire."

"Did you hear any order to fire prior to this?"

"I did not hear an order to fire, and I did not give an order to fire."

"No one under your command?"

"One of the highway patrol officers told me that we had been fired upon, that's what."

"Do you remember his name, who he was?"

"Inspector Jones," Magee answered. "I asked him if he gave orders to fire. He said he did not, that we had been fired upon."

•

The next officer called upstairs to the conference room was Charles Little, a city policeman assigned to Thompson's Tank. Officer Little walked into the room accompanied by two attorneys, Edward Holderfield and Charles Wright. The three sat facing the conference table.

Officer Little told the committee there had been two snipers at Jackson State: one on the north side of the Lynch Street campus and another on the south.

Little said he had been in the tank with eight other men. He sat right behind the driver in the van's first row of seats. The motor was running, the police radio was on, and men were talking and walking about in the tank. As the tank pulled up in front of Alexander Hall that night, Little said, he looked out the tiny window to his left and saw bricks and bottles flying. A cursing crowd of nearly four hundred students were in front of the dorm, he said, and several officers outside were hit by missiles. Little said that one man inside the tank had all but uncapped a tear-gas cannister to launch it at the dorm if ordered.

Little said he had spotted "a colored male" in a stairwell window in Alexander Hall. "There were several students in front of him," Little testified. "He pushed them out of the way. He had a pistol in his hand. He busted a pane out with the butt of the pistol, stuck the weapon down almost point blank at the men on the ground, and fired. He fired once and I—they have portholes on the side of the tank—I tried to yell at one of the patrolmen standing beside it that the man had a gun. Evidently they had already seen him."

A second sniper appeared, Little said. "Then one of the officers inside on the right side of the tank yelled, 'There is another somebody shooting from one of the other buildings on the south side of the street.' He said it appeared to be a rifle, judging from the blaze from the end of the gun."

"Could you tell us what officer that was?" Little was asked.

"I—I do not—I don't know, sir. It was—all I know is he yelled it. I don't know as to which one it was. It could have been either one of the five on that side. I don't know how many rounds the student fired, but I do know that he stuck the gun out and fired it. Then is when the return fire started and mass confusion started."

After the shooting stopped, the police got out of Thompson's Tank. Little noticed TV newsmen Bert Case and Jack Hobbs. "One of the reporters, I don't know which one, physically threw his TV camera and went under the tank," Little said. "And the only thing I heard him say when he came back out was that they had almost gotten him. They were definitely close on us."

"Did you see officers firing?" Little was asked.

"No sir. I didn't."

•

Police Sergeant Charles Lee, a squad leader, was called next to testify. Officer Lee had been on the department's two-man sniper team at Jackson State. That night he had carried an AR-15 rifle and a walkie-talkie while standing in the skirmish line in front of the men's dorm, Stewart Hall. Lee's job was to watch the windows above for sniper fire. Like Lieutenant Magee, Lee was standing with the other policemen near the west end of the line—the end opposite that of the highway patrolmen. And like Magee, Lee had heard gunfire at the men's dorm, but he had seen no sniper.

"We had been there just a very short time—hardly got placed good—when you could hear occasionally what sounded like a gunshot," Lee recalled. "I never did see anybody shoot. I didn't never see them, but it sounded like gunshots."

Lee testified that after only a few minutes at Stewart Hall, the lawmen followed Thompson's Tank east up Lynch Street to Alexander Hall. The tank halted in the street facing east, while the police lined up toward the front of it. To the rear of the tank was the patrol. Bricks were flying all around him in the street, Lee said, and one man, Officer Claude Gholson, staggered after he was struck by a rock.

Sergeant Lee was asked if he had seen gunblasts before the officers began shooting. Lee said no. "I heard some—I did not see any. No sir," Lee said. "I never could pick out any flashes or anything to tell me right where it was coming from. Then all of a sudden, all of a sudden, all of this other gunfire broke out. I never did give my men the command to fire."

"Did any of your men fire?"

"I'll say this, I never saw any of my men fire. . . . Now I couldn't sit here and swear that none of them did or didn't shoot, because like I said, I was watching these buildings more than I was watching my men. I say this, I did not fire. I can tell you that. I was out there two nights and I have not fired. I hadn't even come close to firing, you know."

"Did you hear the cease fire order?"

"Well, I even hollered one time myself, because I hadn't ordered anybody to fire."

"Did the firing catch you by surprise?"

"It did," Lee said. "It startled me."

"Did you see anything or any act that might have triggered this round of firing, anything that in your opinion might have caused the shots to be fired?"

"I don't know what started it," Lee said. "I really don't. I wish I did, because quick as it ceased, I asked several men. I said, 'Who gave the command to fire? Who gave the command to fire?' I went around and nobody said anybody did, you know."

"Did you ask each of your men whether or not they had fired?"

"I did," Lee said.

Lee told the committee he asked every one of his men for the eight buckshot shells they had been issued earlier at headquarters. That is, Lee asked every many except those assigned to Thompson's Tank.

"But see, the tank men—we hadn't issued them any, because their equipment is in the tank," Lee said. When Lee asked his other men for their eight rounds, each officer returned exactly eight rounds.

"I went by each man's chair and said, 'Show me your shells,' " Lee testified. "I was going to see how many shells they were missing. And I checked them, and I would put a little—if he wasn't short any—I would put an aught down. And I went all the way around, and I didn't find a man short. Every man showed me eight shells."

•

The other member of the sniper team, Police Sergeant Truitt Beasley, mounted the winding staircase and entered the conference room. Beasley confirmed the major elements of Sergeant Lee's testimony. Beasley said that he too thought he had heard gunfire down at the men's dormitory, Stewart Hall. And like Lee, Sergeant Beasley said that, nevertheless, he had seen no sniper there. Nor had he seen a sniper at Alexander Hall.

Beasley told the committee that while in front of the women's dorm, he had been looking south into the shadowy park across the street. At that moment, Sergeant Lee had been looking in the opposite direction, toward Alexander Hall. Like Beasley, a line of highway patrolmen also had faced the park, he said. That was the side of the street where James Green was killed in front of the dining hall. Beasley said he had seen no sniper fire from this direction.

"Did you observe any student getting actually hit, or see anybody fall?" Beasley was asked.

"I did not," he replied. But Beasley had noticed one youth—it was James Green—on a stretcher near the dining hall. "I didn't examine that body, but the man there appeared to be dead."

•

Having questioned key police witnesses, the mayor's biracial committee turned its attention to the reports that police had written on the night of the killings. Attorney Francis Bowling flipped through the reports, highlighting them for the rest of the committee.

Bowling told the committee that Lieutenant Magee's written report was essentially the same as the testimony he had just given. However, Bowling noted that Magee's written report included a statement that Jack Hobbs and Bert Case of WJTV had seen sniper fire from a fourth-floor window in Alexander Hall.

"Then he describes the wounds to Gibbs, Phillip L. Gibbs, twenty-one years old, Ripley, Mississippi, a student at Jackson State," Bowling said, surveying the sheaf of papers before him. "A bullet hit Gibbs just about the lower edge of the left eye and came out about one inch in front of the left ear. He was also hit under the left armpit." The other dead black youth was "James Earl Green, 17, a student at Jim Hill High School," Bowling added. Green, who lived two blocks from Jackson State, had been walking home after work that evening. He had been hit by a slug three inches below the nipple of his right breast.

Though a complete accounting for all the wounded was not ready, Bowling listed the injuries to eight students and one nonstudent whom police had questioned. Leroy Kenter, a male student, was hit by one slug in the left leg and listed as fair. Fonzie Coleman, in critical condition Friday, was shot in the leg. He was now in fair condition. Redd Wilson, in fair condition, was hit in the upper leg. Lonzie Thompson, fair, shot in the thigh. The slug could not be removed. Bowling concluded the list of five wounded males with the name of a thirty-year-old nonstudent, Willie Lee Woodward, who remained in critical condition, shot in the left chest. His lung had collapsed.

All of the wounded women were listed in good condition: Andrea Reese, hit in the right arm by a slug; Stella Spinks, struck in the arm and back by ricocheting bullet fragments; Climmie Johnson, hit by a buckshot slug penetrating her scalp over the right eye and exiting an inch and half to the rear of the slug's entrance. Gloria Mayhorn was hit in the head and back by ricocheting buckshot, and her right shoulder was pierced by a buckshot pellet.

Four more women were treated for hysteria: Eddie Jean McDonald, Marion Buchanan, Carol Marie Bingham, and Gladys Dinkins.

After reviewing these reports, the committee decided to end the questioning of police witnesses. The committee had questioned five city policemen, three of them the top-ranked officers at the scene. Not one of the three officers in charge had seen sniper fire. Only two policemen had made that claim: Officers Charles Little and Joseph David Griffith, who also testified before the committee. At the time of the barrage, both Little and Griffith had been inside Thompson's Tank.

After the morning's session ended, the committee members drove to Jackson State to examine the bullet-scarred campus. It was quiet. FBI agents were at the college, conducting their own investigation. The agents collected slugs embedded in the walls, ceilings, and doors of college buildings. They photographed the blood stains where the wounded had fallen. They even examined the angles of the bullet holes in the dorm's steel panels to learn exactly where the officers had stood while firing.

FBI Director J. Edgar Hoover had sent extra agents to Jackson to conduct this investigation. He did this at the request of President Nixon's attorney general, John Mitchell, who would soon visit Jackson State. Meanwhile, the FBI's Jackson office had developed a code word for their investigation of the Jackson State slayings. It was a code word that hunters could appreciate for its special irony. It was "Jacktwo."

6

YOKNAPATAWPHA IN BLACK

When a feller has to start killin' folks, he 'most always has to keep on killin' 'em. And when he does, he's already dead hisself.

—William Faulkner, Sartoris

Both front doors of the tiny red-brick church were open. In their Sunday best, the crowd of black churchgoers stretched from the shadows indoors, down the concrete steps outside, and onto the wide sunlit lawn of St. Paul's Methodist Church. It was Sunday in the village of Ripley, Mississippi, but the people were not here for the Sabbath. They were here to pay their respects to Phillip Gibbs, the student shot three days before at Jackson State College, two hundred miles south of Ripley. Nearly a thousand mourners had come, crowding the pews and lining the aisles. Those who arrived last had to stand outside the church and strain for a glimpse of the ceremony. They could hear the organ music as the choir began to sing:

Fair are the meadows,
Fairer the woodlands,
Robed in flow'rs of blooming spring;
Jesus is fairer,
Jesus is purer,
He makes our sorrowing spirit sing.

After the service, a group of young black men in suits and ties emerged from the church with the coffin of Phillip Gibbs. Grim-faced, they scuffed down the steps and crossed the lawn to the hearse. Cars lined the winding roadway in front of the church, and the drivers followed the hearse as it moved slowly through the quiet, tree-shaded streets of Ripley. The procession would end just a mile away in the town's black burial ground.

Blacks could not recall the last time so many had turned out for a funeral here. Phillip Gibbs's hometown lay in peaceful country less than forty miles south of the Tennessee border. It was a land of rolling green hills and roadsides covered with kudzu vines. The cotton fields were dusted by Piper Cubs that swooped from the sky and rose to the sun, leaving their mist over long green rows.

Only about thirty-five hundred people lived in Ripley, and nearly 20 percent of them were black. Everybody knew everybody and neighbors in pickup trucks tooted their horns and waved when you passed, even if you were a stranger. The dusty village square had a drugstore, a florist's shop, a theater, and a cafe. The focal point of the square was the red-brick courthouse of Tippah County. Old men in faded overalls sat in its shade all day, just talking and whittling away at pieces of wood. In the afternoon, farmers pulled up in their pickup trucks and lowered their tailgates to sell okra, cucumbers, tomatoes, and squash.

People came to Ripley's town square from Tennessee and across Mississippi on the first Monday of each month—bargain days for buying farm equipment, dry goods, and even land. That was what Phillip Gibbs's hometown was famous for—"First Monday." That, and the Falkners. For this was Falkner country, inspiration for the fictional Yoknapatawpha County. The great novelist's family had taken root in Ripley, and here its patriarch, Confederate Colonel William C. Falkner, had started his plantation and his railroad. In the village square one day, he was gunned down by a rival.

A century later, in 1970, old scores were still settled with the gun in Mississippi.

• •

Who was Phillip Gibbs?

One view was summed up in a front-page headline in the *Jackson Clarion-Ledger*: "J-State Victim 'Drunk.' " Citing a coroner's report, the *Ledger* emphasized that Gibbs had a .27 percent alcohol content in his blood on the night he had died at Jackson State. The *Ledger* reported Gibbs had been "very drunk."

The *New York Times*, however, depicted Gibbs in a more positive light. A *Times* story headlined, "Slain Youths Lacked Time for 'Politics,' " said that Gibbs had not been the type to get involved in protests. Like James Green, the other youth killed at the college, Gibbs had been too busy

Phillip Lafayette Gibbs.

"working or studying and . . . had little time to be militant." The *Times* described Gibbs as a quiet young married man with an eleven-month-old son, and as merely an "onlooker" to the civil rights ferment in his hometown during the 1960s.

But Phillip Gibbs's story was far more complicated than either the *Times* or the *Ledger* had indicated. Though the *Times* proved more charitable than the *Ledger,* neither newspaper gave an accurate impression of young Gibbs.

Phillip Lafayette Gibbs was born on September 1, 1948 to Ozell and Louise Gibbs. The son of a sharecropper and an elementary school teacher, Phillip was raised in Ripley with a brother and two sisters until he was three years old. Then in 1951 the Gibbs family left Mississippi for the Midwest. They were part of the great black tide that for decades had swept north from the segregated South. Only about a year after leaving Mississippi, Phillip's parents were separated. While his father settled and worked as a laborer in Davenport, Iowa, Phillip lived with his mother and the other children in Milwaukee. But in 1962 when Phillip was thirteen, the Gibbs children returned to Mississippi to live with grandparents in Ripley. The children were orphans, for both their mother and father had recently died after long illnesses.

Phillip grew to dislike Mississippi. The schools were segregated and black boys were taught never to touch a white girl. They were warned that if you even looked at one the wrong way, the whites might cut off your penis. Folks still talked about Emmett Till, the black fourteen-year-old who was fished out of a river in Money, Mississippi back in 1955. Some said that young Till had talked fresh to a white woman. Phillip told friends in Ripley that it had been different up in Milwaukee. In grade school he used to sit right next to a white girl, and on winter mornings they pulled each other's boots off.

Few things squared with the way Phillip thought they should be in Ripley. At the Kream Kup dairy bar, for instance, blacks had to order at the window. They could not sit with the whites inside. The same went for Renfrow's Cafe on the village square. Blacks could enter by the back door only, and had to eat in the kitchen. Across the street at the courthouse there were toilets and drinking fountains set aside for whites only. For blacks, swimming in the town pool was banned, and to see a movie in the Dixie Theater they had to sit in the balcony. Black boys in Ripley were brought up to say, "Yes, Cap'n" or "Yes, sir" whenever they spoke to white men. They learned at an early age there was no sense in getting yourself killed by fighting every white man who called you "nigger."

Phillip resented the whites who lived by these codes, but he rejected the views of his grandparents as well. They were strict disciplinarians who reminded him that he was "colored," that he should "stay back and be black."

> "Our grandparents taught us to say 'yes, ma'am,' and 'no, ma'am,' and 'yes, sir,' and 'no, sir' to whites," Phillip's oldest sister Nerene recalls. "But it wasn't in me, and it wasn't in Phillip either. Maybe it was because of our Milwaukee upbringing. I remember that my grandmother didn't want me to work as a maid for white people in town, because she was afraid I wouldn't know how to act. Now Phillip—he believed in equal rights, and that just sums it up. He wanted that for everyone."

At fifteen, Phillip Gibbs got the chance to do something about the injustices he saw in Ripley. It was 1964, the year of "Freedom Summer," when black activists joined hundreds of northern white students to fight segregation in Mississippi. After nightriders had burned the Antioch Baptist Church, Phillip and his friends worked with white students rebuilding the church. And when the activists planned a campaign to end segregation in Ripley, Phillip joined them.

"Phillip was never one short of bravery," recalls Roland Colom, a Ripley native who was Phillip's roommate at Jackson State. "One thing I remember about Phillip was that he was one of the first blacks to integrate a place in Ripley called Renfrow's Cafe. I remember that I wouldn't have walked into the place for $550,000 during that time. I remember that if anybody black would go in there, it was two people that I knew: my brother Wilbur, or Phillip. At that place they [the customers] hated black folks, and they didn't let it be any secret about what they would do to you. Even though I don't believe they ever did anything, except maybe burn churches and things like that. But they would let you know from the start: 'If you come up here, you put your life in the hands of God.' "

Not only did Phillip and his activist friends integrate Renfrow's Cafe, but one day they jumped into the town swimming pool, ignoring the whites who scurried from the water and yelled until police arrived to pluck the black youths from the pool. Phillip and his friends also staged a sit-in at the Kream Kup, and still another at the Dixie Theater.

"Phillip and I and a couple of other friends went to the movie theater," recalls Wilbur Colom, the brother of Phillip's college roommate. "We went downstairs and we sat down, and white people threw popcorn and soda at us as we tried to watch the movie. Because he was a Yankee, Phillip had a greater tendency to strike back than most of us. He couldn't stand the insults and the abuse in the movie theater. That really hurt. At the time, I thought that was about it for Phillip. If you lived in the South and were born seeing black people picking cotton and washing floors and getting off sidewalks so white people could pass—these injustices wouldn't seem unusual. But Phillip was a Yankee. He wasn't used to it. I remember he was boiling constantly. Once we were getting everybody in line to march single file up to the courthouse and Phillip said, 'To hell with this and all the organizing and stay-in-single-line stuff! If they want to arrest us, to hell with it! Let them arrest us.' Phillip was impatient with the whole process of sit-ins and passive resistance."

In the mid-1960s, Mississippi extended "Freedom of Choice" to black students who wished to attend the white public schools. The blacks who took advantage of that plan, of course, did so at their own hazard. So, like most black students in Ripley, Phillip Gibbs remained in a black school. At the Line Street Consolidated School he was a member of the varsity basketball team and a favorite with the girls. Slim and about five-feet-ten, Phillip was a handsome boy with a square jaw and coffee-colored skin. He was popular with both students and teachers.

> "He was a good student," recalls F. L. Spight, Phillip's principal and a distant relative. "Science at first was his main interest, but social studies kind of swayed him away from that. He read all the political things. Phillip wasn't angry, but he was concerned about the ways of life for blacks. He didn't just want to be assigned something—he was always hunting for something to read. And all the girls went wild over him. He could get whatever girl he wanted to. He had a face as pretty as a girl's. He was the type—always a leader in school, without teachers and others telling him what to do."

At the Line Street School, Phillip learned racial pride. He learned to sing "The Negro National Anthem" at the school, where Black History Week was observed each year. Phillip's teachers often discussed Richard Wright, Mississippi's great black novelist, and William Faulkner (who added a "u" to the family name), born just twenty miles south of Ripley in New Albany. Every schoolchild in town—black or white—had heard the tale of the white novelist's great-grandfather, Colonel William C. Falkner, who settled in Ripley during the 1840s. The colonel had slaves, a two-thousand-acre plantation, and a law office on the village square. He organized and led the "Magnolia Guards" to fight for the Confederacy and built the railroad linking northern Mississippi to Memphis, Tennessee.

Though Colonel Falkner wrote poetry and novels, he was no reclusive man of letters. Twice he killed a man in a scuffle. On election day in 1889, while campaigning for the state legislature in Ripley's town square, the colonel came face to face with an old rival: the town's wealthiest citizen, R. J. Thurmond. Apparently thinking that Falkner was reaching for a gun, Thurmond shot Falkner in the face. The colonel won the election that day, but he lost his life.

More than a thousand mourners showed up for Falkner's funeral in Ripley. In the town's cemetery for whites, they laid him in a vault of brick that held him above the yellow Mississippi clay. A pretentious white statue of the colonel—two stories high and made of marble—was later placed beside his grave.

More than Falkner lore, the importance of religion was stamped into the mind of young Phillip Gibbs. On Sundays he attended services at St. Paul's Methodist Church and sang in the choir led by high school principal F. L.

Spight. Phillip loved sacred music and found in Christianity the conviction that all people were equal.

> "It was kind of strange: even though Phil was no angel, he mentioned God to me almost daily," remembers Roland Colom, Phillip's college roommate. "That's something I always admired about him. He did have Christian beliefs. He believed in the Divine Creator and he believed there's got to be a better way. He sang spiritual music—he was singing it all the time, even though he could not sing a drop. We'd always talk about church. I remember Phillip once said, 'The God I believe in would not let his children believe that they are masters over the blacks.' He said, 'You know what the white people would do to us if you or I tried to get into their church? They would throw us out—you know that's what they would do.' He said none of the people going to those churches would ever see God's face. Their god was Satan. He couldn't understand why white people acted like white people."

While Phillip was a high school senior and living with his married sister Nerene, he began dating Dale Adams, a sophomore at Falkner High School. She was tall, light-skinned, and slim. She attended the white school under Mississippi's token "Freedom of Choice" plan. That plan did not guarantee she would be happy there. On opening day at Falkner High, only a handful of black students had entered the school with Dale. They were escorted by FBI agents. White students shouted "niggers" at the black students, and Dale could never forget what one white boy told her that day: "The government might have put your black ass down here, but it's not gonna keep me off your back!" Dale decided to return the next year to the Line Street School, the black school where she had met Phillip Gibbs.

Phillip first showed interest in Dale while she was still dating his friend, Roland Colom. Phillip could see that relationship was in trouble, so he decided to make a move.

"Hey, I'm coming to your house," he told Dale.

"No you're not," she said.

Dale was shocked when Phillip showed up at the front door of her family's white wood-frame house on Terry Street.

"You know why I came to your house that first day?" Phillip asked her afterwards.

"No, why?"

" 'Cause you said I couldn't," he answered, grinning.

But in the fall of 1967, Phillip left his sweetheart in Ripley to go to Jackson State College. Hoping to become a lawyer, Phillip decided to major in political science.

"He was full of life, but he had serious moments," his oldest sister Nerene remembers. "He had big dreams. He had a goal in life and that was to be somebody. What I mean by that: not just go to high school, get married, have a family, and go to work in a factory. That wasn't it. He wanted to be something. Like I told you—Roland and Wilbur Colom and all—they were all buddies of his. Roland wanted to be a dentist. Now, from Ripley, he is the only black dentist that I know. And Wilbur is an attorney. They wanted to do something, and be someone."

But free and away from home for the first time, Phillip failed to buckle down and meet the challenge of college studies. Though he dreamed of becoming a successful lawyer and leaving Mississippi forever, he lacked self-discipline.

"He was on and off probation at school more than one or two times," recalls Roland Colom. "He had the ability, but he never had the concentration. He just never had it. He would go in spurts. He would study hard, like I don't know what. I mean, he would spend hours on hours studying during the end of the semester. But I guess everybody gets into it then."

During the fall of 1968, Phillip learned that Dale, seventeen at the time, was pregnant. Phillip was twenty and still clung to his dream of becoming a lawyer. Though he had little money, he decided to marry Dale and try to remain in college. Since the death of his parents he had received Social Security checks, so he would try to stretch that money and wages from a part-time job to support his family.

Just before Thanksgiving vacation in his sophomore year, Phillip wrote Dale that he was determined to support her and their child.

Nov. 10, 1968

Dear Dale,

"Everything wouldn't be so bad if I
knew for certain that you are ready
for this."

—Dale Adams

For the truth, I don't know if I am ready or not, but that is not the problem. I am not ready to take on the responsibility of a baby and a wife. I don't have the money to keep you and the baby up, but I am willing to go ragged and hungry trying. Dale when I was home I told you how I felt. I love you more since you have the baby than ever before. I can't express myself with a pen well enough to let you know how I feel about you and the baby. It's true that I am afraid, but I think that I have the courage to see this through, just remember that (*I love you*).

I am sending you this money order so we will have some money when I come home thanksgiving. If you need some money, take it. . . . I don't like my job, but I will put up with it for the baby's benefit.

I didn't have the money to come home last weekend. You know I have to save my money.

Just remember I love you!

Bye Love.

Dale and Phillip married during his Thanksgiving vacation. For several months after Phillip, Jr., was born, they lived in a small, eighty-dollars-a-month apartment in Jackson. But it was impossible for Phillip to attend college, support the family, and keep his 1964 Chevy on the road—all on his Social Security checks and earnings from his part-time job. Sometimes the refrigerator was empty, and all he and Dale had to eat for dinner was popcorn. Eventually they admitted that living together as husband and wife while Phillip remained a student could not work. So Dale returned to Ripley to live with her parents, while Phillip stayed at Jackson State. On weekends he drove home to live with Dale and her family, but that, too, was not easy. Ever since Dale's father had learned she was pregnant, he had had few kind words for Phillip Gibbs.

The weekend commuting solved few problems. Dale worked part time as a teacher's aide, yet they were poor. In Phillip's junior year at Jackson State, he often talked of going to law school, but to make ends meet he considered entering the Air Force. He was opposed to the Vietnam War, and he mistrusted the military establishment. Still, he needed a way to support his family.

Phillip discussed money and entering the Air Force in a letter he wrote to Dale the week after Christmas vacation. He wrote in a hasty scrawl:

Jan. 6, 1970

Dear Dale,

How is my little ole man? Have he been sick or had an bad cold. Last sunday I did not want to come back to school because I wanted to stay with you and my little wooly headed baby. Dale have you been feeling well? I've been thinking about you being sick during the Xmas holidays, but I can only say that Xmas will be here in an another year and I hope and believe that we will have an enjoyable Xmas then.

Did you go to work Monday? I have figured out a way how I will be able to eat during the week after the 12th when my meal card runs out. You can send me a box of food with can goods and things like that to eat.

I have been trying to get me a job in the school lunch room. If I do we may be able to meet some of our many bills becaus I know that you are getting tired of working and not being able to get anything for your self.

I really don't want to go to the air force but I want you and my man to be staying with me. If the air force offer me an apartment I will be willing to accepted an enlistment.

. . . I love you and my little man. And dont let him get cold at night, let him sleep with you.

Phillip

Living nearly two hundred miles apart was enough of a strain on Phillip and Dale's relationship, but his interest in other women complicated the situation. In the spring of 1970, Phillip was living in an off-campus apartment and dating other students. Sometimes he double-dated with one of his roommates, Roland Colom. Like Phillip, Roland was also from Ripley and married to a young woman back home.

"There was something about Phillip and women," Roland Colom recalls. "He loved them all—ugly, fat, short. He loved all women and all women were crazy about him. He used to tell me, 'If there's any weakness I've got, it's women.' He loved his wife and his family and all this, but he would admit to this weakness for women. I wasn't that much different from him. I didn't drink as much—I couldn't stand a can of beer at all—but I liked women. I liked having a good time."

By May of 1970, Phillip Gibbs's personal affairs were in a desperate tangle, and he looked in vain for a way out. He faced the prospect of having to support yet another child, since he had impregnated a Jackson State student. Furthermore, his draft board had classified him 1-A, which made him eligible for a stint in Vietnam. Perhaps Phillip was reclassified because his grades had not been good. Roland scolded him sometimes for ignoring his studies and reading instead a book about the Black Panthers or some other radical subject. Roland told Phillip to read books for his political science classes, and to forget the left-wing propaganda. But Phillip ignored the warnings, and as the spring term drew to a close, he became increasingly worried about his grades.

Phillip began acting in ways that mystified friends. He often wrote poetry or stared silently into space. On the week before final exams, he asked a life insurance salesman to stop at the roach-infested, one-room apartment he shared with Roland and two other roommates. It was on Pearl Street right behind the Jackson State campus and had a few stools, one big bed, and a couch with springs that poked through the upholstery.

On Tuesday afternoon, May 12, 1970, a white insurance agent walked into the dreary apartment. He said he worked for State Life Insurance Company of Indianapolis, Indiana. Looking around the room, the insurance agent could see there had been some drinking going on. Wine bottles were strewn about and one student lay drunk on the bed in a corner. But the salesman sat down at the kitchen table anyway and tried to sell life insurance to Phillip and Roland.

> "The guy was from Booneville, Mississippi, a white guy," Colom remembers. "I think the insurance premiums were something like five-hundred-and-some-odd-dollars a year. You just started paying after you finished college. And I said to Phillip, 'Well five hundred dollars is like a million dollars to me.' I think it was a forty-thousand-dollar double-indemnity policy. And Phillip said, 'I believe I will take that policy,' so the guy wrote him up. I thought this guy was a crook. He looked kind of shiftless. I could just look at him and tell that, because there was this big sales pitch, and Phillip was just biting for it. Later I remember asking Phillip, 'Man, what's wrong with you? You're acting kind of funny around him. You're doing funny things.' Because he was sitting and staring off by himself. That wasn't him, to just sit and look. So I figured there were some money problems, or something wrong at home, because he didn't have any real family. I don't know. But he said, 'There's nothing wrong. It's all right. It's all right.' "

Death had been the subject of a talk Phillip had had with Dale just the previous weekend in Ripley. They had been sitting on the porch of Dale's parents' house while Phillip had played with his "Man," his "milky-mouthed baby," as he called Phillip, Jr.

> "He had Phillip, Jr. at the time, who couldn't walk, and he was trying to teach him," Dale Gibbs recalls. "He just worshiped the kid. And Big Phillip loved this little outfit—that's why I put it on the baby—he had on red pants with a little elephant on the front and little white shoes and little white socks. Big Phillip said, 'Oh my little Man is looking cute

today.' And he said, 'When I die, don't keep me out of the ground too long. Light-skinned people turn dark if you keep them out too long.' Now Phillip was a fair-skinned black man, and he said: 'I want to look just like I look now.' "

At night on Tuesday, the same day that Phillip had signed the life insurance contract, he and Roland drove to Alexander Hall. They were picking up their dates: Diane Royce and Janine Johnston (not their real names). The four were to go swimming at the Ross Barnett Reservoir, a man-made lake about ten miles east of Jackson State. The two couples double-dated from time to time. It was nothing serious, since both men were married and usually staying with their wives on weekends. But while in Jackson, Phillip and Roland sometimes brought their dates to the reservoir for a moonlight swim. Often they brought a picnic of sandwiches and beer. Other students also liked to go to the reservoir for a beer and a swim on a warm spring night. But for Phillip Gibbs, that Tuesday evening was no normal night at the reservoir.

"When we went swimming, there was a place in the reservoir where we would go—it was real wide, about three hundred yards," Roland Colom recalls. "Well, Phillip asked one girl, 'Would you believe I can swim across this thing—over and back?' So I said, 'Man, don't be playin' no jokes.' He could swim, but he couldn't swim that good. So he ran and jumped in the water and started swimming out and got about halfway there, and I could tell he was giving out. He kept going. So I hollered, 'Git to the other side and stay!' He went all the way over to the other side and could just barely pull himself out. Then he turned around, jumped in again, and started back. He got halfway across that reservoir, and I knew that he was gone. I mean, I just knew it, because he kept going under and would come back up. I started out to the water to go and see if I could get him, and he kept coming just a little bit closer. I said to myself, 'Well, I'm going to stay back from him and see what he does.' He did come out. But to me, that incident was just a sign that something was wrong, man. He didn't do things like that."

The next night, Wednesday, a "miniriot" erupted at Jackson State. Phillip and Roland watched some of the rock-throwing on Lynch Street. They could see it as they stood near the water tower on the hill behind their apartment on Pearl Street.

"Let's go over there and watch and see what's going on," Roland said.

"No, I'm staying away from that," Phillip replied. "I'm not even going over there."

Instead, they headed for Alexander Hall to visit Diane and Janine. The two couples left the campus together, but they returned a little while later to sit and talk in the lobby of the women's dorm. Roland watched as Phillip talked to his youngest sister, Mary, also a Jackson State student. She lived in Alexander Hall.

Before the dorm's midnight curfew, Phillip and Roland said goodnight to their dates and left. They walked east toward the Lynch Street bar strip and stopped at the Penguin for a hot dog. Afterwards they went home and to bed.

"I personally don't think there was anything raunchy going on between Phillip and Diane," Roland Colom says. "Diane and Janine were just nice people to us. It was real fun. I was just as wild as anyone at that time. I was not an angel or anything. But it never did, between Janine and me, come to a sexual thing. Phillip never did say there was anything deep going on between him and Diane. We spent a lot of time with them, okay? We'd go out to the reservoir together. We were just having a really good time. There was nothing like an orgy going on. If we could have got one going on, we would have tried it, but they weren't too interested in it. They were just killing time. We would often pick at each other and say, 'Why are we fooling around with these women?' Because they were nothing special. Janine was fair, and Diane was below average. We used to say, 'Why are we fooling with these two and spending our little nickels we have on these women?' Now Phillip was not the kind of guy to hide his conquests. We talked all the time about things like that, and I just can't remember him ever saying anything serious about Diane. And I know about Janine—I got zero with her."

At the spur of the moment the next day, Thursday, May 14, Roland decided to go home to Ripley. He had heard a rumor that classes were cancelled because of the miniriot.

"Hey, how about let's going home?" he said to Phillip in the apartment.

"No," Phillip replied, adding that he had classes.

"Well, we're not having no classes," Roland told him.

"I'll probably come home Friday," Phillip said.

"But, you know, we can go home together. Come on and go now," Roland urged him.

"No, wait so we can go together on Friday."

"No, I can't wait," Roland said. Again he thought that Phillip was acting strangely.

> "That really surprised me," Colom recalls. "Any time you talked about going to Ripley to him—zip—we were gone. But he was more studious then than I had ever known him to be. I mean, he was really concerned. That was one of the reasons why he didn't go home—one of the reasons he gave me—because he wanted to study. He was afraid that he was going to fail."

After Roland left Jackson alone, Phillip telephoned Dale in Ripley. He told her he had a class and some studying to do, so he could not make the trip home with his roommate. Things were getting bad at the college, with all the rock-throwing and the trouble at the ROTC barracks, but Phillip reassured Dale that late the next night he would be home.

Yet instead of cracking the books that Thursday afternoon, Phillip joined friends who drove out to the reservoir for a picnic. They played football and later went to the Psychedelic Shack on Lynch Street for a few beers. Afterwards, Phillip drove to Alexander Hall to pick up Diane Royce. She could see he had been drinking, though he didn't seem stumbling drunk. Friends said that Phillip had a knack for looking sober while under the influence.

After leaving Alexander Hall, Phillip drove Diane around Jackson for awhile. They parked on Lynch Street and went into the Psychedelic Shack. They drank and talked with friends. Then they left and Phillip drove back to the campus.

> "Phillip was a very fine, understanding person," Diane Royce remembers. "He was a very respectable person. He was nice when he was with me—a gentleman—just a nice person. I was only a friend, someone he could talk to. I think he was lonely and needed someone to talk with, but he never really confided in me. He never told me intimate details about his personal life."

As Phillip drove east on Lynch Street, he saw a police roadblock in the glow of the WOKJ radio sign just ahead. He stopped. The policeman told him to park and walk if he had to get back to the campus, so Phillip left his car in a gas station lot nearby. Then he and Diane began the quarter-mile walk east down Lynch Street toward the campus. It was getting late, and she had to be back in Alexander Hall by the midnight curfew. They hurried.

When Phillip and Diane arrived at a second roadblock on Lynch Street, they were stopped by a white policeman who was fat. Phillip smelled smoke in the air, so he asked the white officer if someone had fired tear gas. No, the officer said. Phillip asked whether it was safe to go on. The white officer said that if he were them, he would not.

But Phillip and Diane decided to move on anyway. Once they arrived at Alexander Hall, they talked awhile in the lobby. At about midnight, someone flicked the lights on and off. All men had to go. Phillip must have been high, because he seemed beery and sentimental and kept right on talking. To Diane, that seemed out of character for Phillip. She was embarrassed and anxious to go upstairs to her room. "Well, I have to go now," she kept saying. "I have to go now."

> "He said some things that night that were kind of weird," Diane recalls. "He said he wanted to get divorced, and that he loved me and that he wanted to marry me and go to church with me Sunday. Well, he was a married man. We were just friends. I don't know what he felt for me, but I didn't love him. He was just a friend."

Diane stepped into the elevator to go up to her room, while Phillip turned to go. He walked outside into the dark yard, cutting across the lawn toward a crowd of shouting students near the west wing doorway. There were men in blue helmets standing in Lynch Street, and the students were jeering them. Phillip heard gunblasts, and he ran. In the roaring darkness something slammed into his face. Phillip fell.

• •

On the Sunday afternoon three days after Phillip Gibbs died, the hearse bearing his body climbed the hill to the Ripley Cemetery. The hearse passed the trim lawns and monuments of the white cemetery. It stopped at the black iron fence of the burying ground for blacks. The pallbearers made their last wobbly-kneed walk with the body of their friend.

> "I've heard the extremes," Roland Colom, one of the pallbearers, recalls. "On one side people say: 'He was real quiet and a real nice guy. This guy never did go anywhere or do anything. The only reason he'd gone to the women's dormitory was to pick up his sister.' Then I heard the other

> side that said: 'This guy was wild. He was a big drinker, a rowdy, and a cut-up.' Hey, neither side was telling the truth. He was somewhere in between. He was in the norm with a great deal of other people during that time, during that sixties generation. The wine, the anti-this and anti-that feelings, antiwar, anti-Establishment—he was in that group with all the rest of them, the majority of them. But he wasn't at any extreme."

The pallbearers laid the coffin in the grave near the black fence. They lowered their heads and prayed.

A few paces away, in the white cemetery, stood the white marble monument to W. C. Falkner, slave owner, Confederate colonel, and patriarch of the great Falkner line. The eyes of his white effigy had grown dark with moss, and his grave was surrounded by its own fence of black iron.

7

CRISIS

We have been believers feeding greedy grinning gods, like a Moloch demanding our sons and our daughters, our strength and our wills and our spirits of pain.

—Margaret Walker

Monday morning, May 18, 1970. Jackson, Mississippi was in turmoil.

Five hundred black children from schools across the city walked out of their morning classes, converging downtown to picket the Governor's Mansion. Meanwhile, dozens of Jackson State students were picketing stores in the capital to enforce a boycott of white businesses. Jackson's white merchants were seething. Since the campus shootings on Friday, three of their stores in black neighborhoods had gone up in flames.

Jackson's black leaders, too, were enraged. Dr. Aaron Shirley, a black pediatrician widely regarded as a moderate, had warned the next time lawmen shot at students, the black youths might not die so peacefully. Dr. Shirley belonged to the Mississippi United Front, a civil rights group that talked of forming a paramilitary Defense League to arm and protect blacks.

There were others thinking of guns. According to news reports, gunshops in Jackson were doing a brisk business. Even Jackson State students were threatening to buy guns to protect themselves. Responding to talk like that, black leaders were trying to keep the students busy with the boycott in the daytime and at church rallies at night.

"They were very militant," former NAACP Field Director Alex Waites recalls. "They were ready to burn down Capitol Street, and our fear was that their fervor was going to get them killed. We were afraid those kids were going to do something in a disorganized fashion and end up killed, because the city police were anticipating something violent."

Even the Sunday sermons the day before in Jackson's churches had reflected the racial discord. White preachers had railed against the godless communism on the campuses, while black preachers had called for a boycott of white-owned businesses. Jackson had not been so tense since the assassination of Medgar Evers back in 1963. In such a volatile atmosphere, the Jackson office of the FBI feared for the safety of Attorney General John Mitchell, scheduled to arrive on Monday afternoon. To maintain order, Governor Williams had ordered the National Guard on stand-by alert at the state fairgrounds downtown.

Fanning the flames of racial unrest was the Hederman press. The *Jackson Daily News,* for instance, printed the fiction that for more than a year the city police had known that Jackson State students "maintained an arsenal of rifles, pistols, shotguns, ammunition and other weapons on campus." The *Daily News* added that "many" reporters had confirmed police reports of snipers at the college.

Fortunately, the Hederman press had no monopoly on the news about the Jackson State killings. Accounts of the shootings had appeared on the front pages of the nation's major newspapers. In an editorial, *The New York Times* condemned "the terrible succession of official gunfire and death" at Kent and Jackson State. The *Washington Post* described the slayings on the two campuses as "horribly the same in the essential details." The nation's television networks focused on the Jackson State slayings night after night on their evening news shows. For many viewers, pictures of black students staring through the shards of glass in Alexander Hall were almost as familiar as the film of guardsmen firing M-1's at Kent State.

Criticized for reacting coolly to the Kent State tragedy, President Richard Nixon released a statement to the press that he and Mrs. Nixon were "deeply saddened by the death of two students at Jackson State College."

Students across the nation responded to the campus slayings in Mississippi by organizing memorial services and demonstrations. Peaceful rallies were held at the University of Chicago, University of Southern Mississippi, University of Utah, North Carolina State, Memphis State, Georgia State, New York University, and Claremont College in California, among others. A few of the protests were less than peaceful. When a thousand black students from Morgan State College blocked traffic on the busy streets of Baltimore, police tear-gassed the crowd. The black youths responded by pelting lawmen with rocks and bottles. Students at the University of Alabama held a quiet candlelight march to protest the Kent and Jackson State shootings, but after the services, thirty-seven were arrested for defying a police order to disperse.

One-fifth of the nation's campuses had closed in the wake of the Kent State tragedy. Still others cancelled classes after the Jackson State killings. These included predominantly black schools such as Bowie State College and Knoxville College in Tennessee, Morgan State in Maryland, Lincoln University in Pennsylvania, and Howard University in Washington, D.C. Predominantly white schools cancelled classes as well, including Northern Illinois University, the University of Cincinnati, and the University of Washington in Seattle. To honor the youths shot at Jackson State, students raised money for scholarships and memorials at City University of New York, State University of New York at Stony Brook, Washington University in Seattle, and Kent State.

Still, the nation's black students complained that after the Jackson State killings, white students did not reveal the same degree of outrage they had shown after Kent State. They were correct. Weary of more than two weeks of demonstrations, most students had left the picket lines either to study for final exams or to head home for an early summer vacation.

By the third week of May, only a handful of campuses each day were disrupted by violent protest. The turmoil of May '70 was subsiding, and with it the student antiwar movement and the political idealism of the 1960s.

• •

It was just after 10:00 A.M. on Monday, May 18, when WJTV anchorman Bert Case loped up the winding staircase in city hall to face questioning by the mayor's biracial committee. Case was carrying his cassette tape recorder. Because finding every reporter who had witnessed the shootings might take days, the committee decided to call on Case first. After all, he was the man with the tape recording of the officers' barrage.

Case had grown up in a neighborhood about a mile north of Jackson City Hall where his father made a business of renting apartments. Rooted in Case's memory of his father and the old neighborhood was his abhorrence of the Old South's racial customs. Case could never forget that when he had turned thirteen, his father had ordered him to stay away from black friends. "You can't play with them anymore," his father had told him, so that was the end of the sandlot ballgames with the neighborhood's black kids. In time, Case learned to ignore the impulses of boyhood, and he adopted the more complicated ways of the adults' caste system.

Two decades later, anchorman Case was a respected journalist in Jackson. But there were those who regarded him as a flaming liberal, and some were asking Case why he had not reported sniper fire at Jackson State. As Case sat facing the committee, he was ready to answer questions like that. Yet as a journalist, Case was determined to stick to the facts.

Case began by explaining that he was at home on Thursday night, May 14, at about 10:20 P.M. when his phone had rung. It was Jack Hobbs calling from the TV studio to ask whether Case wanted to check things out at Jackson State. Case replied that he had already checked the campus at about 9:30 P.M., and everything had seemed calm. Yet Case agreed to meet Hobbs near the college anyway.

Arriving on Lynch Street, the two TV newsmen found a police roadblock in front of radio station WOKJ. A black officer there told the reporters that three blocks ahead, Jackson State students were throwing rocks and bottles at cars. Case and Hobbs hoped that black cameraman Martel Cook—who was also a Jackson State student—would manage to get some good pictures. Cook was on the campus with Hobbs's portable light.

Hobbs and Case decided to circle the college, taking side streets to avoid the rock-throwers. Case wanted to see whether Mayor Davis had set up a command post at the corner of Rose and Lynch Street as he had on the night before. But when the newsmen arrived, they discovered Davis was not there. Instead, they found two policemen at a roadblock. There, a quarter mile east of the campus, Case heard what sounded like shots.

"I couldn't say where, only just in the general direction of south," he told the mayor's biracial committee. "Nothing happened after the shots. It was just dead silence. And I said to the policemen, 'You guys are fools sitting out there by yourself. You ought to have some help.' Then I went on back over toward the car. Quite frankly, I didn't want to be a target at that barricade."

So Hobbs and Case again circled the campus, returning west to the roadblock in front of radio station WOKJ. They found National Guardsmen assembling there in the middle of Lynch Street. While Case stood beside a police squad car, he overheard a police radio report: "We're being fired upon up here!" That was Police Lieutenant Magee, three blocks to the east in front of Stewart Hall dormitory. As the National Guard prepared to march toward Magee's position, Hobbs put on his shoulder-mount TV camera and Case noted the time on his portable tape recorder: four minutes before midnight. A fellow reporter who worked for the Associated Press, James "Hank" Downey, joined Hobbs and Case as they followed the guardsmen. It was a five-minute, three-block march to the Jackson State campus.

At the corner of Lynch and Prentiss Street, near two men's dormitories, the guardsmen halted. Case, Hobbs, and Downey walked past the troops and continued up Lynch Street where they could see lines of officers in the road. Case said he feared sniper fire, but at Hobbs's urging, Case joined in the walk up Lynch Street toward the officers' lines in front of Alexander Hall. When the reporters arrived at the women's dorm, they learned the officers were city police and highway patrolmen who had come with Thompson's Tank.

"I wanted to stay behind that tank for protection," Case said. "I could hear students yelling—just a terribly loud noise. It sounded like hundreds and hundreds of students yelling."

Case then drew a diagram for the committee (see figure 2). He drew an unmarked line to the east, in front of the tank. This represented a group of officers he could not identify. The parallel arrows he sketched alongside the tank showed where he and Hobbs had walked for a better view of the crowd in front of the dormitory. To the west, behind the tank, was a line of pa-

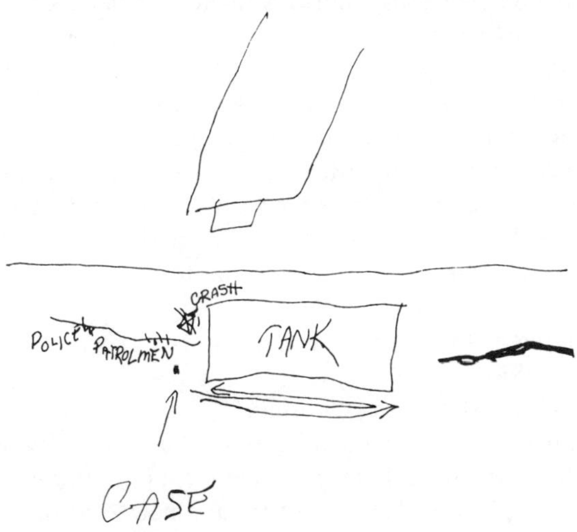

Figure 2. Facsimile of WJTV reporter Bert Case's sketch of the shooting scene.

trolmen and perhaps a few city policemen, Case recalled. He drew a dot and labelled it "Case" to show where he had stood. Hobbs had been right in front of him. Case wrote "Crash" and an asterisk, pointing out where a bottle had landed in the street.

When this bottle shattered, the two reporters had been standing among the lawmen only two or three minutes, Case told the committee. Just seconds before the bottle shattered, Case had asked Hobbs: "Are you shooting?" That is, "shooting" film.

Hobbs had replied, "yes," Case testified. The bottle broke on the pavement near the lawmen, "and the next thing I remember, they were firing."

"Did you hear any shots before the officers fired?" Case was asked.

"I did not hear any shots."

"Did you hear any window breaking before the barrage?"

"No sir."

"You said you had expected sniper fire," Fred Banks, a black attorney, said. "Was this because the police had reported they were being fired upon earlier?"

"That was one reason, Fred," Case replied. "Another reason was that I have heard from various sources since 1967, that if there is ever another situation at Jackson State like there had been at least two times before, they were going to shoot back."

"But they hadn't shot back Thursday night?" Banks asked.

"Not to my knowledge," Case said.

Case was asked about claims that a bullet had whizzed past Jack Hobbs's head. The committee wanted to know whether Case first learned of that before or after the lawmen opened fire.

"It was something he told me afterwards," Case replied. "Jack said to me, 'Did you hear that bullet zing past my head?' And I said, 'No, I didn't.' "

"Did you see Hobbs make any motion before the barrage?"

"No," Case said, "but I was not looking at him."

"Where were you looking?"

"I was looking at the dormitory," he replied. "There was a bunch of students in that door."

"Was that where Hobbs was shooting?"

"He was aimed generally in that direction," Case said. "But then when I heard these shots, and when I turned and looked, I saw the weapons aimed up. My first thought was, 'That's got to be a new kind of tear-gas gun. Surely, they are going to shoot tear gas.' And then the next thing I saw, windows were breaking and I kept expecting to see tear gas come, a cloud of tear gas come up in the windows. It never did come, and it finally dawned on me, you know, like five to ten seconds into the barrage, that this was not tear gas. This was real, live ammunition."

Case said the upper-floor windows in the dorm broke first. Then the lower-floor windows. At first the officers fired high, and then they lowered their weapons.

"Did you see any city policemen firing?"

"I did not," Case said.

"Did you see any highway patrolmen firing?" black co-chairman Reuben Anderson asked.

"That is all I saw fire, Reuben: highway patrolmen."

"Did you see any highway patrolman who was not firing?"

"No, I did not," Case said.

"Who seemed to be in charge of the police units there?"

"I didn't know at the time—I didn't," Case said. "You couldn't tell. Officers were just milling around there. . . . Now afterward it became clear to me that apparently Inspector Lloyd Jones was in charge of the highway patrol."

The committee asked Case if he saw students in the windows on every floor of Alexander Hall's west stairway.

"I was not conscious of the fact that there were students in those windows. I was conscious of the fact that there were a lot of students concentrated in that doorway below. And I remember either right at the latter stages of the firing, of just after it stopped, . . . they just piled up. They were on top of each other. It looked like everybody was trying to get into the door, and it just became a pile of humanity, just moving from everybody trying to get in."

"Bert, did any of your film that you all shot that night come out?"

"No, not good film," he said. "We sent it to Memphis for special processing to try to force it and all. You can tell there is the lighted doorway there, but the rest of it is just blackness."

"Tell us about how long it was after this bottle crash and the volley started."

"Oh, just a couple of 'beats' as we call it in the news business," Case replied. "It's just, just like this," he added, slapping the conference table a couple of times. "Then it went off."

"I think it was said that you or Jack Hobbs—one or the other—dived under the tank. Is that correct?"

"No sir," Case said, adding that at one point he had dropped the microphone of his tape recorder and stooped to pick it up.

"Did Hobbs drop or throw his camera at the time of the volley of shots?"

"No, he did not," Case said.

The committee asked Case about a second sniper, since police had claimed there was another gunman in Ayer Hall, the women's dorm in the park across the street from Alexander Hall. Case was asked if he had seen evidence of gunfire from that direction.

"I did not," Case replied. But he added that a patrolman named Rex Armistead had told him of shooting from that direction. "He pointed to a building considerably behind us—pointed high," Case said.

"Who is Rex Armistead?" Case was asked.

"He is, I believe, the chief investigator of the highway patrol."

"And this was said immediately after the shooting?"

"A few minutes after, yes," Case said.

"Did he or anybody else attempt to do anything about the sniper over there?"

"Well, after the shooting, the officers were asked to move back against the wall—this concrete wall on the south side of the street," Case said. "And at one point I remember several officers wheeled around and pointed their guns in that direction, just pointed their weapons in the direction of south. Nobody fired."

Case was asked if the students were throwing rocks at the officers before the shooting began.

"Prior to the volley of shots, the only thing that I know of was the bottle thrown," Case said.

"Did you see any gestures by anyone, the crowd in general, or anything that in your opinion seemed to initiate the thing?" he was asked.

"Well, of course you know that the Mississippi Highway Patrol, and for that matter the Jackson police—although I am not saying Jackson police fired, because I didn't see them fire—these men are going to be infuriated by Negro students yelling, 'You white son-of-a-bitches' and 'you white pigs.' Now I can imagine that—and this is strictly opinion now—it's my opinion that this would make a Mississippi highway patrolman really tense up, and really feel like he wanted to fire."

"But you can't go to a specific act like a crowd movement or something like that, that seemed to touch off the incident?"

"Not other than the bottle," Case said. But then Case told the committee about the tape recording he had brought with him. On Thursday night, Case's eyes and ears had led him to believe there had been no sniper, but something on this mechanical device led him to wonder if there just might have been a gunman.

Case placed his portable tape recorder on the conference table. He explained that since he had dropped his microphone just as the barrage began, the first few pops on the tape might not be gunfire at all. Case was not sure. As he pushed the "play" button on his machine, the five attorneys listened intently. First, there was the din of young shouting voices, and then Case's nervous yell to cameraman Hobbs: "Are you shooting?" Hobbs replied, "Yah!" Then a pop, another pop, the shattering of glass, and then thundering blasts that blotted out the students' yells. After twenty-eight seconds, the fusillade ended as a megaphoned voice yelled, "Cease firing!"

> "Why? I've asked myself that a thousand times," Bert Case says, looking back over more than a decade since the slayings. "And what I always come back to—my own personal belief—and this is nothing more than opinion. I believe that the whole shooting thing was triggered by one bottle being thrown, a bottle that was tossed right into the middle of us and that I felt sprinkle my leg, and I think probably hit highway patrolmen also. I know I heard one say that it did. My own theory—my own opinion is—that was enough in that tense atmosphere to touch off one guy shooting. Others followed."

•

In a plaid sports coat and thin tie, Jack Hobbs entered the conference room.

Hobbs was weary. He had been covering the Jackson State story around the clock: interviewing students, writing scripts, chasing public officials around town for comments, appearing on the daily newscasts, and facing endless questions from FBI agents and fellow journalists. Hobbs found himself in a dizzying position. He was a key source in a news story that he was still trying to cover. When pressed by other reporters, Hobbs said he did not know whether there had been a sniper at Jackson State, and he was not sure that a sniper's bullet had whizzed by his ear that night.

Peering through his dark-rimmed glasses at the mayor's biracial committee, Hobbs testified that during the shooting he had stood with Case near the rear bumper of Thompson's Tank. They were in the middle of Lynch Street near a manhole cover. As they faced Alexander Hall, lawmen were all around them. While Hobbs aimed his TV camera at the dorm, behind him was Bert Case, and farther back along the sidewalk there was a fence atop a concrete retaining wall.

Hobbs sketched the scene for the committee (see figure 3). He printed *X*'s to represent the patrolmen standing in front of him and to his left. He

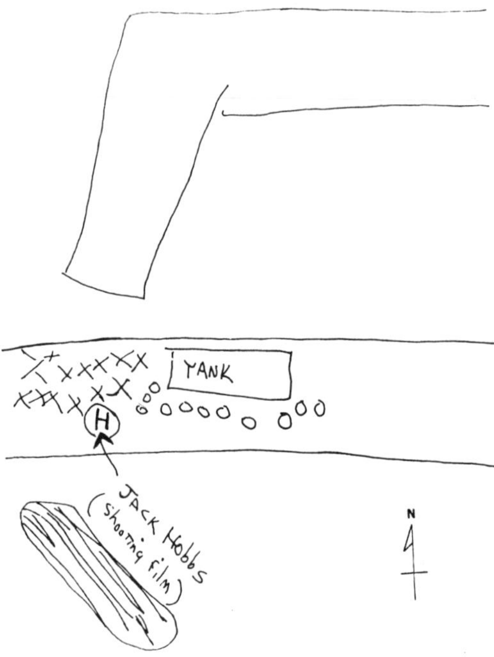

Figure 3. Facsimile of WJTV reporter Jack Hobbs's sketch of the shooting scene.

added *O's* to denote the city police to his right and alongside the tank. He circled an *H* to show where he had been filming.

"I had my camera shoulder-mounted," Hobbs told the committee, "and I was shooting at the stairwell windows, and I was shooting film of the doorway."

"The west entrance of Alexander Hall?"

"Yes," Hobbs replied.

"Did you think you had enough light to be shooting?"

"No, but you shoot anyway," Hobbs explained.

While filming, Hobbs heard glass shatter near his feet. "I was standing sort of spraddle-legged, bracing myself because I was shooting film. I was shooting at the second-to-the-top window of the west entrance of Alexander Hall. . . . The next thing that happened was almost split-second. I heard the bottle shatter. I heard what sounded to me like a shot."

"One or more?"

"One," Hobbs said. "It appeared to me that it came from the direction of the dormitory. I don't know to the right, to the left, or where from."

"You're speaking of Alexander Hall, immediately north of where you were standing?"

"Un-huh," Hobbs answered affirmatively. "What I am saying is that I heard a report from this general vicinity."

"You're indicating the entire Alexander Hall vicinity?"

"And to the west of the dorm," Hobbs added. "It could have been the vicinity between Alexander Hall and the Student Union Building next door—I don't know. All I know is I heard the report, and the noise I heard came from in front of me. Either to my right or to my left. And as I say, it was all split-second. I heard that sound, I heard and felt something zing past my ear."

"Immediately after the shot?"

"It was—this was all split-second," Hobbs said. "I heard the noise, I felt the wind, and heard the zing of something go past my left ear, and heard it ricochet off the fence or the wall behind me."

"Now go ahead—how long was this before the volley by the officers."

"Immediately after that, in a matter of one or two seconds, I heard the first shotgun blast go off to my left," Hobbs said.

"Did you observe what officers: city police, patrolmen, or what?"

"From my observation it was patrolmen, because patrolmen were to my left."

"Approximately how many patrolmen fired? Could you say?"

"My estimate of how many were out there is between twenty and thirty, but as I say, I was concentrating on shooting film," Hobbs replied. "To my estimation, a great majority of them fired. . . . After the initial blast that I heard to my left, there was another in a matter of maybe a second or two before the entire barrage started. When it erupted, it came from my left and from my right, and I was sort of standing in the middle of it. . . . It was coming from behind me, to the side of me, all around me were firing."

"Did you see any Jackson City Police fire?"

"No," Hobbs said.

Though Hobbs had seen no policemen shooting, he was convinced they had used their weapons. Hobbs had heard firing all around him, and that included from the officers to his right—the city police. But Hobbs did not offer this opinion to the committee. He felt that he was in enough hot water with the city's blacks for saying a shot had whizzed by his ear. Hobbs did not want to take more heat for accusing the police of pulling their triggers.

Continuing his story, Hobbs said that when the shooting began, he was looking through the viewfinder at the top two windows of Alexander Hall. Then he glanced to his left and saw patrolmen firing with guns raised. At first he thought they were just firing into the air, but then he glanced through the viewfinder again and saw windows breaking in the women's dorm.

"Could you see any persons standing in those windows?"

"There were people in all of the windows . . . ," Hobbs said. "The two or three students that were standing in the top windows had sort of disappeared and the curtains had been blown out and were dancing from the blast."

"In the minutes immediately before the shooting started, what sort of actions did you observe from the crowd of students around the dormitory—just shouting?"

"It was just a lot of shouting, screaming, calling names, and yelling obscenities," Hobbs said.

Hobbs was asked whether bricks and several bottles were thrown at the officers.

"I don't recall any before that bottle shattered," Hobbs said. "I don't recall any bricks or anything being thrown."

"Could you tell whether the people you saw in the windows were men or women?"

"Men and women," Hobbs said.

Other than law officers, Hobbs was the only witness to state unequivocally that males had been in Alexander Hall before the barrage.

"Now as you looked at these windows, did you see whether any were broken prior to the volley?" Hobbs was asked.

"I couldn't say."

"Are you sure that the bullet that passed by your ear struck the fence behind you?"

"I am not sure that what passed by my ear was what struck the fence," Hobbs said. "There is no way to tell."

"I'm a little hazy on it," white attorney Francis Bowling said, "but it seems to me like there was a notation in a police investigation report that you saw someone break a window—a dormitory window with a pistol or some other object. Is that so?"

"I haven't talked to the police," Hobbs said. "I have given them no statement."

"Jack, did you get down and hide under Thompson's Tank?"

"No."

Hobbs was asked whether anything unusual had happened behind him on the south side of Lynch Street, where a second sniper was alleged to have fired from Ayer Hall, a women's dorm.

"No," Hobbs answered. But then he recalled what he had seen the officers do after the barrage—after they heard Hobbs say that a shot had whizzed by his ear.

"After a time, I don't know how long, someone gave the order that everyone get back against the wall, which was the retaining wall behind us," Hobbs said. Several officers pointed their guns south toward Ayer Hall, and Hobbs heard one patrolman say, "There is a sniper up in that window." Another officer approached Hobbs with a flattened piece of lead.

"He walked up to me and he said, 'This is probably one of the kinds, one of the types that went past your ear.' "

Hobbs was asked if he could suggest another witness the committee should question about the killings.

"I would recommend Hank Downey, of course, of the Associated Press," Hobbs said. "He was not with us all the time, but he was in the same general area. I would also recommend the big, heavy-set guy that was with him. I think Bert knows who he is. Hank knows who he is. I don't. I had never met him. Those are the two I would recommend, outside of law enforcement people. We were the only ones in there—the four of us."

> "I was the only person who made a statement that in any way justified the shootings," recalls Jack Hobbs, convinced that a bullet from Alexander Hall had zoomed past him that night more than a decade ago—but unconvinced by the lawmen's claims there had been two campus snipers. "I think that what I had said was later used as a justification. But there was only one person there who could say that somebody shot at him. And that was me."

•

Associated Press reporter James "Hank" Downey took a seat in the sunny second-floor conference room to testify before the mayor's biracial committee.

Downey was a twenty-five-year-old native of Hattiesburg, Mississippi. Thin and about six-feet-six, Downey almost always carried a two-way radio to contact Associated Press headquarters. He was an energetic and bright young reporter, a liberal Mississippian. But whenever Downey talked publicly about the killings, he sought to omit his personal views.

Facing the five attorneys at the conference table, Downey said that when the shooting erupted he had been standing with TV reporters Jack Hobbs and Bert Case in front of Alexander Hall. It had been dark, so dark he could hardly tell the city police from the highway patrolmen, Downey said. While he was just a few paces behind Bert Case that night, officers with shotguns were standing behind both of them. When Downey looked up at Alexander Hall, he could see students crowding the lighted windows of the west stairwell.

"I heard a bottle break," he told the attorneys. "It was somewhere near me—I didn't see it. . . . Just probably a second or two later, I heard a report. In my news story, I said it sounded like a firecracker or a small-caliber weapon—either one. . . . Almost immediately the officers opened fire on the dormitory."

As the lawmen were firing, Downey crouched and scrambled behind them to the white concrete retaining wall along the Lynch Street sidewalk. Squatting beside the wall, he used his two-way radio to dictate a bulletin to AP's New Orleans office. Downey reported that nearly seventy-five officers had just opened fire on about a hundred black students in front of a women's dormitory.

"Did you see anyone in the windows there above the entrance break a window and fire out?" co-chairman John Kuykendall asked.

"I did not," Downey replied.

"Just recall whether or not, in your opinion, if such an occurrence had happened, you would have seen it."

"I believe, had there been any fire from the windows of the west wing of Alexander Hall facing us—I think I would have seen it," Downey answered.

"The first 'report' that you stated you heard—could you tell us from what direction it is your impression that it came from?"

"No sir, I can't," Downey answered. "And it's not because I haven't tried. . . . My only impression is that, in all honesty, I don't feel it came from the windows in front of us on the west wing of Alexander Hall."

"Did you see any officers struck by any objects thrown by the students?"

"I did not."

"Did the students indicate they were going to harm these officers?"

"No, not that I saw," Downey said. "I saw no overt threat to the officers from the students in front of the dorm."

"Do you know just how far you were from Bert Case and Jack Hobbs?"

"No, sir, because I had been talking with them on and off for the few minutes we had been there. As best I recall, I had talked with them just a moment earlier, and had stepped back. I had met a man that I was to meet down there, and as best I recall, I had stepped back and talked with him."

"Could you tell us who that was?"

"That was David Boone," Downey said, naming a tall, fat white man who was a friend. "He is a sports writer for the *Jackson Daily News.*"

"David Boone?"

"Right, David Boone."

•

David Boone was young, just twenty years old, and he was big. He weighed about three hundred pounds and stood six-feet-five. Boone was the fat white man in the dark suit who, just before the shootings, had walked alone down Lynch Street and right past Alexander Hall, drawing the jeers and rocks of the black students.

"I had a number of bottles and a number of rocks thrown at me," Boone told the mayor's biracial committee. "At one point I heard somebody in the crowd at the dorm shout, 'Whitey! Let's get him!' But I thank my lucky stars I'm fairly well known on the Jackson State campus, and somebody else shouted, 'Leave him alone. He's all right.' "

That night was not the first that Boone had walked alone on the Jackson State campus. As a sports writer for the *Daily News,* he often covered the games at the college. A native Jacksonian, Boone was impressed by the black teams and thought it unfair they received so little attention in the Hederman press. So Boone tried to give Jackson State more sports coverage than it had received in the past. But he felt he had to accept the fact there would never be a big, eight-column story about Jackson State sports in his paper. Still, Boone loved his job at the newspaper, and on the night of May 14 he had been drawn to the troubled black campus by the prospect of a good story.

Arriving on Lynch Street, Boone looked for fellow reporter Hank Downey, but he could not find him. So the sports writer walked west down the middle of Lynch Street toward Jackson State. As he passed Alexander Hall, he ducked the rocks thrown by the crowd of students there. He pressed on toward the fire he could see about a block down the sloping street. A dump truck was ablaze. Boone watched as firemen put out the flames. After the city police and patrolmen left the scene and marched to Alexander Hall, Boone stood with them in the middle of Lynch Street. There he joined WJTV reporters Bert Case and Jack Hobbs, as well as his friend, AP reporter Hank Downey. The four reporters were surrounded by lawmen with shotguns and rifles. Case and Hobbs stood near the middle of the street behind Thompson's Tank, while Boone stood back, closer to the sidewalk, with Downey. All four reporters faced the black students as they jeered the officers from behind a chain-link fence.

"The highway patrol had formed in what appeared to me a pretty worked-out routine—what I would describe as a rough semi-circle formation toward the front of the dorm—just a rough half-circle," Boone said. He saw Lieutenant Warren Magee, bullhorn in hand, moving toward the shouting crowd.

"I presumed he was going to take over some sort of instructions to the students," Boone said. "But before he could move up, a bottle came crashing from somewhere and hit on the street. Just a split second behind the bottle came some kind of loud report. . . . Without apparently any visible command, the highway patrol opened fire on the dormitory."

When asked about the first "report" he had heard, Boone testified he did not know where it had come from, or who had fired it. It had followed the crash of the bottle and it sounded like a loud firecracker. A split second later, the crowd of officers opened up.

After the shooting had stopped, Boone testified, he had muttered, "It just wasn't called for—there was just no reason for this to happen." Then a tall, heavy-set patrolman had approached him.

"He confronted me and demanded to see my press credentials, which is rather an unusual move," Boone testified. "And of course I showed them to him. . . . He said, 'You young punk. Do you want to know what really happened out here? Or are you just going to use your own opinion?' And at this time I was—I was getting a little fearful, because there was a small group of highway patrolmen ganging up on me. This officer turned to his companion and told him to show me something. The guy pulled out of his pockets two shells that he said he had picked up on Lynch Street. And he remarked to me something to the effect of, 'What are we supposed to do? They have been out here shooting at us for over thirty minutes.' "

•

After more than a week of hearings and sifting through police reports, the mayor's biracial committee could not agree on the form of its final report. Both the committee and Mayor Davis had come under heavy fire from hard-line segregationists. The critics had complained that two committee members were black and that police had been subjected to questioning.

The three younger attorneys on the committee—the two blacks and William Pyle, a white—were determined to submit a final report to Mayor

Davis. They wanted this report to draw conclusions from the testimony of the twenty policemen, reporters, college officials, and wounded students they had questioned. But Attorneys Kuykendall and Bowling, both established white attorneys, opposed such a report. They recommended sending only the transcripts of the hearings to the mayor. As a result of this impasse, the three younger attorneys drafted a majority report and submitted it to Mayor Davis.

The majority report concluded that the students at Alexander Hall had posed no threat to the officers and had thrown few, if any, objects at them. The three attorneys also found the lawmen had made no serious attempt to protect themselves from sniper fire, and there was no credible evidence of a campus sniper. Finally, the report concluded there was no evidence that city police had taken part in the fusillade.

To arrive at these conclusions, the attorneys had relied heavily on the four newsmen's testimony. But the reporters' knowledge was limited. They could not know, for example, that FBI agents had discovered number-one buckshot in front of Alexander Hall. And that only the Jackson Police had been armed with number-one shot on the night of the killings.

• •

It was about eighty-five degrees and the tarmac shimmered in the late-afternoon sun as the Air Force jet touched down on Allen Thompson Field in Jackson. The jet from Washington taxied to a halt, and out the doorway and down the stairs stepped Attorney General John N. Mitchell, the man who had run President Nixon's campaign in 1968—the same man who once had called militant students "stupid bastards."

With his left hand in his pants pocket and his right swinging as he walked, the balding attorney general approached a sedan surrounded by FBI agents. One agent opened the back door just as a flock of reporters and TV cameras closed in on the attorney general. A reporter shook Mitchell's hand to delay him long enough to ask why he was in Jackson.

"The purpose, of course, is to evidence concern and see what we can do about taking care of the situation here that everybody is so uptight about and fraught with danger," Mitchell said.

"Sir, who'll be at the meeting?" another reporter asked.

"I'm not quite certain," Mitchell replied. "There'll be Mayor Davis and Dr. Peoples, and who else I don't know."

Mitchell began to duck into the back seat of the sedan to put off further questions. But as he placed just one foot inside, a reporter asked another question.

"Let me ask you why you're coming here to personally investigate this incident and you did not go to Kent State?"

"There's that much concern over this incident here," Mitchell said impatiently.

"Is this the most serious one yet?"

"It could possibly be," Mitchell said, turning to face the reporters again. "We hope not." Mitchell got back into the car and closed the door, and the sedan pulled away from the tarmac.

After a two-hour meeting downtown with Mayor Davis and President Peoples, Mitchell stood in front of Alexander Hall, puffing on his pipe. President Peoples pointed out the fence where the students had stood Thursday night. He also pointed out the Lynch Street pavement where the lawmen had stood firing.

"And only twelve were struck?" asked Attorney General John Mitchell as he conferred with Jackson State College President John Peoples in front of bullet-sprayed Alexander Hall. (UPI/Bettmann Newsphotos)

Squinting in the sunlight, the attorney general looked up at the shattered windows and the shredded curtains stirring in the breeze. More than 250 bullet holes had been drilled into the steel panels and concrete walls of the stairwell above him. To the reporters watching him, Mitchell appeared shocked by what he saw.

"And only twelve were struck?" Mitchell asked Peoples.

An hour later, Mitchell was on a plane flying to Cleveland, Mississippi in the soil-rich Delta region more than a hundred miles north of Jackson. There he addressed the annual convention of the Delta Council, an elite organization of white planters and businessmen. Mitchell congratulated the council for a resolution supporting Nixon's Cambodia incursion. On the topic of student unrest, he told the Mississippians:

> There can be no greater evidence of disorder in society than the sound of gunfire on a college campus. From Santa Barbara to Kent State to Jackson State, we have seen the citadels of reason turn into fortresses of force, and as a result, the nation has witnessed the saddest semester in the history of American education.

Back in Washington four days later, Mitchell had some more remarks on the subject. They were intended, in part, for the Mississippi Highway Patrol, which still refused to cooperate with the FBI's investigation of the Jackson State killings. Lawmen who refused to answer questions about campus shootings would be subpoenaed, Mitchell warned. "One can recognize the provocations which often accompany disorders," he added, "but trained law enforcement personnel have a responsibility to keep their cool."

8

MAJESTY OF THE LAW

If I were the sheriff and a negro fiend fell into my hands, I would run him out of the county. If I were governor and were asked for troops to protect him, I would send them. But if I were a private citizen, I would head the mob to string the brute up.

—James K. Vardaman, Mississippi governor, 1904–8

Tuesday, May 19, 1970. On a highway in southern Georgia, civil rights marchers followed three mule-drawn wagons on a hundred-mile march to Atlanta. On each of the three wagons was a coffin with a sign: 2 Killed in Jackson, 4 Killed in Kent, 6 Killed in Augusta. In New York City, public schools closed to honor the students slain at Jackson State. And in Washington, the "front runner" for the Democratic presidential nomination, Senator Edmund Muskie, announced he would join a congressional delegation at the funeral of James Green in Jackson on Friday.

While the nation continued to focus attention on the campus slayings in Mississippi, another confrontation between students and lawmen pushed Jackson to the brink of renewed violence.

At 7:30 A.M., state construction trucks pulled up along the Lynch Street curb in front of Alexander Hall. State workmen and agents of the highway patrol's crime lab got out of the trucks, walked to the dormitory, and entered the west-wing doorway. They began removing the shattered doors and windows that appeared night after night on local and network television—an embarrassment to the state of Mississippi. But the students on watch alerted their comrades, and as the white workmen boarded up the west-wing doorway, a crowd of more than a hundred black youths closed in on them. The students ordered the white men off their campus. The whites moved from the doorway, walked back to their trucks, and left Lynch Street.

It was the second time in twenty-four hours that workmen and state investigators had tried to enter the dorm, and the second time Jackson State students turned them away. The black youths posted a sign at the west-wing doorway: "No Evidence Is To Be Removed." Fearing a coverup by the state of Mississippi, the students called upon other blacks to help guard the campus. They passed out handbills in the Lynch Street neighborhood:

> The state highway patrol is trying to take our evidence out of Alexander Hall West Wing. We can not let them do this. They are trying to destroy the evidence. . . . The FBI wants it so they can tell the world the truth. Let's show them we know what they are trying to do. Please give us your support. Meet at Alexander Hall at Jackson State immediately.

In front of Alexander Hall, the crowd of blacks swelled to about three hundred, and they picketed the campus along Lynch Street. After President Peoples learned of the protest, he hurried to the dorm and spoke to a group of student leaders. Reporters watched as Peoples, underscoring his words with open palms, urged the students to calm down and let the state take the evidence.

"The only thing left here is of symbolic value," Peoples told the students. "It is of no investigatory value since this has been done by the FBI."

"Don't you see what they're doing?" one student said. "They're taking these scars away."

"It's not for repair," Peoples said. "They're taking evidence to the laboratory for investigation. And I would suggest that you young people, the future leaders of this state, do not use yourselves as cannon fodder."

One student complained that there was more to all this than just fixing up a building: "Why do they practically bring in the National Guard to fix up some nigger windows?"

Peoples convinced the students to meet with him in the college football stadium, where they could discuss the issue during a rally. About seven hundred black youths walked down Lynch Street to the stadium. But after the rally, they marched right back to Alexander Hall. On the knoll in front of the west-wing stairwell, the black students defiantly faced the TV cameras set up in Lynch Street. While chanting slogans, the youths waved placards that proclaimed: "Shoot Me, My back Is Turned," "Pigs Watch Out!" and "Deliver Me From John Bell Williams." The blacks told the newsmen their bullet-raked dormitory was a monument to those who had died here. They would eat and sleep here every day and every night, and even die here if necessary.

Black ministers, Jackson State teachers, and leaders of the NAACP mingled with the students in front of the women's dorm. They sympathized with the youths, but they worried that once again guns would be trained on the students.

The black leaders were right to worry. Unknown to them, Governor John Bell Williams had warned the FBI he might declare martial law in Jackson and send ten thousand Mississippi National Guardsmen to Lynch Street. They would seal off both ends of the street and sweep the students from the campus to secure Alexander Hall. Then Mississippi investigators could collect their evidence, and state workmen could repair the dormitory. No evidence would go to the FBI, Williams told federal agents. All would go to a grand jury of Mississippians.

• •

Wednesday morning, May 20, 1970. A young black minister with a bullhorn addressed a crowd in front of Alexander Hall. He was Reverend W. L. Jenkins, a former Jackson State student. Behind him was a sign on the west stairwell door: "No Evidence Is To Be Removed."

Surrounding the young minister in front of the dorm were network television crews and a crowd of about three hundred black demonstrators. Using the bullhorn, the young minister read to them a federal court order: "The court concludes that the removal of said evidence should be left to the discretion of the State authorities, whose property it is. . . ."

To show their contempt for the order, Jackson State students ripped copies and threw them in a small pile on the sidewalk. They lit the papers, which blackened as they burned. Reverend Jenkins declared: "We plan to hold out until we bring white Mississippians to their senses, or we bring them to their damned knees!" The students cheered and raised fists in the Black Power salute as the TV cameras panned the crowd and the burning papers.

The demonstrators at Alexander Hall were protesting a federal court order issued by Judge J. P. Coleman, a former governor of Mississippi. A moderate on racial issues, Judge Coleman had flown to Jackson from New Orleans the night before to hold an unusual 10:00 P.M. hearing on the controversial repairs to Alexander Hall. A group called the Concerned Students of Jackson State College had petitioned Coleman to prevent Mississippi from seizing evidence in the dorm. The students had argued that the same agency that had fired on the dorm, the Mississippi Highway Patrol, was trying to remove the evidence of the shootings. The students also had

After state workmen attempted to repair Alexander Hall and remove evidence of the shootings, Millsaps College students joined the Jackson State students blocking entrance to the dorm. (*The Kudzu*)

asked Coleman to delay repairs to their dorm for three days, until after the funeral of James Green on Friday.

But at 7:00 A.M. the following morning, after conferring with Governor John Bell Williams, Judge Coleman issued his handwritten decision: the state of Mississippi could repair Alexander Hall whenever it deemed necessary. However, all evidence must be turned over to the FBI.

The Jackson State students resented Coleman's decision. First, because they did not trust Governor John Bell Williams to turn over all evidence to the FBI. Second, because they did not want the state to repair the dorm before the funeral on Friday. Senator Muskie and about ninety other congressmen and civil rights sympathizers were to attend the service. The Jackson State students wanted these officials and the journalists with them to see their bullet-raked dormitory.

As tensions heightened, Jackson crept closer to the edge. Two more white-owned stores in black neighborhoods had been firebombed in the early hours of Wednesday morning. Two city hospitals had received bomb threats. About twelve hundred fresh National Guard troops entered Jackson and bivouacked in a city park near Jackson State, on the state fairgrounds downtown, and at a nearby armory. Mississippi's game wardens were guarding the capitol and other state buildings downtown, while officials of the Justice Department's Civil Rights Division ran a rumor clinic to ease tensions. Tales of racially motivated rapes and beatings were sweeping the city.

By mid-afternoon Wednesday, more than eight hundred student protesters had amassed in front of the Alexander Hall's west wing. They carried signs that declared: "JSC Is Not Vietnam," and "Honkie Hogs Must Go." Black youths from local high schools and about twenty-five white students from Millsaps College had joined the protest. The crowd stirred as a small congressional delegation led by Senators Walter Mondale of Minnesota and Birch Bayh of Indiana entered the yard in front of Alexander Hall. Student leaders led the congressmen into the dorm's west stairwell. Network television crews followed. They scuffed through the shattered glass inside and went upstairs to see the blood-stained walls.

Returning to the knoll outside the dorm, reporters surrounded the congressmen to get their comments.

"From what you understand," one reporter asked Senator Bayh, "do you feel the police reaction was excessive, even if there was a sniper?"

"Well, first of all, I've heard no evidence of a sniper," Senator Bayh replied. "Second, I think we've learned, as long ago as the terrible Detroit riot, that if you do have a sniper, you don't just shoot everything in sight."

"It's a new national syndrome—the unfound sniper," Senator Walter Mondale added. "Every time there's an overreaction, that unfound sniper always gets blamed."

• •

The White House, Wednesday afternoon, May 20. President Richard Nixon was sitting at a large oval-shaped table with fifteen presidents of black colleges. Legs crossed, slumped comfortably in his chair, and holding a pen to his chin, President Nixon listened as the black educators explained why they had asked for this meeting.

A bald, broad-shouldered black man named Dr. Herman Branson sat across the table from Nixon. The president of Central State University in Ohio, Branson told Nixon the nation's black students felt alienated from the White House. One reason was the careless rhetoric of Nixon's closest advisers, especially Vice President Agnew, Branson said. He also criticized Nixon for courting the right-wing vote with his "Southern Strategy" and for nominating two southern conservatives to the Supreme Court: G. Harold Carswell and Clement F. Haynsworth. Branson also faulted the president for neglecting America's crumbling cities and for failing to use his "moral influence" to unite the nation.

To the other black educators in the room, Nixon's face seemed to redden as Branson spoke. But the president said nothing.

Dr. Branson presented several recommendations to Nixon: hold a conference with black student representatives; bar lawmen with guns from college campuses; issue guidelines on the use of weapons for crowd control; and involve more blacks in domestic policies.

The president declined to make any promises. "Judge me by my deeds," Nixon said calmly, "not by my words."

Among the college presidents at the oval table was Dr. John Peoples of Jackson State College in Mississippi. Also there was M. Maceo Nance of Orangeburg State College in South Carolina. On Nance's campus in 1968, three black students had been killed and thirty wounded by state and local police trying to quell student protests. Lewis C. Dowdy of North Carolina A&T also sat at the oval table. During the late 1960s, lawmen had shot and killed a student on his campus as well.

Dr. Peoples spoke about the recent shootings at Jackson State. He told President Nixon that his students had stood in front of a girls' dormitory and had cursed city and state policemen as they lined up in the street. These lawmen were "not used to being cursed by blacks," Peoples said, so when they "tired of the name-calling," they opened fire. Peoples handed Nixon several photographs of bullet-raked walls and windows in Alexander Hall. Nixon's eyes appeared to widen and he looked appalled as he examined the pictures.

Nixon said that he did not understand. When he was young, relationships between students and police had been friendly.

• •

It was Thursday, May 21, the night before the funeral of James Green, the black high school student killed at Jackson State. At nine o'clock, Governor John Bell Williams appeared on TV screens in living rooms across Mississippi. Williams's aides had set up an emergency TV network so the governor could address the issue of Jackson State and warn against violence at the funeral.

"Ladies and gentlemen," the governor began, "my fellow Mississippians: one week ago the city of Jackson and Mississippi suffered one of the most traumatic nights in our history." Williams told the viewers that until now he had deliberately refrained from commenting on the shootings." It would have been "highly improper" to prejudge the case, the governor said, and he would not now "place blame or seek exoneration for anyone who may have participated in the events of last Thursday night."

But then Williams did just that. The governor reassured his listeners that Jackson police and highway patrolmen were "well trained" and "not hotheads." He said they had been pelted by rocks at Jackson State, and there was "evidence of sniper activity." To prevent more violence, Williams warned, he would throw the full weight of Mississippi's might against any troublemakers at the next day's funeral. He said that thirteen hundred National Guardsmen were in Jackson, "all possessing the latest equipment available, all well trained, all ready to go in a matter of moments." Ten thousand more troops were on alert.

"The next few days are going to be days of great tension. It's going to be a test for the people of Mississippi, and I hope that the people, neither black nor white, will permit themselves to be led further by the pied-pipers of anarchy and insurrection—that they will obey the law, and that they will accept the fact that this is a state which is governed by law and not by men, nor by mob violence. But as your governor, I will tell you here and now that the majesty of the law will be upheld."

9

SHOWDOWN

For if they do this when the wood is green, what will happen when it is dry?

—Luke 23:31

Senator Edmund Muskie stood in the aisle of a Boeing 707 to address the congressmen, black leaders, and journalists seated before him. "Two young black men are dead," Muskie said, using the stewardess's microphone. "They died during a senseless display of violence at Jackson State College. Black Americans are all too often required to live in fear, fear often from the possible illegal overreaction of police authorities. From the facts at hand today, we seem to have yet another example of black lives not being valued."

Whitney Young, Jr., the husky black director of the National Urban League, rose in the jet's aisle to speak. "I am attending the funeral of the slain black youth in Jackson, Mississippi, because I want to help dramatize the sickness in our society that led to this tragedy. We are today a nation divisible with guns, and invective for all."

On Friday, May 22, 1970, Jackson was indeed a city divided by guns. Though guardsmen in jeeps were patrolling black neighborhoods, yet another white-owned store had been firebombed—the sixth such incident in a week. Troops were now stationed at Poindexter Park, about a mile north of Jackson State, and at Battlefield Park, a mile to the south. All leaves were cancelled for city police, and officers guarded most intersections along Lynch Street—the route of James Green's funeral procession. In addition, about 350 highway patrolmen were on alert in Jackson. At the Governor's Mansion downtown, twenty patrolmen stood guard with shotguns.

In keeping with Jackson's martial spirit, the morning's *Clarion-Ledger* bragged that special riot equipment had arrived overnight for the city police: new Buco riot helmets, new bullet-proof vests, and "new, super-strength" Pepper Fog, a tear gas that was "the most potent ever made." The *Jackson Daily News* also declared that the northerners flying to Jackson for James Green's funeral were "fanning fires of vulturous politics over a corpse." Governor John Bell Williams, too, had heaped invective on the visitors from Washington. Williams called them "self-appointed experts" who had "found the people of Mississippi guilty before they ever left Washington."

At about 1:00 P.M., a chartered Boeing 707 touched down in the ninety-degree heat at Thompson Field. Senator Muskie and the other dignitaries from Washington filed down the steps to the tarmac and boarded three air-conditioned buses parked nearby. Among the group were Senators Thomas Eagleton, Charles Percy, Ralph Yarborough, Daniel Inouye, Claiborne Pell, and Harold Hughes. From the House were Congressmen John Anderson, Adam Clayton Powell, Charles Diggs, John Conyers, Henry Reuss, and Abner Mikva. The group included Ambassador to the Soviet Union Averell Harriman and representatives of the NAACP, the U.S. Civil Rights Commission, and two students from Kent State University. In all, it was a delegation of nearly ninety civil rights sympathizers, one of the largest such gatherings since the funeral of Martin Luther King, Jr. two years before. Accompanying the dignitaries were journalists from *Newsweek, Time,* the *Washington Post,* the *Baltimore Sun,* the *New York Amsterdam News* and other news organizations.

At about 1:40 P.M., the three buses pulled up in front of Alexander Hall and the politicians stepped out to see the bullet-scarred dormitory. As they approached about thirty black students guarding the west doorway, the reporters and TV cameras pressed close. The students told the white politicians they would never yield the evidence inside to Mississippi authorities. But Republican Senator Charles Percy tried to reassure the students, promising them a federal investigation that would mean "absolute justice in this."

Senator Muskie added: "There isn't any worry that we can have confidence in the results."

At about 2:00 P.M., Senators Muskie and Percy and the rest of the delegation walked east down Lynch Street toward the Masonic Temple. Black neighbors crowded the front porches and lawns along the street to watch the famous visitors pass. When the delegation arrived at the Masonic Temple, a tangle of cars and buses clogged the traffic on Lynch Street. A crowd of four thousand inched through the front doors of the Masonic Temple to take seats in the auditorium.

This was the same auditorium where the funeral of Medgar Evers had been held one hot June day in 1963. After the service, a procession from Lynch Street to downtown Jackson nearly had ended in a riot. A crowd of blacks had tossed rocks at the police, patrolmen, and sheriff's deputies guarding the Capitol Street business district.

"We want the killer!" the mob had shouted that day at the lawmen who faced them with guns and attack dogs. Dodging flying bottles, one white man stepped between the blacks and the officers. He shouted that his name was John D-O-A-R, and that he was an attorney with the Justice Department, and that this was not the way to get what they wanted. A black youth stepped beside Doar and yelled, "This man is right!" The bottle-throwing stopped, and a tragedy was averted.

Still, white Jacksonians never forgot what had happened at that funeral in 1963. That was why nearly seven years later, on the day of James Green's funeral, police were in riot gear and guarding the intersections along Lynch Street.

In the Masonic Temple on Lynch Street, mourners filed by the open casket of James Green. They had been doing that for three hours. They were little black girls in starched white frocks, young men in black ties and white shirts, and old men in loose-fitting gray suits. The flower-banked coffin lay at the foot of the auditorium's stage. Three thousand black mourners sat in metal chairs and fanned themselves with their funeral programs. The air-conditioning system chugged noisily overhead.

After the auditorium filled, the mother, the stepfather, and the brothers and sisters of James Green walked up the center aisle and took seats in the front row. The bright lights of the network TV cameras swept the family staring at the casket.

On the stage, the visitors from Washington looked out on the black faces and fluttering white programs and the crowd of standing mourners that stretched into the hallway. After the coffin was closed, "Nearer My God to Thee" was sung, and an old black preacher approached the microphone that whined as he spoke: "When one of our children is taken from us, all we can think about is our loss. We're selfish, aren't we? Don't we know anymore that when we lose someone, we haven't lost them at all—that they are reborn in His glory?"

Despite the words of the preacher, Mrs. Myrtle Green Burton was inconsolable. President Nixon had called and sent a telegram, and Senator Edward Brooke, the black senator from Massachusetts, had visited her home on Tuesday; but James had been her liveliest and favorite child, and now he was gone. She had raised James and her eight other children in a small wood-frame house on Aberdeen Street. James and his best friend, Amos Patton, grew up together on that street, where they used sticks and drilled holes in their backyards to play golf. And ever since they were nine, both James and Amos worked as car hops at a corner store on Lynch Street called the "Wag-a-bag."

On a typical day at work, Amos and James would sit on the soda crates in front of the store, waiting for cars to pull into the lot for curb service. The boys would take the customers' orders and return to the cars with the groceries. Most customers tipped, but not all of them. To get those who did, Amos and James often played tricks on each other. When James spotted a nontipper coming, for example, he would stroll into the Wag-a-bag. That way Amos had to take the order, while James got a chance at the next.

> "James was a likable person," Amos Patton recalls. "He was liked by everybody he worked with. He was not the type of person to get involved in no big arguments or nothing like that. I would say he was the type of person that anyone could come to for advice. If he could help in any way, he would do it."

White men often gathered in the Wag-a-bag's back room to talk and drink beer. Sometimes they griped about "niggers." But to keep their jobs, James and Amos had to ignore that kind of talk. Now and then one of these men got rough with the boys, but Frank Dantoni, the friendly white store manager, intervened. Dantoni also protected Amos and James from the cornerboys who tried to steal their tips. Once, when a cornerboy pulled a gun on James, Dantoni helped scare off the man.

> "James was a good kid, one of the best kids I ever had working there," Dantoni recalls. "Everyone liked James. Most of our customers were really high-class white people then, and they all liked James Green. He was a jolly kid, I'll tell you that. On the counter during Christmas, the carhops would put cigar boxes wrapped in white paper, and put their names on them. James always got more tips than anybody else, because everybody liked him."

James was a senior at Jim Hill High School, just five blocks south of the Wag-a-bag. It was a new, two-story brick school, yet clearly not intended for white youths. Built on marshy land near the railroad tracks, the high school overlooked Willow Park Cemetery, which was for blacks. There was no fence around that cemetery, and after the city schools were integrated in January, friends of the new white students drove motorcycles over the black graves.

That made the black students angry, and Principal Emmitt Hayes, who was black, asked the city to build a fence around the graveyard.

• •

Principal Hayes, a tall black man, approached the microphone in the Masonic hall. He looked down on the coffin of James Green, which would be buried in the black graveyard in front of his school.

Hayes told the mourners that James had been a student of average ability who had trained hard as a one-mile runner on the track team. "He was never a discipline problem, and was well liked by both teachers and pupils," Hayes said. "Our hope is that the person or persons responsible for his death will be brought to justice under just laws."

Though James was on the school track team and dreamed of winning an athletic scholarship to attend college, he did little studying. Some teachers said James may have felt he was just too poor to afford college. In his senior year, James was in the second lowest quarter of his graduating class, managing to earn B's in only gym and driver education. But on his report card, faculty evaluations of James' character were glowing.

> "James was quiet, reserved," recalls Alberta Bingham, his English teacher. "I remember him as a child who sat kind of in the corner toward the front of the room. He always sat slouched at his desk, smiling. I think he smiled half the time. I don't remember a sad expression on his face ever. I sure don't. He was a kid who took to me, one of those kids who just hang onto you. I don't know, but I may have been pretty close to the youngest teacher at Jim Hill at that time. He'd come by, and if the door was opened, he would always peep in, just drop in. He was an average achiever, I would say. His ability was better than he showed to me, and I'd attribute that to his economic situation."

The long hours James put in at the Wag-a-bag were one reason he did poorly in school. He worked almost every night after classes, from about

James Earl Green.

four in the afternoon until ten at night. James earned about twenty-five dollars in wages and tips each week, and he knew that if his family of five brothers and three sisters was going to make it, he had to help out. Each week he spent most of his earnings on his family, saving only a few dollars for himself. He had a small charge account at the Wag-a-bag and brought food home when the family was hungry.

> "James had a little something different from my others, and I don't know what it was," remembers Myrtle Green Burton, his mother. "I didn't have trouble from none of them, but he was different. He was close to his mother. He was the kind of boy that didn't have time to think about a lot of junk. He was working, he was on the track team, and he was in school. He wanted everything tidy. He managed money like a little man. Most kids would squander it. He didn't, he shared. I really depended on that money. I really did. When you have a family as big as ours, you need it."

The death of James was not the first blow that his family had had to face. In 1957, when James had been only five, his father had died of a stroke. His mother married a laborer, Matt Burton, whose wages helped keep the family together. But in January of 1970, the house they rented on Aberdeen

Street was destroyed by fire. James climbed to the smoking roof with a water hose that day, but without success. His brothers and sisters managed to drag an old stereo and TV set from the fire, but the clothes, dishes, bedding, and everything else were consumed by the flames.

The family moved to a neighborhood one block from Jackson State. Dalton Circle was a narrow, horseshoe-shaped street of dilapidated shotgun houses. As with most shotguns, theirs had just three rooms, and James shared a bed with three brothers: Wesley, Alfred, and Charles. Like matches in a box, all fourteen members of the family were packed into this hovel, including James's sister Mattie and her three children. At first, James's mother resisted the move to Dalton Circle. There were too many divorced and unwed mothers there for her liking.

Though James then lived nearly a mile from his job, he continued working at the Wag-a-bag as usual. He was there on Thursday night, May 14, 1970, the second evening of rock-throwing at Jackson State. In recent days, James had had several things on his mind, including the senior prom and graduation. And lots of people were talking about the trouble at Jackson State. Since James now lived about a block south of the college, he had to walk through the campus every night on his way home from work. At about 9:45 P.M. Thursday, just after the rock-throwing had erupted on campus, James and his friend Amos were finishing work at the Wag-a-bag. They swept the floors and filled the beer boxes, and they watched several police cars pass the store. Four blocks down Lynch Street, in front of radio station WOKJ, there was a roadblock.

> "We said, 'There's something wrong up there,' and sure enough, there was," Amos Patton recalls. "It had been going on for a couple of nights, the way I remember it. So I asked him, 'James, what are you going to do? You've got to go home.' He said: 'I won't be staying out this way no more. I'm gonna go up through there and cut through the campus.' By cutting through the campus, he got a straight angle to his house on Dalton Circle. It was a shortcut he was taking every night when he walked home."

At 10:00 P.M., store manager Frank Dantoni turned out the lights and locked the front door of the Wag-a-bag. He and the two boys stood out front on Lynch Street.

> "I told them both to go on home and not to fool around because all that stuff was going on on Lynch Street," Dantoni recalls. "So Amos went on towards his house—I watched him—and James went on to his."

James headed toward the campus about a half mile down the street. He stopped near Stewart Hall dormitory, apparently to watch all the excitement. A friend of James later told the FBI that he and James had stood near the dorm. They heard gunfire and it frightened them, so they scurried up the knoll near the dormitory. They jumped over a fence, and for several minutes stayed there. Finally, they decided to go to their homes in opposite directions.

For James, that meant going back to Lynch Street and walking east toward Alexander Hall. He would cross the street and cut through the commons park to his home. But when James got as far as Roberts Dining Hall near the darkened park, there was a crowd of students shouting in front of Alexander Hall. Blue-helmeted officers with guns were lined up in the street and facing the crowd. Though most were watching the shouting students in front of the dorm, a few officers faced the park and the dining hall on the opposite side of Lynch Street, where James was standing. A sudden burst of gunfire lit the shadowy park. James ran. A shotgun slug ripped through his chest, and he fell in the dark.

• •

"How long, oh Lord, will our white brothers continue to destroy us?" Charles Evers asked, as he stood on the stage above James Green's casket. Evers leaned toward the microphone and looked out at the rows of black faces fanning themselves in the Masonic hall.

"To this kind of unbelievable murder, I don't know what I can really say at a time like this. But all of you who come from Washington—you've come because you cared. Because you're concerned. . . . We want you to go back to Washington and do one thing for us: you see that we get an investigation. You've got to go back this evening, and you've got to get up tomorrow morning and let everyone know, and make sure that this kind of murdering happens no more."

The funeral of James Green ended at 3:00 P.M., and the northern visitors returned to their air-conditioned buses on Lynch Street for the trip back to Thompson Field. Outside the Masonic Temple, James Green's mother and his stepfather, Matt Burton, stepped into a car for the mile-and-a-half procession up Lynch Street to the cemetery. Burton was a short, thin, balding man who worked for a grocery wholesaler in town. But since the death of his stepson James, the future seemed uncertain for Burton and his family.

After the shootings at Jackson State, Burton's foreman approached him. It was not just to extend his condolences.

> "He said, 'Matt, was that your stepson that got killed?' I said, 'Yes.' So he said, 'You must feel pretty big with all those senators and reporters coming to the house.' I said, 'No, I feel like just regular people.' They laid me off—said they'd call me back later. But they never did. I went down there two or three times trying to get my job back, but I never did. Charles Evers called the company two or three times for me, but no luck. I wasn't angry, just hurt for a time, because I didn't have no work to do. After seven years down there they told me I was the best on the conveyor line. I wasn't fired, they told me, or so they said."

The hearse bearing James Green's body pulled from the curb in front of the Masonic Temple and moved slowly west on Lynch Street. A crowd of mourners marched behind the hearse, forming a procession about a half mile long. The blacks passed police with shotguns at the corner of Dalton and Lynch near the Jackson State campus. The marchers followed the hearse past bullet-raked Roberts Dining Hall, where James Green had fallen. Across the street in front of Alexander Hall, the students guarding the dorm raised their fists in the Black Power salute.

When the procession reached police barricades in front of radio station WOKJ, the long black line turned south on Valley Street. An officer on a motorcycle followed as the marchers passed Bailey's Grill and the Delta Cotton Oil and Fertilizer plant. They crossed the railroad tracks and approached Jim Hill High, James Green's school. In the black graveyard in front of the school, the procession came to an end.

A crowd of about three thousand surrounded the grave site. After a black minister read the Twenty-third Psalm, James Green's coffin was lowered into the Mississippi clay. While the mourners were leaving the cemetery, a black workman in short sleeves sank a shovel into a pile of clay. He tossed the yellow clods into the grave.

• •

A full moon hung in the chilly twilight over Alexander Hall. On blankets in front of the dorm's west doorway were more than 150 black students. It was near dawn, Saturday, the morning after James Green's funeral. At 5:00

Fayette Mayor Charles Evers, brother of slain civil rights leader Medgar Evers, stands in the crowd of mourners at the cemetery where James Green was buried. (*The Kudzu*)

A.M., U.S. marshals, FBI agents, and Justice Department officials approached the students at the dorm. The federal agents had come to tell the black youths the state of Mississippi would soon take control of their campus.

Governor John Bell Williams had told the FBI he would not seize Alexander Hall for two days after the funeral. But apparently encouraged by the peaceful funeral on Friday, Williams decided to reverse his decision and swoop down on the campus at dawn Saturday. "It is a poker game," Governor Williams said, "and a showdown is necessary."

The FBI had warned Attorney General John Mitchell that such a confrontation would lead to bloodshed. To prevent more violence, Mitchell sent Deputy Attorney General Jerris Leonard to Jackson. It was three o'clock Saturday morning (Eastern time) when Leonard boarded a U.S. Air Force jet in Washington. At about 4:00 A.M. he landed at Thompson Field in Jackson. He met immediately with local reporters and federal agents to assess the situation at Jackson State.

An hour later, in the pink glow of the Mississippi dawn, Deputy Attorney General Leonard approached the black youths guarding Alexander Hall. In wire-rimmed glasses and tailored suit, Leonard asked Fayette Mayor Charles Evers and Student Government President Warner Buxton to confer with him on the sidewalk across the street from the dorm. Reporters and federal agents were allowed to join in the huddle and observe the negotiations.

"With John Bell Williams in the Mansion, nobody was very confident that this would be anything but a disaster," recalls Wilson Minor, a former *New Orleans Times-Picayune* reporter. "I thought it was going to mean more bloodshed. Yet Jerris Leonard negotiated well that early morning. The terms were that the students would let the state take down

Network TV crews and local reporters cover the confrontation between students and state officials over the repair of Alexander Hall. With the megaphone is Student Government President Warner Buxton. To the left and holding a pipe is U.S. Deputy Attorney General Jerris Leonard. In the baseball cap is Cecil Yarbro, the head of Mississippi's Building Commission. In front of Yarbro and holding a microphone is WJTV newsman Bert Case, a witness to the shootings. (*The Kudzu*)

the bullet-riddled panels, if, after the FBI inspected them, they were returned to the students to be used as they saw fit—as a memorial."

After the deal was made, three state construction trucks pulled up along the curb in front of Alexander Hall. From one truck emerged a short, fat man in a yellow jacket and baseball cap. He was Cecil Yarbro, director of Mississippi's Building Commission. Yarbro's job was to remove the evidence from Alexander Hall. Leonard approached Yarbro and told him of the agreement he had just reached with the students to avert a confrontation.

> "The man who was the head of the State Building Commission—I knew Cecil Yarbro pretty well," recalls Jerry DeLaughter, a former *Memphis Commercial-Appeal* reporter. "Well, I learned that Cecil told John Bell Williams that as head of the Building Commission, he would be glad to handle the problem out at Jackson State. Cecil said, 'I understand the niggers. After all, I own a lot of property on Lynch Street.' "

As the sun rose above the horizon, Yarbro, Leonard, and student leader Warner Buxton approached the chain-link fence that separated the white officials from the black youths blocking the west doorway to Alexander Hall. TV cameras and reporters with notepads surrounded the three men at the fence as they faced the students blocking the doorway only a few feet away.

"I have instructions here," Yarbro announced with a bullhorn, "which are a court order for my workmen and me to remove this glass and these panels and turn it over to the FBI."

As the short, pudgy man in the baseball cap spoke, the students grunted "oink-oink-oink." They yelled that Yarbro should read the court decision ordering them off the campus. Yarbro opened a copy of Judge Coleman's decision and read, emphasizing one passage as a warning:

> All parties to these proceedings, and all others who may be informed of them, are hereby expressly enjoined, upon the penalties of contempt, from in any manner whatever interfering with, hampering, or hindering the removal of said evidence and the preservation thereof.

Deputy Attorney General Leonard took the bullhorn and announced that all evidence, including the shattered windows and bullet-pocked panels, would go to the FBI—not to the state of Mississippi.

"I want to assure everyone here," Leonard said, "that it's my understanding that as the paneling is removed, that it will be marked, that it will be placed in the cardboard boxes that are on the trucks, and that the panelling will be placed in the boxes under the supervision of the bureau, and that all boxes will be marked and turned over to the FBI as the court order requires."

The student leader at the fence, Warner Buxton, took the megaphone to address his fellow students. Buxton feared they might not accept the compromise he had worked out with the white officials.

"We want to prevent the destruction of this," Buxton said, nodding toward Alexander Hall. "That's why we're here in the first place. I want to make sure that all evidence is passed over to the proper authorities and will not under any circumstances be destroyed. We are here not to cause further bloodshed, and we are not here to fight their armies, because they outnumber us anyways. But like good warriors, we're going to retreat."

Turning to Yarbro, Deputy Attorney General Leonard said he could now enter the dormitory. But Leonard reminded Yarbro that all materials were to be "turned over immediately to the FBI."

"Boss man," Yarbro said testily, "if I tell you I am going to put them in a box and turn them over to the FBI, that's what I'm going to do."

The students blocking the dorm grumbled at Yarbro's remark, but they stepped aside anyway and walked to the opposite side of Lynch Street. From the sidewalk, they watched as the state's work crews entered the dorm. The white workmen took down the shattered windows, the glass doors, and the green steel panels riddled by gunfire. They placed all the evidence in labelled boxes on the state trucks. Stored in a local warehouse, the boxes were later turned over to the FBI.

The evidence in these boxes soon would be studied by a presidential commission, two grand juries, and a civil court. Perhaps then, it was hoped, the full truth about the Jackson State killings would be known.

10

NIXON'S COURT

That Justice is a blind goddess
Is a thing to which we black are wise:
Her bandage hides two festering sores
That once perhaps were eyes.

—Langston Hughes

Biloxi, Mississippi. Resort town of palm trees, white antebellum mansions and beachfront motels facing the brown silty waters of the Gulf of Mexico. In 1972 it was a hustling town of strip joints, seedy bars, Keesler Air Force Base, and marinas. A wave-swept and battered city, Biloxi had survived Indian raids, Yankee conquerors, and killer hurricanes like Camille, which in 1969 had sucked away 157 lives and smashed 36,000 homes and 400 businesses along Mississippi's Gulf Coast.

Just 80 miles east of New Orleans—but more than 160 miles south of Jackson—Biloxi seemed more a part of Louisiana than Baptist Mississippi. Settled two centuries ago by the French, it was a Roman Catholic city of fifty-thousand (14 percent black). It had its own Mardi Gras festival, and like Bourbon Street, its own strip of nightclubs with girly shows and spirits flowing until the wee hours. Things were a lot quieter in the rest of Mississippi, where many towns had no bars at all, and those that did sell liquor closed the bars at midnight.

But Biloxi was the Sodom of Mississippi, a tolerant, easy-going resort town that had no great quarrel with a little vice and the racial peace that helped keep the tourist trade humming. True, Biloxi was the resting place of Mississippi's own Jefferson Davis, president of the Confederacy. And once there had been segregated buses and segregated water fountains here, as well as beaches for whites only. But during the sixties, there had been none of the lynchings and church-bombings that had erupted in other parts of Mississippi.

In February 1972 the students wounded two years before at Jackson

State came to Biloxi for justice. They and the families of Phillip Gibbs and James Green had filed suit in the U.S. District Court for the Southern District of Mississippi against the State of Mississippi, Patrol Inspector Lloyd "Goon" Jones, and the forty-two patrolmen he had led to the Jackson State campus. The blacks also had sued the City of Jackson and Police Lieutenant Warren Magee, as well as the five policemen who had admitted firing on the campus. The blacks alleged the lawmen had been poorly trained and had opened fire "maliciously, recklessly, and without just regard for life and safety." The black plaintiffs demanded 13.8 million dollars in compensation for their pain, anguish, and medical expenses.

Though litigation over the Jackson State case had begun two years before, the black plaintiffs had found the results discouraging. In June of 1970, a special federal grand jury had convened in Jackson to investigate the killings. Attorney General John Mitchell had requested this grand jury after the highway patrol, with Governor John Bell Williams's blessing, had refused to speak to FBI agents or submit weapons for lab tests. The federal judge who convened the grand jury was William H. Cox, notorious for having called blacks "chimpanzees" and for once having said from the bench: "The intelligence of colored people don't compare ratio-wise to white people." On June 29, 1970 in a federal courtroom in Jackson, newsmen from across the country were stunned by Judge Cox's biased remarks on the Jackson State shootings. In his instructions to the grand jury, Cox said:

> In your consideration of the Jackson State College incident, you will understand that nobody—black or white—has any right conferred upon him by Congress, or by any section of the federal constitution, to engage in a riot, or rebellion, or to set fire to real or personal property of another, or to shoot at peace officers, or to throw bricks or bottles or rocks at policemen, firemen, State Highway Patrolmen or National Guardsmen.

Judge Cox added the warning that his district would not "provide safe sanctuary for militants or for anarchists or for revolutionaries of any race." Not surprisingly, the federal grand jury declined to indict any of the officers who had opened fire at Jackson State.

A week after Cox had addressed his jury, Judge Russel D. Moore III convened the Hinds County Grand Jury in Jackson. In his instructions to the county jury, Judge Moore paraphrased portions of Cox's remarks, emphasizing that no one, "black or white," has a right to riot, and that lawmen may open fire on rioters. After questioning witnesses, the county grand jury called for the indictment of a black male on charges of arson and inciting riot at Jackson State. He was Ernest Lee Kyles, a twenty-one-year-old nonstudent. But the charges against Kyles were later dropped for lack of evidence.

In Washington, D.C., President Nixon yielded to demands for an investigation of the Jackson and Kent State killings. Nixon established the President's Commission on Campus Unrest and named William W. Scranton, a former Republican governor of Pennsylvania, as chairman. By September of 1970, the commission's report was ready. It called the shootings at Kent and Jackson State "unjustified." The commission concluded there was no convincing evidence of sniper fire at Kent State, and "no physical evidence of small arms fire in the area around Alexander Hall" at Jackson State. Having studied the evidence gathered by the FBI, the commission added that at Jackson State there was no evidence of a bullet ricocheting off the concrete wall behind TV newsman Jack Hobbs, as Hobbs had reported.

The presidential commission's report gave Jackson State students some satisfaction, but it did not bear the weight of law. To redress their grievances, the students wounded at Jackson State, as well as the families of Phillip Gibbs and James Green, had just one more opportunity: the civil trial in Biloxi.

• •

On Monday, February 28, 1972, Judge Walter Nixon addressed the all-white jury of nine men and three women in the jury box. A dark-haired, forty-three-year-old Biloxian, Nixon told the white Mississippi jurors they should view the facts of this case "without bias, without sympathy for any party or parties."

"All persons stand equal before the law," Nixon added, "and are to be dealt with as equals in a court of justice." Nodding toward the plaintiffs' table in the wood-panelled courtroom, Nixon called for opening statements to the jury.

Ralph McAfee, a white attorney for the black plaintiffs, approached the "podium," the wooden lectern facing Judge Nixon. McAfee worked for one of the best law firms in the nation—Cravaith, Swaine and Moore—the Wall Street firm often hired by such powerful corporations as IBM. But on this case, McAfee's firm was working without fee to assist civil rights attorneys in Jackson. At the podium microphone, Attorney McAfee addressed Judge Nixon and the jury: "May it please the court, your honor, ladies and gentlemen of the jury, around midnight on May 14, 1970, a Thursday, forty-three members of the Mississippi Highway Safety Patrol and twenty-six members of the City of Jackson Police Department moved into a position generally in front of the west wing of Alexander Hall. After a very brief time—a very brief time—they opened fire on that women's dormitory."

McAfee said the patrol and policemen who had fired were undisciplined and had been poorly trained. He said the lawmen had nothing but excuses for what they had done. McAfee predicted the officers would blame the students for the shootings by accusing them of cursing and throwing rocks and bottles. But the lawmen's chief justification for firing, McAfee told the jury, would be sniper fire from the windows of college dormitories. Since there was no conclusive evidence of snipers at Jackson State, McAfee asked the jurors to imagine there had been a gunman. "Now let's think about whether or not that's a justification under the circumstances I've outlined to you," McAfee said. He asked the jurors whether a sniper at a window upstairs in Alexander Hall could justify killing students outdoors on the ground.

McAfee told the jury that officers had fired their weapons even before the alleged gunfire from Alexander Hall. "There had been a shot fired, or two shots fired, or perhaps even three, into one of the rooms in Stewart Hall—I believe number 421. Now we have heard that the defendant Lloyd Jones, who was in charge of the highway patrol here, was at least in this area at the time when this firing occurred. No one was hit, but he or one of his men fired one or more shots from an alleyway up into room 421. And that's a very interesting fact to play with."

•

"If it please the court, I will make the opening statement on behalf of the defendants," Attorney Robert Nichols said to Judge Nixon. Nichols was a white attorney defending Police Lieutenant Magee, five other policemen, and the City of Jackson.

Nichols began with the events of May 13, 1970, the night before the campus slayings. He said the rock-throwing on Lynch Street had been "dangerous in every form" for motorists passing the Jackson State campus. There had been an attempt to firebomb an ROTC building, Nichols said, and when officers had arrived to restore order, they had been "subjected not only to a barrage of brick-throwing, but every known type of filthy, disgusting epithets that that crowd could toss at them."

The next night, May 14, again police and patrolmen had been summoned to the campus to stop more rock-throwing. "It reminds me of what Gilbert and Sullivan said about policemen," Nichols said. " 'A policeman's life is not a happy one.' "

Nichols told the jury the officers sent to Jackson State "are not ill-equipped yuks that they sent out there to shoot people." These men confronted "riotous conditions" on the campus, he said, and rocks and obscenities "kept flying at the police." As the officers watched the windows of two women's dormitories that night, they noticed gunflashes, he said. The police working the searchlight inside Thompson's Tank were warned of gunfire from Ayer Hall dormitory, he said. At about the same time, "a colored male" with a pistol began shooting from a top-floor window in Alexander Hall, Nichols said. "We will show you that there was actually a sniper in that building."

•

"Would you state your full name please?"

"Vernon Steve Weakley."

The man asking the question was George Taylor, a white attorney in the Jackson office of the Lawyers Committee for Civil Rights under Law, a national organization that takes civil rights cases. Taylor was working with the New York attorneys representing the black plaintiffs.

Weakley was the first witness for the plaintiffs and one of twelve students wounded at Jackson State. Speaking into the microphone in a low voice, Weakley told the court he was a member of Omega Psi Phi fraternity, and that he worked part time in a post office in Jackson. After work at 9:30 on Wednesday night, May 13, 1970, he had gone to the Jackson State campus for a fraternity meeting. Weakley said students were throwing rocks at cars that night, and a crowd attacked an ROTC building.

Attorney Taylor asked if Weakley had been involved in the violence.

"No, I wasn't," Weakley replied.

On the next night, Weakley testified, again he had returned to the Jackson State campus after work. He and some friends had left the campus for awhile to have a beer at the Red Carpet Lounge on Lynch Street. At about 11:30 P.M., they had returned to the college, and Weakley had stood talking with friends near the chain-link fence in front of Alexander Hall's west wing. He recalled seeing lines of officers marching east up the street toward the dorm.

"As the police and highway patrolmen arrived," Weakley said, "you had an officer with a white shirt on, whoever he was, with the bullhorn talking. . . ." Students were cursing and three or four tossed rocks at the lawmen, Weakley recalled. "At that time, I saw a bottle thrown. It seemed to me as if it came from the opposite side of the street." The bottle shattered in Lynch Street.

"It seemed to me as soon as it hit behind the officers—they were facing Alexander Hall, you know—they just started shooting," Weakley said. "I turned around to run, and the next thing I know I was hit and knocked down. I was hit in the right leg and I was bleeding real bad and my leg was burning."

"Did you hear any sniper shots at all at that point coming from any area on the Jackson State campus?" Attorney Taylor asked.

"No, I didn't."

•

The next witness was Mrs. Myrtle Green Burton, a short, frail, light-skinned woman of forty-five and the mother of James Green. Mrs. Burton told the court she was a housewife, and since the death of her son James her husband had been unemployed. She had raised nine children, she said, and James had been her fifth.

"Did your family and did James use the campus as a passageway from your home to the other side of town?" Attorney McAfee asked. "Specifically, did he walk from where you lived, normally, through the campus over to the grocery store to work?"

"Yes he did," Mrs. Green answered. "We all did, until that happened."

"What time did James Earl normally return from work at night?"

Mrs. Green said he usually left work at 10:15 P.M. after cleaning up the store. Then it would take thirty or forty minutes to walk the mile east from the Wag-a-bag and through the campus to the family's shotgun house on Dalton Circle.

"Did you wait up for him at night?" McAfee asked.

"Every night I probably would lie down on the bed," she said, "but I wouldn't go to sleep until all of my children was in, and then I would go to sleep. But I couldn't go to sleep until they was inside."

"How did you hear that your son had been shot?"

"I heard the shooting when it occurred," Mrs. Burton recalled. She testified she had been in bed when she was startled by gunblasts. She got up and started walking about the house. She found all of the children but James were watching television.

"I didn't want to tell them that I was upset, because I figured that some of the oldest children might try to see what it was all about," Mrs. Burton testified. "I just kept hoping and looking for James. And that's when I heard that he had been killed—it was on the news when they were looking at TV. It came over the news and then one of the children said, 'Did you understand what they said?' I was so upset then, I couldn't believe it. I said, 'No, he is not dead, I am sure. He must be wounded somewhere. He couldn't be dead.' "

•

Tuwaine Davis Whitehead took the stand. A thin, twenty-one-year-old junior, she majored in special education and commuted to Jackson State from Canton, her hometown twenty-eight miles north of the campus. Since she had always been a commuting student, Whitehead testified, it was only by accident that she had been in Alexander Hall on the night of May 14, 1970.

"We was going to have a final physical education examination that night from six to eight, so we had to stay over," Whitehead said.

Lacking a ride home after her exam that night, she had gone to Alexander Hall to see friends on the third floor of the west wing. The group was listening to records and playing cards in the dorm when she heard a yell: "They are marching in front of the dorm!" She and her friends scurried down the hallway to the west-wing stairwell. On the landing between the third and fourth floors, they found other female students crowding the windows overlooking Lynch Street. From these same stairwell windows, according to the highway patrolmen, a male sniper had opened fire.

"When I got to the windows," Whitehead told the court, "I went to look out, but I only got a glance. That's when someone shouted that the officers was fixing to shoot. . . . I turned to run and I got halfway down the stairs, and I felt something hit me in my back. I fell down the stairs and I crawled behind a wall and there I stayed up until the shooting had stopped. . . . While I was behind the wall I noticed that my arm was bleeding. It had been cut open, and I could see buckshots, or whatever they was, bouncing all around me, and glass and everything falling around me."

"You were hit in the arm?" Attorney McAfee asked.

"In the arm and in the leg and back."

"How did you feel while this shooting was going on?"

"I was scared to see all this coming around me, coming straight at me. I could hear this noise like shooting going on and bullets bouncing all around me and everything. I was just scared to death, because I just knew I was dead. Wasn't nobody up around me or nothing, I just knew I was dead."

"Did you see a man, a sniper there firing shots out of the broken window?"

"No, not at all."

"Up to the shooting, had you seen a man anywhere in the dormitory?"

"No, not at all."

•

Leroy Kenter, Jr., was the next wounded student to testify. He was a tall, muscular youth with a beard—a sophomore back in 1970. After he had been shot at Alexander Hall, Kenter had lain in traction for nearly two months. Kenter's left thigh bone had been shattered and the leg shortened by a half inch. Bullet fragments remained in his right leg.

Kenter told the court that on the night of the shootings he had been talking with friends in front of Alexander Hall just after saying good night to his girlfriend. Like many other students, Kenter had never seen the dump truck ablaze two blocks west in front of Stewart Hall, and he had not heard the patrol shooting in the alleyway alongside the men's dorm. When the peace officers began marching up Lynch Street toward Alexander Hall, Kenter said, he had no idea who they were: the guard, the patrol, or the police. He recalled seeing objects tossed over his head and toward the lawmen when they turned to face the students at Alexander Hall.

"Then the front line dropped down to their knees," Kenter testified. "They leveled down in order for the back line to see over them. . . . That's when I ran. . . . The bullet knocked me out. I was laying there and I didn't really think I was shot. I figured I was hit with a blank bullet, because I couldn't believe that people would shoot live ammunition into a girls' dorm. So I said to myself that I was going to lay there until they got through, but after they had stopped, I tried to get up. I couldn't, . . . and that's when I reached down and felt my leg, and that's when I came up with a handful of blood."

"Had you heard any sniper shots immediately before these police officers started aiming their weapons?" Kenter was asked.

"I hadn't heard any shots."

•

Dale Gibbs, the widow of Phillip Gibbs, was sworn in and took her seat in the witness box. Her hair was shoulder-length and she wore a lavender dress. Mrs. Gibbs was the nineteen-year-old mother of two boys now; unknown to Phillip, she had become pregnant only a week or two before her husband had been killed. Her oldest boy, two-year-old Phillip, Jr., had sat in the courtroom with her since the trial's beginning.

Mrs. Gibbs told the court that she and Phillip had married and lived together in Jackson for nine months while he was a student at Jackson State. She said that Phillip had worked part time and received Social Security checks, yet the money had not been enough, so she and Phillip, Jr., had moved back to Ripley to stay with her parents. She said that before Phillip had been killed, he had made the two-hundred-mile drive north to Ripley almost every weekend to stay with her and their son.

"Did you love your husband?" attorney Taylor asked.

"Yes," Mrs. Gibbs answered.

"Did he love you?"

"Yes."

"Did he help you take care of the child when he was home on the weekends?"

"Yes, you know, diapers and getting bottles and all," Mrs. Gibbs replied.

Rufus Creekmore, a white attorney for the Jackson police, approached the podium to cross-examine Mrs. Gibbs. Creekmore drew attention to Mrs. Gibbs's sex life by indirectly questioning the legitimacy of her youngest child. He asked her for the exact dates of her marriage and the births of her two children. As Mrs. Gibbs told him each date, Creekmore repeated it for the benefit of the jury. Then he asked her what sort of drinking habits Phillip had had.

"He drank," Mrs. Gibbs replied.

"And would he frequently get drunk when you were living with him?"

"No."

"Now if you read the autopsy report," Creekmore said, "you know that the doctors found in his blood .27 percent of alcohol by weight. Do you know that?"

"That's what I read, yes," Mrs. Gibbs replied. "But I am not sure."

"If he had .27 percent," Creekmore said, "and if .15 percent makes a man drunk, he really had plenty to make him drunk, didn't he?"

•

Redd Wilson was a slim, wiry Jackson State senior studying to become a social studies teacher. He had been shot in the upper left thigh on the night of the killings. After taking the witness stand, Wilson testified that on the first night of unrest, May 13, 1970, he had been among the crowd charging across the campus and shouting, "Let's burn the Rotsy buildings!" The crowd had thrown stones at the ROTC barracks, Wilson said, but he had not. He was there just to watch, he said, and he never saw the firebombing attempt later in the evening.

"Excuse me," Judge Nixon said to Wilson. "Why were rocks being thrown at the ROTC building, and why was there talk of burning the ROTC building down?"

"Because there are some students who resent an ROTC branch on the Jackson State campus," Wilson replied. "They feel it is a branch of the military."

On the next night, Wilson testified, he had been talking with friends in front of Alexander Hall after just saying goodnight to his girlfriend. When the lawmen arrived at the dorm, Wilson was standing near the west wing. Students were shouting, "We are not going to run!" Staying to face the guns was a matter of courage, Wilson told the court. That was why the students had not run from the police.

Only "a couple of seconds" after the officers had arrived, Wilson testified, a bottle flew from the crowd of students. It burst like a .22 shot on the Lynch Street pavement.

"Immediately after that happened," Wilson added, "they started to shoot."

•

As the testimony of the wounded continued, the jury learned how the other students had become tangled in the events at Jackson State.

Lonzie Thompson stopped to talk with friends at Alexander Hall after finishing a night's work at a local grocery store. When the lawmen arrived in front of the women's dorm, Thompson saw a brick and a bottle sailing from the crowd toward the white men. The next thing he knew, he was shot in the right thigh. Pat Sanders was also in front of the west wing, just "talking and looking and waiting" with friends. She was hit in the right shoulder. Climmie Johnson Murry was upstairs, reading in the dorm's second-floor TV lounge. As the shooting erupted, she was struck in the head by buckshot. Stella Spinks, a commuting student, was in Alexander

Hall only to borrow a book. Standing near a west stairwell window, she was hit in the arm and back by buckshot fragments. She said she saw no sniper in the stairwell. Montie Rose Davis, daughter of a Hattiesburg minister, was also looking out a stairwell window when she felt ricocheting buckshot burning her arm. She, too, said she had seen no sniper.

In all, nine of the twelve wounded students testified before the all-white jury in Biloxi, though just three of them had filed suit against the lawmen. Five other student witnesses told what it had been like that night at Alexander Hall. While cross-examining each of the students, the attorneys for the lawmen focused on the students' prior scrapes with the law, their allegedly poor study habits, their drinking habits, or their failure to stop the rock-throwing on their campus.

The students' testimony agreed on one chief point: there had been no snipers at Jackson State. Except for that, their stories were a hodgepodge of contradictory facts. Some students thought the man with the bullhorn, Lieutenant Magee, had addressed the crowd at Alexander Hall. Others said there had been no time for that. Some students said the officers had fired as soon as they had stopped near the dorm, while others said the white men had been there several minutes. Some students said the officers in the front line had fired from the hip. Others said they had knelt.

The students' contradictory testimony reflected their blurred memories and fragmented perceptions of a nightmarish evening two years in the past. The testimony of the lawmen would be clearer and more consistent.

• •

Highway Patrolman Thomas Latham was sworn in and sat in the witness box. He told the jury that on the night of the killings he had been armed with a nine-millimeter submachine gun. Latham had been one of two patrolmen on the campus with such a weapon, which could fire seven hundred rounds per minute.

"How many times did you fire this submachine gun?" Attorney McAfee asked.

"I don't know, sir," Patrolman Latham answered.

"Could you give us an estimate?" McAfee asked.

"I fired one short burst, probably eight or ten rounds," Latham said.

"And at what target did you aim that weapon when you fired that burst?"

"Across the top of Alexander Hall, the west wing."

"Why did you fire there?"

"Someone hollered that there was a sniper up top of the dormitory," Latham testified. "I looked up. I saw some flashes of fire after the shooting had already started—the other officers had started shooting. And I shot at what I thought was in the direction of where this sniper was, across the top of the building. I was looking up through some power lines."

Deputy Attorney General William Allain, the state's defense attorney for the patrolmen, began cross-examining Patrolman Latham. Allain's approach with Latham would be nearly the same for every officer he questioned—the apple-pie approach. Allain asked Patrolman Latham whether he was married. Latham said he was. Allain next asked how many children he had. Latham said three. Allain then asked whether Latham had attended classes beyond high school and how long he had served in the patrol and in the armed forces.

Allain also asked Latham, who had been armed with a submachine gun, if he had been afraid for his life at Jackson State.

"Yes, sir, I was," Latham said. "I thought I was going to die right there in that street."

•

Rex P. Armistead, a field investigator for the highway patrol, took the stand. A plainclothesman, Armistead told the court that even before arriving at Alexander Hall, he had heard shots on the Jackson State campus. At Stewart Hall, he testified, he had heard gunfire all around him: from behind Stewart Hall to the north, from Alexander Hall two blocks east, and from the ROTC buildings across the street to the south.

But there had been other gunfire at the men's dorm that night—gunfire from the patrol. Investigator Armistead's memory of this shooting proved imperfect.

Attorney McAfee asked Armistead if he had heard shooting in the alleyway alongside Stewart Hall.

"Yes, sir," Armistead replied.

"What kind of gunfire was that?" McAfee asked.

"I think it was shotgun," Investigator Armistead said. "I'm not sure, because there was so much noise that I couldn't determine what it was."

"And you didn't go around to ascertain whether one of the patrolmen had fired his shotgun?" McAfee asked.

"That's not my duty, sir," Investigator Armistead replied.

Continuing his story, Armistead said that after the officers had arrived at

Alexander Hall, they had lined up to face the dorm. He had stood about four yards to the rear of Thompson's Tank while Police Lieutenant Magee had tried to calm the students.

"The mob at that point had become so violent, and there was so much debris being hurled at us, that I couldn't hear anything Lieutenant Magee said," Armistead testified. "I observed a black male with a weapon in his hand—a hand weapon or a revolver—it could have been an automatic—but it was a hand weapon, firing two shots at the police officers and the highway patrolmen."

Armistead said the gunman had been in the west stairwell window, second from the top, where the glass had been broken out. Armistead said there were two flashes of gunfire from that window, and a bullet passed to his right and struck the concrete retaining wall behind him.

"Did you then fire?"

"Immediately upon being fired at the first time, I returned fire to the third floor."

"How many times did you fire?"

"Five times."

Armistead testified that he had considered firing again after seeing yet another gunman, a black male in red pants and armed with a pistol. This man in red pants, Armistead said, had stood among the students on the knoll in front of Alexander Hall. But Armistead said he had never fired at this gunman, since the man was surrounded by students.

Armistead added that he had witnessed one more sign of sniper fire that night: a city policeman had yanked open the back door of Thompson's Tank and yelled that every man should get down—sniper fire from the south. Armistead said he had turned around and pointed his shotgun south, the direction of Ayer Hall dormitory for women. But he could not see this sniper.

•

It took more than a week for the forty-three highway patrolmen to finish testifying before the all-white jury in Biloxi. Their stories were monotonous. Not just because they dragged on for so long, but because one patrolman's account sounded just like another's. In lawyers' lingo, the patrolmen's testimony was "sing-songy."

Patrolman Joseph Braun, for example, said he had seen two "muzzle flashes" from the window second from the top in Alexander Hall's west stairwell. Armed with a submachine gun, Braun raked the window with about ten bullets, he said. Patrolman Jimmy Taylor saw a "muzzle blast" from the same window and fired his .308 rifle twice at it. Patrolmen Emmit Edwards and Claude Daniel said they also saw "muzzle blasts" from the west stairwell. So did Patrolman Donald Bray. So did Patrolmen Jerry Jones, Jerry Butler, John Myers, and Charles Langford. And each said he had just returned the fire.

Thirty-eight of the forty-three patrolmen admitted opening fire on the Jackson State campus. They testified they had fired no less than 127 shots. Though nearly all of the patrolmen admitted using their weapons at Jackson State, two-thirds said they had fired toward a window on the second-from-the-top floor in the west wing stairwell. Most of the other officers said they had shot into the air or along the roofline of the dormitory. Not one officer admitted to firing at ground level, even though eleven black youths had been wounded there, two of them fatally.

Clearly, the patrolmen's testimony amounted to a coverup.

•

The last patrolman to testify was Inspector Lloyd "Goon" Jones, who had worn two pistols and carried a shotgun on the night of the campus killings. As Inspector for Patrol District 1, Jones had been the officer who had radioed the number of "niggers" shot that evening at Alexander Hall. After Jones settled his six-foot-three frame in the witness box, he told the court that he had once been a farmer, a mail carrier, and had worked for a butane company. He had served in the hospital corps of the U.S. Navy.

Attorney McAfee asked Jones about the first time lawmen had opened fire on the campus on May 14, 1970—at Stewart Hall. It was crucial to understand what had happened there, since those who claimed there was sniper fire had pointed to a radio report that Police Lieutenant Magee had made while at Stewart Hall. Magee had radioed: "We're being fired upon up here!" But the shots that had startled Magee may well have come from patrolmen instead of from snipers.

"How many shots were fired by your men, and by you, at Stewart Hall that night?" McAfee asked Jones.

"The best I remember, sir," Jones said, "I was the only one that fired, but I did not shoot at the building or at any person. I fired a shot when Assistant Inspector Vinson got hit on the head with a jug, and I fired a shot straight up in the air. We were about halfway up in the alley, and we were about two or three feet from the side of the building."

"Well, let me read to you your sworn testimony before the President's

Commission on Campus Unrest," Attorney McAfee said. Turning to page 592 of the hearings transcript, McAfee read Inspector Jones's testimony, which suggested that several patrolmen had opened fire while at Stewart Hall, and at two different times:

> We moved up to the burning dump truck. We were being thrown at with everything, and some of the students came down near an alley and threw at all of us—all the men in the city police and patrol. Some one or two shots were fired up over the heads of the ones that were in the alley as they went back up the alley. The fire truck came up and started putting the fire out. We went back up the alley. I went up the alley myself to see if any students were up back of the building. Two or three men went with me. . . . When we were going up the alley, the men were hit by a jug out of the window. Two or three of us fired up in the air. . . .

"Is this true and correct as I've read it here, and as it appears in this sworn testimony?"

"Yes, sir," Jones replied.

When the patrolmen had opened fire in Stewart Hall's alleyway, Police Lieutenant Magee had been standing around the corner with his men where he could not see the shooting in the alleyway. So the sound of patrolmen's gunshots, instead of sniper fire, may have startled Magee.

Turning to the shootings at Alexander Hall, Attorney McAfee asked Jones about Lieutenant Magee's efforts to keep the peace. "Was he having any luck getting the people to move and go into the dormitory?" McAfee asked.

"They were moving some. Yes, sir," Jones replied. "I remember him saying up there, 'Ladies and Gentlemen, please go back in the buildings,' and that's the last I remember hearing him say over the bullhorn that night."

"Then what happened."

"The shooting started."

"What did you do?" McAfee asked. "Did anyone give a command to fire?"

"No, sir," Jones said. He added that students had been throwing rocks, so he approached an officer with a tear-gas cannister on his belt.

"I got it from him and was fixin' to pull the pin when I turned around to face the crowd again," Jones said. "I heard a shot—saw a flash and heard a shot—and the shooting by the officers started, and I never did get to throw the gas."

•

Officer Billy Dwight Till was the first Jackson policeman to take the stand. Till was one of five city officers who admitted firing while at Jackson State.

Police Officer Till told the court that according to his training, if a mob threatened city policemen, the officers were to fire high into the air. But only if ordered. Next, they were to lower their guns and fire into the ground, but only if ordered. Finally, they were to fire into the mob if, ordered. Policeman Till said that at Alexander Hall twice he had fired into the air. Because other officers had been shooting, Till said, he had assumed the order to fire high had been given.

"Did you hear any shots prior to the barrage?" Attorney Taylor asked, referring to possible sniper fire.

"Yes, sir," Officer Till said. "I did."

"Would you describe those?"

"They sounded like—I heard two shots," Till testified. "You could hear them when they zinged. They sounded like a small-caliber weapon. I heard the shots hit the concrete and then ricochet."

Till added that one shot had come from the north, the direction of Alexander Hall, and another from the south, the direction of Ayer Hall, also a women's dorm.

"What did you do immediately after the shooting?" Taylor asked Officer Till.

"Well, I didn't know what was going to happen next," Till answered. "Somebody said there were some more shells in the tank and went to the tank and got some more shells."

"That's shells for your shotgun?"

"Yes, sir," Officer Till said.

Drawing on the surplus ammunition in Thompson's Tank, Till and four other policemen who had opened fire were able to return eight unused rounds to their superiors. That had made it look as though they never had pulled their triggers.

"Did you inform anyone after that night that you had not fired your weapon?"

"Yes, sir. I did," Police Officer Till admitted.

"Who did you tell?"

"I told—I don't remember who the two FBI agents were—but I told them I did not."

"Why did you tell them that?"

"Because we hadn't been interviewed by counsel, and because our department hadn't made an investigation, and I just didn't have an idea what to do."

After Officer Till's testimony, four other Jackson policemen took the stand. Each admitted to having fired his weapon while at Jackson State. But the policemen's version of the campus shootings differed somewhat from the highway patrol's. For instance, no policeman claimed to have seen a "muzzle blast," as the patrolmen had. And not one policeman claimed to have spotted a gunman in the second-from-top window in Alexander Hall's west stairwell.

But again, there was a striking similarity in the testimony of all five city policemen who had fired. Police Officer Robert Austin testified that before the barrage at Alexander Hall, he had heard two small-caliber shots. Both shots seemed to come from Alexander Hall, he said, and he fired only once—straight into the air. Police Officer Carl Penson testified that he also had heard two small-caliber shots from the direction of Alexander Hall, and one shot "zinged" off the concrete wall behind him. Penson said that he too had fired into the air. Officers Wayne Simpson, Jr., and Billy Rowzee testified that they, too, had heard two shots before firing into the air.

The city policemen claimed they had fired only because they had believed the order to "fire high" had been given. Three of the policemen admitted to taking extra ammunition from Thompson's Tank. Four of them admitted deceiving the FBI agents who had questioned them about firing their weapons at Jackson State.

•

Lieutenant Warren Magee, the officer in charge of both the police and patrolmen at Jackson State, was the last policeman to testify.

Lawyers for the black plaintiffs regarded Magee as their key witness. After all, Magee had been the officer in command, yet he had said again and again he had never seen a campus sniper and had never ordered his men to fire. In pretrial testimony, Magee even had admitted to being startled by the officers shooting right behind him. To ensure Magee would not change this testimony, attorneys for the black plaintiffs had grilled the lieutenant for nearly a month in advance of the trial. They had wanted a precise and consistent record of everything Magee knew about the slayings—a record Magee could not contradict once on the stand.

After he was sworn in, Lieutenant Magee took his seat in the witness box. Magee, forty-one years of age, was not a big man. He was five-feet-ten and wore glasses. His dark hair was thin at the temples. Magee told the court that on the night of the shootings, students at Stewart Hall dormitory had unloaded a "pretty heavy" barrage of rocks on the officers. Nevertheless, the students had moved away from police lines just as he had ordered them, Magee said. But when a fire truck had come to put out the blazing dump truck near the dorm, Magee had heard shots.

"I heard two shots from what sounded like a small-caliber weapon," Magee testified. He added that the shots seemed to come from the general area of Stewart Hall.

"The two shots that you heard, Lieutenant—could you tell whether they were fired at law enforcement officers?" asked attorney Robert Mullen, who represented the black plaintiffs.

"I can't say, sir. I didn't have any men hit by gunfire."

"Did you see the shots being fired?" attorney Mullen asked.

"No, sir. I did not."

This had been the moment when Lieutenant Magee had radioed: "We're being fired upon up here!"

Responding to gunfire at the men's dorm that night, Major General Walter G. Johnson of the National Guard had approached Lieutenant Magee and told him to withdraw his men so the guard could secure the campus. Magee had not known it, but Johnson had just seen the patrol shooting in the dorm's alleyway. To prevent such an incident, Mayor Davis had wanted the guard, known for its rigid self-discipline, to take control of the campus. But that had not happened, despite an agreement earlier that day between Magee and the general.

That agreement had been for Magee simply to withdraw his men to the entrances of the campus, so the guard could march in safely to restore order. But there was one hitch in this plan: it remained unclear exactly who would give the signal for Magee to withdraw and for the guard to take over. Ultimately, General Johnson made the decision to take control at Stewart Hall but not until Johnson had seen the patrol firing in the dorm's alleyway.

When Magee and his men finally moved from the men's dorm, General Johnson did not realize they were heading toward another confrontation in the heart of the campus. Johnson expected Magee merely to withdraw from the campus, as agreed. But Magee could see black youths ahead in the street near Alexander Hall, and since Police Chief Pierce had ordered Magee to clear the street, that was what the lieutenant intended to do.

After his men arrived in front of Alexander Hall, Magee used a bullhorn to order the crowd back from the street. The students jeered the officers but stayed behind the chain-link fence along the sidewalk. Magee moved closer toward the screaming crowd behind the fence. His men behind him, Magee stood near a telephone pole to dodge rocks.

"While you were in front of the crowd prior to the time the shooting started, did you give any order to use the tear gas?" Attorney Robert Mullen asked.

"I didn't think it was necessary at that time," Magee answered. "The people were complying with my request."

"They were withdrawing from the street area and dispersing as you were ordering them to do?" Mullen asked.

"Yes, sir."

Magee said that a rock had struck his bullhorn, but he had heard no small-caliber shots from a sniper. There had been only the explosion of gunfire behind him.

"What did you do?" Mullen asked.

"I ducked, sir," Magee replied. "I flinched and dropped a little bit and looked up. I didn't know where the shooting was coming from. I didn't know what it was. As I looked up I saw a window in the dormitory break, and just about that time something hit that transformer over my head on the pole and it exploded. And I realized the shooting was coming from my rear, and I immediately turned and took the bullhorn and immediately began ordering cease fire."

"How many times did you order cease fire before the firing stopped?"

Magee said he had given the order at least three, four, or five times but the firing went on and on, and it sounded like a skeet range.

•

There were other witnesses in the Jackson State civil trial. Anchorman Bert Case played his tape of the twenty-eight-second barrage. He told the court that he had never heard sniper fire, nor had he seen a muzzle flash before the officers started shooting. Case's cameraman that night, Jack Hobbs, did not appear in court. Instead, his deposition was read to the jury. Hobbs, who had been standing in front of Case, repeated his testimony that a bullet had zinged by his ear and had ricocheted off the retaining wall behind him.

Testimony was also taken from five FBI agents who had examined the bullet-riddled buildings at Jackson State. Their tests showed that all the bullet holes in the screens, windows, and walls of Alexander, Ayer, and Stewart Hall dormitories had been caused by gunfire outside the buildings. And not by a sniper indoors.

In his final arguments for the plaintiffs, Attorney Robert Mullen told the jury that indeed there had been a riot at Jackson State, "a police riot." As for the lawmen's testimony, Mullen said: "It is perfectly obvious they were lying." Mullen pointed out that not one officer had admitted firing at ground level, where eleven black youths had been wounded, two of them fatally. Furthermore, most of the officers claimed to have fired toward a window on the same floor: the second from the top in the west stairwell of Alexander Hall. Mullen told the jurors that if they believed what the officers had told them, they could not believe the FBI's photographs of Alexander Hall, which was sprayed by indiscriminate gunfire.

George Taylor, a white civil rights attorney, spoke to the jurors. Taylor reminded them that this trial was a lawsuit and his clients were asking for 13.8 million dollars. "We want a lot of money, and that's difficult to say when you're talking about the State of Mississippi and the City of Jackson and law enforcement officers," Taylor said. "But that's the only way in this case that you can say, 'No more and never again.' " Taylor told the jury of the fear expressed by Tuwaine Davis Whitehead, a wounded student, who once had said: "If you kill a nigger, ain't nothing going to be done about it no way."

•

Rufus Creekmore, a white attorney for the City of Jackson, began the final arguments for the defense. Creekmore told the jury not to forget that there had been a student riot at Jackson State. He read from the letter that President John Peoples had written to faculty and students after the first night of unrest: " 'This latest riot was perpetrated by a faceless, mindless mob of students and nonstudents bent on doing violence and destruction.' "

Adding to Creekmore's remarks, Deputy Attorney General William Allain said there were two things about this case that were certain: there had been a riot and there had been a sniper in Alexander Hall. Allain argued that the officers had fired in self-defense. He told the jurors that the officers were family men "like you, educated, well trained." Allain warned the jury: "This is a very important lawsuit because it can set law enforcement back a hundred years, if you are going to punish somebody for doing their duty."

• •

Wednesday, March 22, 1972. At 2:20 P.M., the all-white jury of nine men and three women filed past the bench in Biloxi's federal courtroom. They took their seats in the jury box. Finally, after three weeks of testimony and nearly three days of deliberations, the jurors had come to a decision.

"Members of the jury," Judge Nixon said, "I would like to ask you through your foreman if you have arrived at a unanimous verdict in this case?"

The foreman stood and said: "We have, your honor."

"Very well, would you please hand it to the marshal," Nixon said.

The clerk read the decision to the court: "We the jury find for all of the defendants."

The City of Jackson, the State of Mississippi, and the police and patrolmen had made their case and won.

"Members of the jury," Judge Nixon said, "I want to thank you for discharging your duties as citizens of the United States by serving on this jury in this well-tried case."

As the courtroom emptied, the lawmen, the lawyers, and the families of the slain students opened the glass doors of the brick federal building and stepped outside into Biloxi's warm, springlike air. On the sidewalk a group of highway patrolmen capered and sent up a chorus of rebel yells. They had won. They would not have to pay.

For the students wounded at Jackson State, and for the families of the two who had been slain, the jury's verdict had a message. They had heard this message in the past from their black parents and neighbors: if you kill a nigger, ain't nothing going to be done about it no way.

EPILOGUE

The past is never dead. It's not even past.

—William Faulkner

Litigation in the Jackson State case dragged on for more than a decade. In New Orleans in October 1974, the U.S. Court of Appeals ruled there had been a sniper at Jackson State, but that the lawmen's barrage "far exceeded the response that was appropriate." The court added that Mississippi and the City of Jackson enjoyed "sovereign immunity," so they could not be held liable for the "excessive" shooting.

Seven years later in January 1982, the black plaintiffs appealed to the U.S. Supreme Court to reopen the 13.8 million dollar lawsuit against the state and the city. Only Justices Thurgood Marshall and William Brennan voted to hear arguments in the case. After a dozen years in the courts, the Jackson State case was closed.

Nearly three years before this final decision, I flew to Mississippi to begin research on the Jackson State killings. At the time, I was a college writing teacher from upstate New York. Ever since my days as a college student back in the turbulent spring of 1970, the killings at Kent and Jackson State had left a lasting impression on me. A decade later, I was glad that most Americans still remembered Kent State, but dismayed they had long forgotten the killings at the black college in Jackson. That convinced me to go to Mississippi.

It was April 1979 when my jet nosed down and cruised above the pine treetops and the muddy creeks of central Mississippi. The land below seemed strange. The yellow clay looked warm and moist, unlike the frozen ground in upstate New York that April. I took a bus later that day to Jackson State University, as it was now called. The black busdriver pulled up along the curb on Prentiss Street in front of the New Men's Dormitory. On the night of May 14, 1970, students on the dorm's front steps had jeered the police and patrolmen marching by on their way into the heart of the campus.

Like the lawmen then, I walked south to the Lynch Street corner nearby and headed toward Stewart Hall, another men's dorm. On the dorm's front lawn, about two blocks from the site of the killings, I discovered a small memorial dedicated to Phillip Gibbs and James Green. It had been placed there by the class of 1971 and inscribed: "Martyrs of May 14, 1970."

Following the same route up Lynch Street that the officers had taken on the night of the killings, I saw signs of change on the campus: a new science building, a new music center, another dining hall, and a high-rise administration building. In front of Alexander Hall, I found a pedestrian mall of concrete that blocked the Lynch Street traffic and hid the pavement where lawmen had once knelt firing at students. I was the only white man on the mall that sunny afternoon, so I felt self-conscious looking up at the windows in the black women's dorm. But I soon forgot about that when I noticed the bullet holes that remained in the concrete walls of the dorm's west wing. Many of the holes were bigger than silver dollars.

Across the street from Alexander Hall in the commons park, black students were on park benches under the shady oaks. I asked them whether they had seen the bullet holes in their dormitory, and whether they knew about the shootings there back in 1970. No, the students said, they didn't know anything about that. That was a long time ago. When I asked if they had noticed the memorial two blocks away in front of Stewart Hall, some said they had, some said they hadn't. But none could say what that memorial represented. "So many terrible things have happened to my people," a black reporter later explained to me. "After awhile we just try to forget."

Even Jackson State's administration was trying to forget. President John Peoples—who has since left Jackson State—declined to see me, though I had made several visits to his office. He never answered a letter I had written him or returned my phone calls. A librarian at the school made me wait an hour while she checked with a vice president to see if I could examine the library's papers on the killings. Later, a public relations officer warned me that few people here would accept me with open arms if I was writing a book about the killings. That meant bad publicity, the kind the predominantly white State Board of Higher Education wanted no part of.

Despite these and many other frustrations while researching the story of Jackson State, I became fascinated by Mississippi, a land of scorching sun, flooding creeks, and dry piney woods. During summer and January visits over the next four years, I developed a taste for creamed grits, catfish, the Delta blues, and Faulkner. I liked the warmth and hospitality of the people, both black and white. Even in Jackson, by then a city of three hundred thousand, strangers said hello when they passed you on the street.

The Mississippi that I first got to know was the same one that northern journalists see after checking in at the Jackson Holiday Inn. I saw black women driving city buses, instead of sitting in the back of them. I saw black homeowners mowing their lawns in tidy suburban neighborhoods. On television news shows, black newscasters were as common as whites, and even the city's two newspapers had changed their ways, publishing incisive reports on both the problems and aspirations of Jackson's black community. Later I learned that Mississippi had more elected black officials than any other state. In 1986 Mississippi elected its first black congressman since John Roy Lynch back in Reconstruction days.

Unlike blacks at home in upstate New York, those in Mississippi did not seem restricted to the ghetto. Almost everywhere I went in Jackson there were black people: in the grocery stores, in the libraries, in the motels, banks, and theaters. There were whites there too, and there was a free and easy mingling that I had never expected to find in Mississippi. At first, it seemed that racial harmony would take root here long before it would spread to the North.

But eventually I discovered there are really two Mississippis. One is progressive and rejects the bigotry of the Old South, while the other remains mired in the past.

I glimpsed this other Mississippi during my first visit in April 1979. Soon after I arrived, two black boys in their early teens took a trailer truck for a joyride. As the boys careened through the city streets, sideswiping cars, the Jackson police gave chase. When the truck crashed into a car on a bridge, city police opened fire. One boy was hit in the back and the other in the legs and neck. After one of the wounded boys leaped from the bridge, a policeman continued shooting at the boy in the Pearl River below.

Throughout the 1970s and into the early 1980s, city policemen had been quick to use the gun or the club on black Jacksonians. In 1977, the U.S. Civil Rights Commission reported that Jacksonians, especially blacks, feel "they are victimized rather than protected by the police."

For the Mississippi Highway Patrol, the last two decades have brought significant change. Now integrated, the patrol is no longer used to snuff out civil rights activity. Officers spend most of their time patrolling the state highways and face fewer complaints from black Mississippians. My own experience with the patrol, however, has not been all positive. While on assignment for *Mother Jones* magazine in 1979, I investigated reports that patrolmen had beaten the mayor of an all-black town in the Mississippi delta. After brief discussions with uncooperative patrol officials, I received a letter from my editor in San Francisco. He wrote that San Francisco police had been inquiring about me—at the request of the Mississippi Highway Patrol. No longer do patrolmen systematically spy on dissidents as they once did in the 1960s, but the urge to snoop and harass is still there.

I had one other unusual experience that partly involved the patrol. It was in July 1981 while I was in Ripley, Mississippi to research the life of Phillip Gibbs. I was eating in Reaves Restaurant, formerly a dairy bar where Phillip had once participated in a sit-in. A patrolman walked in the front door and sat at a table with male friends wearing baseball caps. Soon a burly, middle-aged white man strode in and joined the patrolman and the baseball caps. This burly white man started complaining about the urban riots in Great Britain that summer. As he railed against British Molotov-tossers, he grew louder and heaped praise on the Jackson police. This burly man said that with Thompson's Tank, Jackson police could deal with rioters far better than a bunch of English bobbies. He praised the Jackson police for cracking down on Jackson State students one May night in 1970. "Now they weren't shootin' high and they weren't shootin' low that night, were they?" the burly man said, snickering.

"No," his patrolman friend replied, "and you haven't had a problem out there ever since, have you?"

Though many white Mississippians today regret their state's heritage of slavery, segregation, and lynching, there are those who remain unrepentant.

My interest in the highway patrol eventually led me to Simpson County, about thirty miles east of Jackson. A man named Lloyd Jones was sheriff there—"Goon" Jones, the county's black residents called him. One steaming July afternoon in 1979, I watched as about 120 blacks paraded through the Simpson County town of Magee, chanting: "Stop 'Goon' Jones—before he stops you!" The blacks complained of brutality on the part of Jones's officers and other local lawmen. The protesters said the officers had beaten a group of blacks attending a birthday party, and that one woman had had a miscarriage because of the incident.

But Sheriff Jones had his supporters that day: about twenty Ku Klux Klansmen with baseball bats and clubs. They carried signs that said: "Support Your Local Police."

Across the street from the Klan a huge, heavy white man stood alone on the sidewalk. His arms were folded and his eyes were squinting in the sunlight as the black marchers passed. It was Sheriff Lloyd "Goon" Jones. When a photographer and I approached Jones, he pawed at the camera.

"What do you think of all those people calling you 'Goon'?" I managed to ask Jones.

"It don't bother me," he said. "They 'bin callin' me that since the Freedom Rider days."

Two decades after the civil rights movement, some institutions in Mississippi seem almost untouched by change in racial attitudes. Most white churches in the state remain, in effect, segregated. White academies founded to circumvent school integration still enroll few, if any, blacks. In some remote rural towns, doctors and dentists still have separate waiting rooms for black and white patients. Although it has been more than twenty years since James Meredith integrated the University of Mississippi in Oxford, the white fraternities and sororities remain segregated.

Anyone who has ever driven through the alleyways of Jackson, or down the arrow-straight, shimmering highways of the delta, has witnessed the major obstacle to racial equality: poverty. Mississippi has the lowest per capita income of any state, and it receives the most food stamps per person. As the state's politicians often lament, Mississippi has remained on or near the bottom of nearly every statistical table compiled by the federal government.

Mississippi also has remained a right-to-work state. Unions are unwelcome and factory workers usually earn abysmal wages. The poorest workers in the state, the blacks, remove the state's garbage, clean the state's motels, cut the state's pulpwood, harvest the state's cotton, and toil in its furniture factories. Yet they still live in stifling shacks with corrugated tin roofs and in rickety shotgun houses without plumbing. Their streets are often unpaved and their children hungry.

Lynch Street reflects the hard times that persist for black Mississippians. Many of its once busy cinder-block storefronts are now closed. Gone are the Magnolia Food Store, Jones' Pharmacy, and the Kon-tiki Restaurant. Lula Belle's dress shop and the Mid-South Barber College have left, too. Black merchants argue the pedestrian mall at Jackson State blocks customers, as well as commuter traffic, from Lynch Street. But others point out that integration has taken its toll on black merchants here and elsewhere in the South. White-owned shopping malls, now integrated, cater to prosperous blacks who avoid shopping in the inner city.

Despite hard times for the Lynch Street neighborhood, the bars are still bustling, and black youths still congregate on the street corners. But no one calls them "cornerboys" anymore, and since there is a detour at Jackson State, no one throws stones at white motorists on Lynch Street. Instead, black youths wave down an occasional white driver to offer drugs or the charms of soft black flesh.

The old street signs on the corners have been changed. Back in March 1973, the city council had felt there was too much confusion over the name of "Lynch Street," this street where black students had been gunned down in 1964, in 1967, and again in 1970. For a time, there had been consternation and confusion regarding the street's name. Some folks recalled the street had been named after John Roy Lynch, a black congressman from Reconstruction days. But others said it was called "Lynch" because of the killing here over the years. To put an end to this disturbing speculation, the white city council had passed a resolution: "NOW, THEREFORE, BE IT RESOLVED that that certain street in the City of Jackson heretofore known as Lynch Street shall be known hereafter as 'J. R. Lynch Street.' "

SOURCES AND METHODS

Abbreviations used in notes

DAH	Department of Archives and History, Jackson, Mississippi, Mississippi Council on Human Relations collection
JSU	Jackson State University Library, Jackson, Mississippi, Gibbs-Green Memorial Collection, 1970
NA	National Archives, Records of the President's Commission on Campus Unrest
SUNYA	State University of New York at Albany, Library Special Collections
TC	Tougaloo College Library, Tougaloo, Mississippi, *Burton v. Williams* collection
VU	Vanderbilt University, Nashville, Tennessee, Television News Archives

MAIN SOURCES

The most valuable source of information for this book was the Federal Bureau of Investigation's twenty-three-volume report on the Jackson State killings (SUNYA). The FBI's report includes summaries of nearly a thousand interviews with journalists, cornerboys, students, teachers, college administrators, firemen, National Guardsmen, and policemen in Jackson. Most of these interviews were conducted within a week of the shootings—many within twenty-four hours. The report includes photographs, charts, handbills, interoffice memoranda, results of ballistics tests, and other documents. Although all interviewees' names had been deleted from my copy of the report, in many cases their identities were easily inferred. I applied for the FBI's report under the provisions of the Freedom of Information Act.

The next most valuable source was the tape-recorded, pretrial testimony given by the newsmen, law-enforcement officers, and city officials involved in the Jackson State tragedy (TC). During 1971, attorneys representing the students wounded at the college (as well as the families of James Green and Phillip Gibbs) took depositions from reporters, policemen, and patrolmen who had witnessed the shootings. These tape-recorded depositions were part of the legal process leading to the civil suit trial (*Burton v. Williams,* 1972) brought against the City of Jackson, the Jackson police, the State of Mississippi, and the Mississippi Highway Patrol. For these recorded depositions, Police Lieutenant Warren Magee and his superiors (including Mayor Russell Davis) were compelled to answer questions under oath. Highway Patrol Inspector Lloyd "Goon" Jones and his superiors also testified under oath. In addition, the black plaintiffs' attorneys interviewed more than 150 students who had witnessed the shootings. However, these interviews were not available on tape. They were in the form of typewritten summaries of the students' remarks (TC). The black plaintiffs' attorneys (from the Jackson office of the national Lawyers' Committee for Civil Rights Under Law) made countless other documents available to me, including an invaluable transcript of the city policemen's radio tapes for the night of the slayings and most of the exhibits furnished the Hinds County Grand Jury in Jackson, Mississippi during the summer of 1970 (TC). These exhibits included such items as the notes and speeches of Mayor Russell Davis, the log of highway patrol radio communications for the night of May 14, 1970, and Dr. John Peoples's report on the slayings to the State College Board.

A truly indispensable source was the tape-recorded radio communications of both the Jackson police and the highway patrol. I was allowed to duplicate copies available in the National Archives (NA). The tapes were indispensable because each was timed; that is, the radio dispatchers recorded the exact time every few moments as they communicated with officers in the field. These tapes allowed me to develop a reliable chronology of the unrest at Jackson State on both May 13 and 14.

Transcripts of government hearings on the killings were invaluable. These included the three-volume transcript of the mayor's biracial committee (TC), which questioned witnesses for the city of Jackson for more than a week after the slayings. In August of 1970, the President's Commission on Campus Unrest held hearings for three days in Jackson, Mississippi. A copy of the two-volume transcript of these hearings (SUNYA) was made available by the National Archives in Washington, D.C. In addition, the National Archives allowed me to review the commission's working papers on Kent and Jackson State and photocopy the typewritten reports of the Jackson Police Department for the nights of May 13 and 14, 1970. (Hereafter, all dates will refer to the year 1970, unless otherwise stated.)

Another invaluable source was the seventeen-volume transcript of *Burton v. Williams,* the civil suit trial held in March of 1972 in Biloxi, Mississippi. A copy of the transcript (SUNYA) was supplied by Cravaith, Swaine and Moore, the Wall Street law firm that joined the Lawyers' Committee in representing the black plaintiffs.

I relied heavily upon the daily newspaper coverage of the Jackson State slayings, drawing information from major newspapers such as the *New York Times,* the *Washington Post,* and the *Los Angeles Times,* as well as southern newspapers such as the *Louisville Courier-Journal,* the *New Orleans Times-Picayune,* and the *Memphis Commercial-Appeal.* I also reviewed accounts in newspapers throughout the state of Mississippi, including the *Meridian Star,* the *Hattiesburg American,* the *Delta Democrat-Times,* the *Tupelo Daily Journal,* and others.

The Television News Archives (VU) loaned videotape recordings of ABC, CBS, and NBC networks' daily newscasts for the spring and summer of 1970.

I conducted more than 120 interviews with persons who had either witnessed the shootings or could shed light on them. I tape-recorded most of these interviews. Among those interviewed were the four newsmen at the scene of the killings and all but four of the twelve wounded students. Among the important potential sources who declined to be interviewed were Mayor Russell Davis, Dr. John Peoples, Lieutenant Warren Magee, and many of the police and patrolmen who had witnessed the slayings. However, the sworn testimony of these men in the courtroom, in pretrial hearings, and before the President's Commission on Campus Unrest provided much insight into their experiences on the night of slayings.

The two most significant studies of the Kent and Jackson State tragedies were *The Report of the President's Commission on Campus Unrest* and *No Heroes, No Villains,* the latter a report written by Robert M. O'Neil and others, sponsored by the American Association of University Professors. Many of the conclusions I reached about the events described in this book appeared first in either or both of these studies.

Over a period of three and a half years, I spent about nine months in Mississippi conducting research for this book. I spent many more months analyzing FBI documents, pretrial depositions, trial transcripts, and commission hearings. I visited virtually every location described in this work.

The text includes many quotations from documents, interviews, hearings, court records, and newspaper articles. For a more engaging narrative, I have omitted scholarly apparatus such as footnotes, and in most cases, brackets. I have edited the oral histories in this book by adding an occasional word or deleting phrases for the sake of clarity and brevity. However, the strictest care was taken to preserve the authentic words of the police and patrolmen in both their official testimony and in their radio transmissions.

Newspaper reports of unrest in Jackson were crucial to this book, even though facts in the local press were often distorted. The information in the newsletters of civil rights activists were often equally tendentious. Disregarding the rhetoric of both sides, I often found agreement on the facts, and usually I could regard these as true. To confirm the information in published accounts, I interviewed witnesses whenever possible.

NOTES

1 Strange Roots

The epigraph for this entire work, appearing on the page following the title page, is cited with the text. The epigraph for chapter 1 is from "Strange Fruit," an antilynching song by Lewis Allan made popular by singer Billie Holiday in the 1950s.

The information about Congressman John Roy Lynch was drawn from his autobiography, *Reminiscences of an Active Life*. Facts on the history and culture of the street named for Lynch have come from interviews that I conducted with tradesmen, clergymen, residents, students, and former civil rights activists in Jackson. Other interviews with Aurelia Young, Lelia Rhodes, and novelist Margaret Walker—all Jackson State faculty—helped establish the historical importance of the neighborhood. The city directory for 1970 was another important source. Facts on the civil rights organizations with headquarters on the street appeared in the following works: William McCord's *Mississippi: The Long, Hot Summer,* August Meier and Elliot Rudwick's *CORE: A Study in the Civil Rights Movement, 1942–1968,* and Clayborne Carson's *In Struggle: SNCC and the Black Awakening of the 1960s.*

Historical background on the civil rights struggle and racial unrest in America during 1961, 1963, 1964, and 1967—years of conflict on Lynch Street—was drawn principally from Robert Brisbane's *Black Activism: Racial Revolution in the United States, 1954–1970.*

To describe Mississippi's first sit-in (March 1961), I consulted Clarice Campbell and Oscar Allen Rogers, Jr.'s *Mississippi, The View from Tougaloo.* The dialogue quoted in the library scene was taken from the *Jackson Clarion-Ledger,* March 28, 1961. This dialogue appears in almost the same form in Myrlie Evers's book, *For Us, the Living.* James Meredith's autobiography, *Three Years in Mississippi,* as well as an interview with Meredith, were important sources. I also consulted accounts of the unrest in the *Jackson Daily News* and the *Jackson State Times* (now defunct, but in its day a daily newspaper with a reputation for moderation on racial issues). Despite its name, the *Jackson State Times* had had no affiliation with Jackson State College.

Information about the unrest in Jackson during the movement in June 1963 comes from three principal sources: Anne Moodie's *Coming of Age in Mississippi,* Myrlie Evers's book (cited above), and John Salter Jr.'s *Jackson, Mississippi: An American Chronicle of Struggle and Schism.* I relied heavily on Salter's account of the clash between civil rights marchers and lawmen on Lynch Street on the day after Medgar Evers's assassination. Salter's book, James Meredith's autobiography (cited above), and the June 13, 1963 edition of the *Jackson Daily News* established that Jackson State students had thrown bottles at city police cars after the Evers assassination.

Details about crowd control equipment acquired by the Jackson police appeared in McCord's *Long, Hot Summer.* For the description of the campus unrest in February of 1964, I interviewed Jackson State College faculty and students, including Mamie Ballard Crockett, the Alexander Hall resident who had been struck by the white motorist's car. I also interviewed Gregory Haygood, a local high school youth shot on the campus.

For the description of the incidents leading to the 1964 shootings, I relied heavily on news accounts in the *Jackson Daily News* and the *Clarion-Ledger.* The quotation from Charles Evers trying to calm the students appeared in the *Clarion-Ledger,* February 4, 1964. The COFO leaflet circulating during the unrest in 1964 and quoted in this chapter appeared in the newsletter, *Voice of the Movement,* February 7, 1964.

To depict the events on Lynch Street in 1967, I relied heavily on interviews with former *New Orleans Times-Picayune* reporter Wilson Minor and activist Reverend Ken Dean. Of special value were Dean's notes on the shooting of Benjamin Brown. These were among the papers of the Mississippi Council on Human Relations (DAH). An interview with Earl Brown, a Jackson State dormitory director in 1967, confirmed that students had been shot by highway patrolmen that year on the campus. An account of the campus shootings appeared in the *F. D. P. News* (published by the Mississippi Freedom Democratic Party) on May 12, 1967. For more information about the shootings in 1967, I relied upon accounts in the *Jackson Clarion-Ledger,* the *Daily News,* the *Northside Reporter* (May 18, 1967), and the *Mississippi Newsletter* (May 12, 1967). For more on Benjamin Brown, see Bruce Hilton's *The Delta Ministry,* and for more on John Otis Sumrall, the black draft resister, see Alice Lynd's *We Won't Go: Personal Accounts of War Objectors,* in which an essay by Sumrall appears. The scene describing Mayor Allen Thompson addressing the crowd near Jackson State was described in both the *Clarion-Ledger* and the *Daily News.* TV news film of the incident is in the WLBT collection (DAH). The leaflet of the Black People's Unity Movement, quoted in this chapter, was quoted in the conservative black newsweekly, the *Jackson Advocate,* May 20, 1967.

For evidence of unrest at Jackson State during 1968, see both the *Clarion-Ledger* and the *Daily News* for the first week of April, and for evidence of unrest the next year, see both newspapers for the first week of May 1969.

2 Mayday in Amerika

This chapter's epigraph is from D. H. Lawrence's *Studies in Classic American Literature.*

The opening scene in this chapter was based on two news stories: one in the Sunday *Clarion-Ledger-Jackson Daily News* (May 10), and one in the *Jackson Daily News* (May 11). I also drew information from interviews with Henry Thompson, the black student who spoke at the rally on May 9, and two self-described "hippies," William Rusk and David Doggett, who helped organize the rally.

The historical facts on Jackson and its antebellum architecture were borrowed from a variety of sources, including W. F. Powell's *Jackson's Early History and 28 Years of Municipal Progress,* David Sansing and Carroll Waller's *A History of the Mississippi Governor's Mansion,* and the two-volume work, *The Story of Jackson, A History of the Capital of Mississippi, 1821–1951* (no author given).

The two speeches by Richard Nixon quoted in this chapter were taken from transcripts in the *New York Times* on the day after the speeches had been televised. To describe Nixon's demeanor during his address on the Cambodia "incursion," I watched a videotape of the speech (VU).

To describe the mood of the nation during the spring of 1970 and the stalemate in the Vietnam War, I studied back issues of the *Washington Post* (May through June 1970) and the *New York Times* (March through June 1970), particularly the Sunday *Times'* "Week-in-Review" sections. I also viewed videotape recordings of the three major networks' evening newscasts for the period of April 15 through August 15, 1970 (VU). George C. Herring's *America's Longest War: The United States and Vietnam, 1950–1975* was a valuable source on the war. For additional information on campus unrest during May 1970, I studied coverage of the protests in the *Los Angeles Times,* the *New Orleans Times-Picayune,* the *Detroit Free Press,* the *Louisville Courier-Journal,* and the *Memphis Commercial-Appeal.* Of particular value on the May '70 demonstrations were studies by the Carnegie Commission on Higher Education (see "May 1970: The Campus Aftermath of Cambodia and Kent State" in Sponsored Research of the Carnegie Commission on Higher Education, 1975) and the Urban Research Corporation (see *On Strike . . . Shut It Down! A Report on the First National Student Strike in U.S. History, May 1970*). The report of the President's Commission on Campus Unrest and the final essay in Milton Viorst's *Fire in the Streets: America in the 1960s* provided valuable insights into the phenomenon of May '70 and the student unrest at Kent State.

Violent confrontations on or near several campuses deserve specific citation. For a news report on the largest mass arrest of students in American history—at Mississippi Valley State College in Itta Bena—see the *Washington Post,* February 19. For an account of the shootings near Santa Barbara, California, see the *New York Times,* April 18, 19, and 22. For a report on the shootings at Columbus, Ohio, see the *New York Times,* April 30 and May 1. For background on the shootings in College Park, Maryland, see the *Washington Post,* May 5. On the shootings in

Buffalo, New York, see the *Washington Post,* May 8, and on the stabbing of students in Albuquerque, New Mexico, see the *Washington Post,* May 9.

To depict the killings at Kent State in Ohio, I consulted a variety of sources, including the working papers (NA) and *The Report of the President's Commission on Campus Unrest*. I viewed outtakes of CBS News film on the Kent deaths (NA). I drew information from the following books on the subject: I. F. Stone's *The Killings at Kent State: How Murder Went Unpunished* (a book that reports extensively on the Jackson State killings as well); James Michener's *Kent State: What Happened and Why;* Peter Davies's *The Truth About Kent State;* Joe Eszterhas and Michael D. Roberts's *Thirteen Seconds;* Joseph Kelner and James Munves's *The Kent State Coverup,* and *No Heroes, No Villains.*

For information about the May 8 antiwar rally at Jackson State, I examined interviews with students in the FBI report (SUNYA) and the testimony of President John Peoples before the presidential commission (SUNYA). In addition, I questioned Aurelia Young, a Jackson State music teacher, and Warner Buxton, the Jackson State student government president. The sign calling for the Cambodia rally, quoted in this chapter, appeared on CBS News (May 15). It was quoted in the *Washington Post* (May 16) as well. The handbill urging a boycott of classes was quoted in *The Report of the President's Commission on Campus Unrest.*

3 The Miniriot

This chapter's epigraph is from Richard Wright's autobiography, *Black Boy,* which is partly about his life as a boy in Jackson, Mississippi.

The city policemen's dialogue in this and the following chapter was taken from Jackson police radio communications. This was available to me in the form of reel-to-reel tapes (NA).

For details regarding the experiences of the city police on May 13 I relied heavily on Police Lieutenant Warren Magee's pretrial deposition in 1971. However, the two quotations of students mocking the police in front of the ROTC buildings were taken from Sergeant Charles Lee's testimony before the presidential commission. Most of the information about the vandalism on the campus that night was taken from FBI interviews with students, faculty, white commuters, and college security guards. These interviews appeared in the FBI's report (SUNYA). More details about the white commuters assaulted on Lynch Street appeared in the typewritten reports of the city police (NA).

Information regarding the Jackson Police Department's discrimination against black officers was based on Mayor Russell Davis's testimony before the president's commission and based on interviews with two former Jackson policemen, Levaughn Carter and Malcolm McMillin. Analyses of the conduct and reputation of the police force were culled from interviews with black students, attorneys, civil rights activists, and reports in the *Jackson Daily News* and the *Clarion-Ledger* during the 1960s and 1970s.

Analyses of the reputation of the Mississippi Highway Patrol were drawn from interviews with reporters, attorneys, black students, and civil rights activists in Jackson. In *Integration at Ole Miss,* Professor Russell Barrett documents the conduct of the patrol during the riot to prevent Meredith from integrating Ole Miss. The details of Patrol Inspector Lloyd "Goon" Jones's experiences in demonstrations over the years have come from Jones himself, as related in his tape-recorded, pretrial deposition.

For more information about Jones, I interviewed two white civil rights attorneys—Suzanne Griggins and Allison Steiner—who worked in Simpson County where Jones was sheriff during the 1970s. For more about Jones, see a feature story on him in the *Clarion-Ledger,* November 1, 1977, and *Let Justice Roll Down* by Reverend John Perkins, in which Reverend Perkins alleges that Jones beat him. Details on Inspector Jones's experiences on May 13–15 appear in his testimony before the presidential commission and before the federal court that tried the civil suit in Biloxi.

Details on the life and political career of Mayor Russell Davis were drawn in part from the news accounts and campaign literature about Davis in the vertical file in the Department of Archives. I also reviewed news accounts of his first mayoral campaign in 1968. Facts on Davis's movements during the night of May 13 were culled from his pretrial deposition in the 1972 civil suit. For background on Davis's administration, I relied heavily on interviews with civil rights activists, black students, and newsmen in Jackson.

The quotation from Georgia Governor Lester Maddox in this chapter was transcribed from news film appearing on the ABC News, May 13 (VU). For the facts on the state of education in Mississippi, see the *Mississippi Statistical Abstract: 1980.* Facts on the history of and equipment in Thompson's Tank appeared in the FBI's report, in a study of the police department by the Public Administration Service, and in a news story on the tank in the *Clarion-Ledger,* January 18, 1981.

The congressional speech by John Bell Williams that is quoted in this chapter was taken from an unpublished collection of his speeches in the Department of Archives (DAH). Other details about Williams were taken from my interview with the former governor, from interviews with local newsmen and civil rights activists, and from news articles about Williams's career, found in the vertical file of the Department of Archives. For accounts of Williams's gubernatorial campaign, see issues of the *Jackson Daily News* and the *Clarion-Ledger* for fall of 1967.

The scene depicting WLBT-TV reporter Corris Collins delivering his report on the unrest of May 13 was based on news film in the WLBT collection (DAH).

4 By the Magnolia Tree

The epigraph for this chapter was taken from Langston Hughes's poem, "Negro."

For an analysis of the Hederman press, I am heavily indebted to James Silver, who wrote on the subject in *Mississippi: The Closed Society*. Silver argues that the Hederman press had been largely responsible for shaping the segregationist ideology of white Mississippians. Silver was also the source of information on the Hederman press coverage of the Evers slaying and the Washington march in 1963. I must acknowledge an equally heavy debt to Ed Williams, author of an excellent piece on the Hederman press in the *Columbia Journalism Review* (Summer 1970), and to Lew Powell, author of an article in the *Nation* (October 8, 1973). For more on the Hederman press, see Robert Hooker's "Race and the Mississippi Press" in *New South* (Winter 1971). I also drew facts about the Hederman family from Robert M. Hederman, Jr.'s booklet, *The Hederman Story: A Saga of the Printed Word in Mississippi*. Interviews with several Jackson journalists, many of them Hederman employees, contributed to my understanding of the city's newspapers. In addition, I reviewed back issues of the Hederman Press throughout the 1960s and 1970s.

For facts regarding the life and career of President John Peoples of Jackson State College, I examined his testimony before the Scranton Commission and the mayor's biracial committee, his report on the shootings to the State Board of Higher Education, and a history of the university written by Lelia Rhodes (*Jackson State University: The First Hundred Years, 1877–1977*). I am also indebted to Stephan Lesher's "Jackson State A Year After" (*New York Times Magazine,* March 21, 1971). To reconstruct the events in front of Alexander Hall after the shootings, I relied on the remarks of President Peoples himself when he spoke to Jackson State students at the tenth-anniversary assembly on May 4, 1980. At this memorial service, Peoples described what he had seen and said while among the crowd of students after the shootings. The accuracy of Peoples's remarks, quoted at the end of this chapter, were confirmed by Gene "Jughead" Young—then a student activist. An interview with Warner Buxton, student government president, also aided in reconstructing the events at the dorm after the shootings.

The experiences of Mayor Russell Davis, as described in this chapter, were taken from his tape-recorded, pretrial deposition. His televised address was transcribed from news film in the WLBT collection (DAH).

All facts on weather conditions in Jackson (in this and other chapters) have come from daily weather reports in the Jackson *Clarion-Ledger,* which reported the temperature and humidity for morning, afternoon, and evening hours. Televised news reports from the WLBT collection (DAH) and the TV News Archives (VU) also helped establish the weather conditions depicted in several scenes in this narrative.

As in the previous chapter, descriptions of the experiences of the city policemen have been based on their public testimony, police radio tapes, and interviews in the FBI's report (SUNYA). Details on the experiences of students, security guards, and other college officials have come primarily from interviews in the FBI's report. I relied heavily on tapes of the Mississippi Highway Patrol's radio communications (NA). Spelling of Inspector Lloyd "Goon" Jones's recorded communications closely resembles that of excerpts that originally appeared in news accounts and in the presidential commission's report.

The accounts of the wounded students' experiences have come from interviews I have conducted as well as from their public testimony and FBI interviews. The scene at the University Medical Center was based on news film (apparently shot by WJTV newsman Jack Hobbs) that appeared on the ABC News (May 15). I also relied on interviews with students, reporters, and Reverend Ken Dean, a minister at the scene. Dr. Aaron Shirley, a physician also at the scene, confirmed the students' accounts of harassment by hospital personnel. An FBI interview with an ambulance attendant documented the Baptist Hospital's refusal to treat the wounded blacks.

The lyrics of "Ain' Gonna Let Nobody Turn Me 'Round" were transcribed from a recording of the song in a Smithsonian anthology of civil rights songs, *Voices of the Civil Rights Movement: Black American Freedom Songs 1960–1966.*

5 Jacktwo

This chapter's epigraph is from Samuel Clemens's *Life on the Mississippi.* Clemens's remark appears in chapter 35 and refers to the government cemetery in Vicksburg, Mississippi.

The damages to the campus buildings depicted in this chapter (and others) have been documented by FBI reports and photographs, as well as TV film shot by local and network TV newsmen. In addition, I examined still photos in the Gibbs-Green Memorial Collection (JSU). I also relied on photos taken by the staff of *Kudzu,* an underground newspaper in Jackson during the late 1960s.

Mayor Russell Davis's speech in city council chambers was transcribed from news film in the WLBT collection (DAH). For facts about Andrew Jackson's role in the history of Jackson, see James Loewen and Charles Sallis's *Mississippi: Conflict & Change,* as well as Eron Rowland's *History of Hinds County Mississippi, 1821–1922.*

Governor John Bell Williams's statement after the killings appeared in the *Clarion-Ledger,* May 16.

The account of the Millsaps College students' protest was based on photographs taken by *Kudzu* photographers and videotape of ABC News, May 15 (VU). I also interviewed history professor Charles Sallis and education professor Jeanne Middleton Forsythe, participants in the march. Other information about the Millsaps students was taken from spring 1970 issues of the *White and Purple,* the student newspaper.

The description of the press conference at the Masonic Temple was based solely on news film in the WLBT collection (DAH). The sketch describing the CBS News coverage of the shootings was based solely on the network's show on May 15 (VU).

The scene describing the disgruntled Jackson policemen in the hallway of city hall was based on newspaper accounts appearing in the *New York Times* and the

Washington Post, both May 17. For background on the mayor's biracial committee hearings, I interviewed all but one of the five attorneys on the committee.

The policemen's diagrams described in this chapter have been adapted from copies appearing with the hearings transcript of the mayor's biracial committee (TC).

6 Yoknapatawpha in Black

The source of this chapter's epigraph was given in the text. The hymn quoted near the opening of this chapter is "Beautiful Savior," translated by Joseph A. Seiss.

The funeral scene was composed after interviews with friends and relatives of Phillip Gibbs. The program of the funeral service was made available by F. L. Spight, a high school principal in Ripley and distant relative of Phillip Gibbs.

Historical background on Ripley and W. C. Falkner was drawn from Andrew Brown's *History of Tippah County, Mississippi* and from an interview with Tommie Covington, unofficial town historian. For more details on Ripley and the Falkners, see Robert Cantwell's foreword in the Signet Classics edition of William Faulkner's *Sartoris*. Additional information about Ripley during the 1960s was drawn from interviews with relatives and friends of Phillip Gibbs.

Most facts about Phillip Gibbs's life were taken from interviews with his relatives and friends. Another important source was the *New York Times* article (May 16) on both Gibbs and James Green (the high school youth killed at Jackson State). The *Clarion-Ledger* article on Gibbs's intoxication was published on June 5. Dale Gibbs Thomas, Phillip Gibbs's widow, provided the letters quoted in this chapter. Gibbs's relationships with other women were documented in the FBI's report and confirmed by my own interviews with Gibbs's friends.

The account of Gibbs's actions on the night of his death was based chiefly on interviews with his female companion and with other students, and on FBI interviews with students.

7 Crisis

The epigraph for this chapter was taken from Margaret Walker's poem, "We Have Been Believers." Walker, a poet and novelist, was a professor of English at Jackson State.

The racial tensions described in Jackson on this day were reported in both the national and local press and in the memoranda from the Jackson office of the FBI to headquarters in Washington, D.C. In interviews with the students themselves, I learned that they had threatened to use guns and start a riot after the shootings. (As stated in chapter 10, there is no conclusive evidence that students did or did not use guns on the campus on the night of the slayings. Furthermore, there is no conclusive evidence that they did or did not arm themselves after the killings.)

Virtually all information about the lives of the four journalists who witnessed the shootings has come from interviews with them. All dialogue between the mayor's biracial committee and the journalists, as well as the newsmen's sketches of the shooting scene, appeared in the transcripts of the committee's hearings (TC). Though most details about the experiences of the four newsmen were based on these same transcripts, some facts from the reporters' later testimony were added to make their accounts clearer.

Evidence of WJTV reporter Jack Hobbs's uncertainty about whether there had been a sniper in Alexander Hall is well documented. In an interview with ABC News (May 18), Hobbs said: "I couldn't say it was a sniper. I couldn't say who shot it [the "bullett" Hobbs thought he had heard]. I couldn't say that it came from the dormitory." In my interview with Hobbs, he told me he had withheld his judgment that city policemen had used their guns on campus. He said his reason for holding back was to avoid generating more controversy.

The conclusions of the majority of the mayor's biracial committee appeared in the report to Mayor Davis. It was dated June 12 and bound with the full transcript of the committee's hearings (TC).

The scene depicting Attorney General John Mitchell at Thompson Field and later in front of Alexander Hall was based on videotapes of all three major networks' news coverage, May 18 (VU). The quotation from Mitchell's speech in Cleveland, Mississippi was transcribed from a videotape of the CBS News, May 19. Mitchell's well-publicized warning to law enforcement officers, quoted at the end of this chapter, was based on a United Press International news story dated May 22.

8 Majesty of the Law

This chapter's epigraph originally appeared in the *Jackson Clarion-Ledger* in 1903, and it was later quoted in Albert D. Kirwan's *Revolt of the Rednecks.*

Details regarding the confrontation between students and state investigators at Alexander Hall have been culled from memoranda of the FBI's Jackson office and from news reports in the local and national press. The handbill calling upon students to guard Alexander Hall was quoted in the *Jackson Daily News,* May 20. The dialogue between irate students and President Peoples in front of Alexander Hall was drawn from several local news accounts, especially from an Associate Press news story (*Clarion-Ledger,* May 20) and another account in the *Jackson Daily News* (May 19).

All placards quoted in this chapter appeared on televised news film in the WLBT collection (DAH), the TV News Archives (VU), or in still photos taken by local news photographers.

Governor John Bell Williams's threat to use ten thousand troops to end the protest at Alexander Hall and keep all evidence from the FBI are documented by an FBI memorandum, dated May 20, in section 1 of the FBI's report (SUNYA).

The scene depicting the burning of Judge Coleman's decision was based on the filmed reports of all three TV networks, May 20. The details regarding the students' petition and Judge Coleman's decision were taken from local and national newspaper reports, but especially from an account in the *Jackson Daily News,* May 20. Quotations from Judge Coleman's decision in this chapter and others were drawn from local news reports and a photocopy of the decision appearing in Section 6 of the FBI report.

All facts regarding the rising tensions in the city (firebombings, troop alerts, rumors, etc.) were drawn from local press reports, FBI memoranda, and interviews with local reporters, civil rights leaders, and students.

The quotations from the congressional delegation visiting Alexander Hall were transcribed from ABC News film, May 20. The quotation from Charles Evers appeared in the *Sphinx* (May-June 1970), the journal of Alpha Phi Alpha Fraternity, Inc., a black fraternal organization.

For my description of the meeting between President Nixon and the black college presidents I must acknowledge a heavy debt to reporter Jack Nelson of the *Los Angeles Times.* Nelson's May 31 account of the meeting in the White House was based on what he had described as "lengthy" interviews with four of the fifteen college presidents present, one of whom had taken extensive notes on the meeting. I also reviewed a May 21 story in the *Washington Post* and another on that date in the *Los Angeles Times.* A CBS News story on the meeting (May 20) was also helpful. For the transcript of President Herman Branson's remarks to Nixon, see the *Sphinx* (cited above).

The working papers of the presidential commission included a transcript of Governor John Bell Williams's televised speech on May 21 (NA). I also listened to an audiotape of the speech (DAH).

9 Showdown

This chapter's epigraph is from the Revised Standard Edition of the Bible.

The quotations from Senator Muskie and Whitney Young, Jr., were taken from a report in the *Sphinx,* which reprinted a news story originally appearing in the *New York Amsterdam News.*

For details on the Green funeral in the Masonic Temple, my most valuable source was Craig Vetter's "Funeral in Jackson," published June 1971 in *Playboy.* The quotation from the black minister's funeral sermon originally appeared in *Playboy.* Other accounts appeared on May 23 in the *Washington Post,* the *New York Times,* the *New Orleans Times-Picayune,* and the *Memphis Commercial-Appeal.* A videotape of ABC News coverage for May 22 (VU) and film from the WLBT collection (DAH) were indespensable. Still photos in the Gibbs-Green Memorial Collection (JSU) and others contributed by *Kudzu* photographers made it possible to depict events in Jackson on May 22, the day of the funeral.

Details regarding the escalating tensions in the city were drawn primarily from FBI documents and news accounts in the Hederman press on May 22.

The quotations from Senators Percy and Muskie were transcribed from news film in the WLBT collection (DAH).

The account of the unrest in 1963 after the funeral of Medgar Evers was based on a variety of sources, including John Salter's *Jackson, Mississippi: An American Chronicle of Struggle and Schism,* Anne Moodie's *Coming of Age in Mississippi,* and Myrlie Evers's *For Us, the Living.*

Information about James Green's life was drawn from interviews with his friends and family, as well as his English teacher, Alberta Bingham, his employer, Frank Dantoni, and his principal, Emmitt Hayes. Paul L. Montgomery's article on both Green and Phillip Gibbs (*New York Times,* May 16) was also used.

The speech given by Principal Emmitt Hayes was taken from a transcript in the Gibbs-Green Memorial Collection (JSU). Mayor Charles Evers's address was transcribed from film in the WLBT collection (DAH). Other information about the speakers and the funeral service was based on the funeral program in the Gibbs-Green Memorial Collection.

The account of Deputy Attorney General Jerris Leonard's intervention in the controversy over the evidence at Alexander Hall was based on national and local newspaper accounts and memoranda in the FBI report. News accounts of special interest appeared in the *Vicksburg Post* (May 23), the *New Orleans Times-Picayune* (May 23), the *Meridian Star* (May 23), and the *New York Times* (May 24). CBS News coverage of the confrontation (May 23) and *Kudzu* photographers' pictures made it possible to depict the scene in front of the dormitory. Dialogue in this scene was drawn from several of these sources, particularly the CBS account.

10 Nixon's Court

The epigraph for this chapter is from Langston Hughes's poem "Justice."

For facts on Biloxi's history, see Hancock Bank's *The Coast of Mississippi: Its Past and Progress,* Hazel Holt's *History of Biloxi,* and *The Buildings of Biloxi: An Architectural Survey* (no author given). For an illuminating article on Biloxi's nightclub scene, see Tom Ethridge's column in the *Clarion-Ledger,* March 21, 1972.

Many of the details on the career of Judge Harold Cox were based on Carol Caldwell's article, "Harold Cox: Still Racist After All These Years," and confirmed by conversations with attorneys and newsmen in Jackson.

Quotations from Judge Cox's instructions to the Special Federal Grand Jury have been taken from a transcript of his charge (NA). References to Judge Russel D. Moore III's instructions to the Hinds County Grand Jury have been taken from a transcript of his charge (NA).

Facts and quotations from the presidential commission's findings at Kent State and Jackson State have come from the text of the report published by Avon Books.

For daily news accounts of the trial's progress, I examined reports in the *New York Times,* the *Clarion-Ledger,* the *Jackson Daily News,* and the *Daily Herald* (a Gulf Coast newspaper). All quotations and dialogue from the trial have been taken from the seventeen-volume court record of *Burton v. Williams* (SUNYA).

The final scene, in which highway patrolmen are described yelling, was drawn from interviews with Attorneys Constance Slaughter and Robert Mullen, and from Mrs. Dale Gibbs Thomas, widow of Phillip Gibbs.

Epilogue

The epigraph from Faulkner was uttered by the character Gavin Stevens in *Intruder in the Dust.*

The quotations from the U.S. Court of Appeals decision in 1974 were taken from a summary of the decision appearing in the *Chronicle of Higher Education,* October 29, 1974.

The account of the shooting of two black youths in Jackson in April 1979 was based on city police reports, photos of one victim's wounds, interviews with city police, and an interview with civil rights attorney Patrick O'Rourke, who represented one of the wounded youths.

For information about police brutality in Jackson, I interviewed activists, reporters, city police, and alleged black victims of brutality. I also examined the Hederman press's coverage of allegations of brutality. Twice in the 1970s the *Clarion-Ledger* published a series of investigative reports on police misconduct. For more details on police misconduct in Jackson, see the investigative report in 1977 by the United States Commission on Civil Rights. Interviews with City Police Chief Ray Pope and his assistant Gary McGee were also helpful in assessing the seriousness of police brutality in Jackson.

Mississippi Highway Patrol officials declined to comment on either the Jackson State tragedy or complaints of brutality after 1970.

For the account of racial unrest in Simpson County, Mississippi and the role of Sheriff Lloyd "Goon" Jones, I interviewed several of the black residents who alleged that local officers had beaten them. I interviewed their attorney, Suzanne Griggins, and her predecessor in the Mendenhall legal services office, Allison Steiner. I examined the complaint brought against Jones and other officers in federal court. I spoke only briefly to Sheriff Jones, who had previously declined to answer other reporters' questions on the subject of the "Magee 19."

For statistics on economic conditions in Mississippi, I drew from the *Mississippi, Statistical Abstract: 1980* and from reports in the *New York Times* (April 14, 1982 and August 18, 1983).

The city council minutes quoted at the end of this epilogue appeared in the minutes for Tuesday, March 13, 1973.

SOURCES CONSULTED

Books

Agee, James. *Let Us Now Praise Famous Men.* Photographs by Walker Evans. 1939. Reprint. New York: Ballantine Books, 1976.

Baker, Ray Stannard. *Following the Color Line.* 2d ed. New York: Harper & Row, 1964.

Bank, Hancock, ed. *The Coast of Mississippi: Its Past and Progress.* Baton Rouge: Moran Publishing, 1982.

Barrett, Russell H. *Integration at Ole Miss.* Chicago: Quadrangle Books, 1965.

Beard, Charles, ed. *1971 Jacksonian.* Jackson State College Yearbook, n.p.

Berry, Jason. *Amazing Grace: With Charles Evers in Mississippi.* 2d edition. New York: Saturday Review Press, 1978.

Brady, Tom P. *Black Monday: Segregated or Amalgamated . . . America Has Its Choice.* Brookhaven, Miss.: Association of Citizens' Councils, 1955.

Brinson, Carroll. *Jackson, A Special Kind of Place.* Jackson, Miss., n.p., 1977.

Brisbane, Robert H. *Black Activism: Racial Revolution in the United States, 1954–1970.* Valley Forge, Pa.: Judson Press, 1974.

______. *The Black Vanguard: Origins of the Negro Revolution, 1900–1960.* Valley Forge, Pa.: Judson Press, 1969.

Brown, Andrew. *History of Tippah County, Mississippi: The First Century.* Ripley, Miss.: Tippah County Historical and Genealogical Society, 1976.

The Buildings of Biloxi: An Architectural Survey. Biloxi, Miss.: City of Biloxi, 1976.

Campbell, Clarice T., and Oscar Allan Rogers, Jr. *Mississippi, The View From Tougaloo.* Jackson: University Press of Mississippi, 1979.

Carson, Clayborne. *In Struggle: SNCC and the Black Awakening of the 1960s.* Cambridge: Harvard University Press, 1981.

Carter, Hodding. *So the Heffners Left McComb.* Garden City, N.Y.: Doubleday and Company, 1965.

Cash, W. J. *The Mind of the South.* 1941. Reprint. New York: Vintage Books, 1969.

Cunningham, W. J. *Agony at Galloway: One Church's Struggle with Social Change.* Jackson: University Press of Mississippi, 1980.

Dansby, Baldwin B. *A Brief History of Jackson College: A Typical Story of the Survival of Education among Negroes in the South.* New York: American Book-Stratford Press, 1953.

Davies, Peter. *The Truth About Kent State.* New York: Farrar, Straus & Giroux, 1973.

DeVries, Walter, and Jack Bass. *The Transformation of Southern Politics: Social Change and Political Consequence Since 1945.* New York: Basic Books, 1976.

Didion, Joan. *The White Album*. New York: Simon and Schuster, 1979.

Eszterhas, Joe, and Michael D. Roberts. *Thirteen Seconds*. New York: Dodd, Mead, 1970.

Evers, Mrs. Medgar, with William Peters. *For Us, the Living*. Garden City, N.Y.: Doubleday and Company, 1967.

Faulkner, William. *Sartoris*. Foreword by Robert Cantwell. 1929. Reprint. New York: Signet Classics, 1964.

Frady, Marshall. *Southerners: A Journalist's Odyssey*. New York: New American Library, 1980.

Franklin, John Hope. *From Slavery to Freedom: A History of Negro Americans*. 3d edition. New York: Alfred A. Knopf, 1967.

Fuller, Chet. *I Hear Them Calling My Name: A Journey Through the New South*. Boston: Houghton Mifflin, 1981.

Haynes, Robert V. *A Night of Violence: The Houston Riot of 1917*. Baton Rouge: Louisiana State University Press, 1976.

Hederman, Robert M., Jr. *The Hederman Story: A Saga of the Printed Word in Mississippi*. New Jersey: Princeton University Press, 1966.

Herring, George, C. *America's Longest War: The United States and Vietnam, 1950–1975*. New York: John Wiley & Sons, 1979.

Hersey, John. *Algiers Motel Incident*. New York: Alfred A. Knopf, 1968.

Hilton, Bruce. *The Delta Ministry*. New York: MacMillan, 1969.

Hodgson, Godfrey. *America in Our Time*. Garden City, N.Y.: Doubleday and Company, 1976.

Holt, Hazel. *History of Biloxi*. Biloxi, Miss.: First National Bank of Biloxi and Activities, 1968.

Kelner, Joseph, and James Munves. *The Kent State Coverup*. New York: Harper & Row, 1980.

Kirwan, Albert D. *Revolt of the Rednecks; Mississippi Politics: 1876–1925*. Gloucester, Mass.: P. Smith, 1964.

Loewen, James W., and Charles Sallis, eds. *Mississippi: Conflict & Change*. New York: Random House, 1974.

Lord, Walter. *The Past That Would Not Die*. New York: Harper and Row, 1965.

Lynch, John Roy. *Reminiscences of an Active Life: The Autobiography of John Roy Lynch*. Introduction by John Hope Franklin. Chicago: University of Chicago Press, 1970.

Lynd, Alice, ed. *We Won't Go: Personal Accounts of War Objectors*. Boston: Beacon Press, 1968.

McCord, William. *Mississippi: The Long, Hot Summer*. New York: W. W. Norton, 1965.

McMillen, Neil R. *The Citizens' Council: Organized Resistance to the Second Reconstruction, 1954–64*. Chicago: University of Illinois Press, 1971.

McWhiney, Grady. *Southerners and Other Americans*. New York: Basic Books, 1973.

Mailer, Norman. *Some Honorable Men: Political Conventions 1960–1972.* Boston: Little, Brown and Company, 1976.

Mars, Florence. *Witness in Philadelphia.* Baton Rouge: Louisiana State University Press, 1977.

Mayfield, Chris, ed. *Growing Up Southern: "Southern Exposure" Looks at Childhood, Then and Now.* New York: Random House, 1981.

Meier, August, and Elliot Rudwick. *CORE: A Study in the Civil Rights Movement, 1942–1968.* New York: Oxford University Press, 1973.

Meredith, James. *Three Years in Mississippi.* Bloomington: Indiana University Press, 1966.

Michener, James A. *Kent State: What Happened and Why.* New York: Random House, 1971.

Moodie, Anne. *Coming of Age in Mississippi.* New York: Dell Books, 1971.

Morris, Willie. *Terrains of the Heart and Other Essays on Home.* Oxford, Miss.: Yoknapatawpha Press, 1981.

Nelson, Jack, and Jack Bass. *The Orangeburg Massacre.* New York: World Publishing, 1970.

O'Neil, Robert M., John P. Morris, and Raymond Mack. *No Heroes, No Villains: New Perspectives on Kent State and Jackson State.* San Francisco: Jossey-Bass, 1972.

Perkins, Reverend John. *Let Justice Roll Down.* 2d. ed. Glendale, Calif.: G/L Publications, 1978.

Powell, W. F. *Jackson's Early History and 28 Years of Municipal Progress.* Jackson: Tucker Printing House, n.d.

Prenshaw, Peggy W., and Jesse O. McKee, eds. *Sense of Place, Mississippi.* Jackson: University Press of Mississippi, 1979.

Redding, Saunders. *On Being Negro in America.* 1951. Reprint. New York: Bantam Books, 1964.

Rhodes, Lelia Gaston. *Jackson State University: The First Hundred Years, 1877–1977.* Jackson: University Press of Mississippi, 1979.

Rowland, Eron O. *History of Hinds County Mississippi, 1821–1922.* Jackson, Miss.: Jones Ptg. Co., 1922.

Salter, John R., Jr. *Jackson, Mississippi: An American Chronicle of Struggle and Schism.* Foreword by Reverend R. Edwin King, Jr. Hicksville, N.Y.: Exposition Press, 1979.

Sansing, David G., and Carroll Waller. *A History of the Mississippi Governor's Mansion.* Jackson: University Press of Mississippi, 1977.

Sewell, George Alexander. *Mississippi Black History Makers.* Jackson: University Press of Mississippi, 1977.

Silver, James. *Mississippi: The Closed Society.* New York: Harcourt, Brace & World, 1964.

Stone, I. F. *The Killings at Kent State: How Murder Went Unpunished.* Introduction by Senator Stephen Young. 2d ed. New York: Random House, 1971.

The Story of Jackson, A History of the Capital of Mississippi, 1821–1951. 2 vols. Jackson, Miss.: Hyer Publishing, 1953.

Summers, Cecil L. *The Governors of Mississippi.* Gretna, La.: Pelican Publishing, 1980.

Viorst, Milton. *Fire in the Streets: America in the 1960s.* New York: Simon and Schuster, 1979.

Von Hoffman, Nicholas. *Mississippi Notebook.* 2d ed. New York: David White Co., 1964.

Werstein, Irving. *The Draft Riots: July 1963.* 2d ed. New York: Simon & Schuster, 1971.

Wharton, Vernon Lane. *The Negro in Mississippi, 1865–1890.* Chapel Hill: University of North Carolina Press, 1947.

Wright, Richard. *Black Boy: A Record of Childhood and Youth.* Afterword by John Reilly. 1945. Reprint. New York: Perennial Classics, 1966.

Articles

Adams, John P. "Guest Editorial: Truth at the Crossroads." *Christian Century,* June 17, 1970, p. 749.

Aptheker, Herbert. "The Negro College Student in the 1920s: Years of Preparation and Protest, An Introduction." *Science and Society* 33 (Spring 1969): 150–67.

Caldwell, Carol. "Harold Cox: Still Racist After All These Years." *American Lawyer,* July 1979, pp. 27–29.

Colom, Wilbur O. "The Trials of a Mississippi Lawyer." *New York Times Magazine,* May 15, 1983, pp. 62–78.

"Cops Murder Youth in Jackson Protest—4 More Shot!" *Hinds County F.D.P. News,* May 12, 1967.

"Cops Murder Youth in Jackson Rebellion." (Tougaloo) *Mississippi Newsletter,* May 12, 1967.

"Dark Day in Jackson." *Newsweek,* May 25, 1970, pp. 35–36.

"Ebony Photo-Editorial: Law and Disorder." *Ebony,* July 1970, pp. 96–97.

"Excerpts from the Appeals Court's Opinion in Jackson State Suit." *Chronicle of Higher Education,* October 29, 1974, pp. 8–9.

Facts on File: Weekly World Digest. April 30-June 3, 1970, February 13-April 1, 1972.

Halberstam, David. "Starting Out to Be a Famous Reporter." *Esquire,* November 1981, pp. 70–81.

Hooker, Robert. "Race and the Mississippi Press." *New South* 26 (Winter 1971): 55–62.

"Hotheads and Professionals." *Time,* August 10, 1970, pp. 42–43.

Hughes, Rubye. "Night of Terror: Jackson State." (Jackson) *Close Up,* June 1970.

"Investigations: Arms and the Campus." *Newsweek,* October 12, 1970, pp. 44–49.

Jackson Advocate. Special Supplement on Black History. Section A, February 26-March 4, 1981.
"Jackson: Kent State II." *Time,* May 25, 1970, p. 22.
"Jackson State Becalmed." *Newsweek,* March 1, 1971, p. 69.
"Jackson State, Scene of Killings, Tries to Shake Haunts of Past." *Chronicle of Higher Education,* December 6, 1971, p. 6.
"The Jackson Story." *Sphinx* 2 (May-June 1970): 17–24.
Lesher, Stephan. "Jackson State A Year After—'We Resent Everyone Ignoring Us Until We Have A Riot.' " *New York Times Magazine,* March 21, 1971, pp. 24–62.
Love, Sam. "Mississippi College Students Challenge the Courthouse Gang." *New South* 24 (Winter 1969): 17–29.
"Mamie Hit!" (Tougaloo, Mississippi) *Voice of the Movement Newsletter,* February 7, 1964.
Marable, Manning. "Down But Not out in the Delta." *Mother Jones,* June 1983, p. 60.
"Mississippi Revisited." *Newsweek,* November 12, 1979, pp. 49–50.
"Mississippi: What the Tape Said." *Newsweek,* August 24, 1970, pp. 22–25.
Montgomery, Paul L. "Slain Youths Lacked Time for 'Politics.' " *New York Times,* May 16, 1970, p. 15.
Neier, Aryeh. "Mississippi Relives Its '60s." *Nation,* September 23, 1978, pp. 265–67.
Nelson, Jack. "Presidents of Black Colleges Baffled by Nixon's Attitude." *Los Angeles Times,* May 31, 1970.
Powell, Lew. "A Bad Press in Mississippi." *Nation,* October 8, 1973, pp. 331–34.
"Seek To Save Voting Rights Act; Called One Hope Against Bullets." *Jet,* July 2, 1970, pp. 6–7.
Sloat, Bill. "Rapid Growth Brings Pangs of Change." *SOUTH Magazine,* January 1979, pp. 31–39.
Tessler, Mark A., and Ronald D. Hedlund. "A Hard Look at Campus Dissent: Students Aren't Crazies." *New Republic,* September 5–12, 1970, pp. 17–18.
Tulsky, Fredric. "Standing up to Fear in Mississippi." *Southern Exposure* 6 (Fall 1978): 68–72.
Vetter, Craig. "Funeral in Jackson." *Playboy,* June 1971.
Whittington, George. "The Conspiracy that Failed in Mississippi." *The Citizen: Official Journal of the Citizens Councils of America 15,* January 1971.
Williams, Edwin N. "Dimout in Jackson." *Columbia Journalism Review* 9 (Summer 1970): 56–58.

Audiovisual Aids

ABC. "ABC Evening News," April 15-August 15, 1970.
CBS. "CBS Evening News," April 15-August 15, 1970.

______. "CBS New Correspondents' Report, Part I: The Nation," December 27, 1970.

______. Outtakes of news film regarding Kent State slayings, May 1970.

Jackson, Mississippi. Farish Street Baptist Church. Audiotape of sermon by Reverend Hickman Johnson, Sunday, May 17, 1970.

Los Angeles, California. Photographer David Doggett. Collection of more than two hundred still photographs of events in Jackson, Mississippi after the Jackson State slayings, May 1970.

METV. Interview with former Governor John Bell Williams, June 22, 1973, Jackson, Mississippi.

Mississippi Department of Archives and History, Jackson, Mississippi. WLBT audiotape of televised statements of civil rights activists Reuben Anderson, Constance Slaughter, and Alex Waites, June 5, 1970.

National Archives, Washington, D.C. Records of Presidential Committees, Commissions and Boards, Record Group 220. Presidential Commission on Campus Unrest. Twelve tape-recorded reels of Jackson City Police and Mississippi Highway Patrol radio communications regarding student unrest at Jackson State College, May 13–15, 1970.

NBC. "NBC Nightly News," April 15-August 15, 1970.

______. "Our House Divided," May 10, 1970.

______. President Richard M. Nixon's speech on the invasion of Cambodia, April 30, 1970.

Smithsonian Collection of Recordings. "Voices of the Civil Rights Movement: Black American Freedom Songs, 1960–1966," 1980.

Special Mississippi TV-Radio Network. Governor John Bell Williams's address on the Jackson State slayings, May 21, 1970.

Tougaloo College Library, Tougaloo, Mississippi. Lawyers' Committee for Civil Rights Under Law. *Burton v. Williams.* Audiotaped pretrial depositions of City Police and Highway Patrol officers, 1971.

WLBT. Outtakes of WLBT news film regarding Jackson State slayings, May 1970.

Reports and Proceedings

Carnegie Commission on Higher Education. *May 1970: The Campus Aftermath of Cambodia and Kent State.* New York: McGraw-Hill, 1975.

Division of Research, College of Business and Industry. *Mississippi Statistical Abstract: 1980.* Mississippi State, Miss.: University of Mississippi, 1980.

Economic Base Study: Jackson Metropolitan Area, Summary. Jackson: Larry Smith & Co., March 1969.

Jackson, Mississippi Planning Board. *Community Goals Survey.* Jackson, August 1970.

Mayor's biracial committee. Unpublished report and transcript of hearings. 3 vols. Jackson, 1970.

National Anti-Klan Network. *The Ku Klux Klan Revival in Mississippi.* Washington, D.C.: National Anti-Klan Network, 1981.

National Black Draft Counselors. *Thirty Years of Selective Service Racism.* Chicago, Ill.: National Black Draft Counselors, 1971.

Public Administration Service. *Jackson, Mississippi Police Department: A Survey Report.* Chicago: Public Administration Service, 1970.

Southern Regional Council. *Augusta, Georgia and Jackson State University: Southern Episodes in a National Tragedy.* Atlanta: Southern Regional Council, Inc., 1970.

Urban Research Corporation. *On Strike . . . Shut It down! A Report on the First National Student Strike in U.S. History, May 1970.* Chicago: Urban Research Corporation, 1970.

U.S. Commission on Civil Rights, Southern Region. "Statement by Bobby D. Doctor, Director." Atlanta, Ga., February 15, 1977.

U.S. Department of Commerce, Social and Economic Statistics Administration, Bureau of the Census. *1970 Census of Population: Detailed Characteristics, Mississippi.* Washington, D.C.: Government Printing Office. Pubn. PC(1)-D26 (1972).

U.S. District Court, Southern District of Mississippi. Transcript of "Myrtle Green Burton et al. vs. John Bell Williams et al." 17 vols. Civil Action nos. 4740, 4897. Gulfport, Miss., 1972.

U.S. Federal Bureau of Investigation. Unpublished report on the Jackson State College killings. 23 vols. Washington, D.C., 1970.

U.S. President's Commission on Campus Unrest. *The Report of the President's Commission on Campus Unrest.* New York: Avon Books, 1971.

———. Unpublished hearings in Jackson, Mississippi. 2 vols. Washington, D.C., 1970.

Newspapers

Blue and White Flash (Jackson State College student newspaper), March 1964; March 1967; February, May, July, November 1968; February 1969; February, April 1970; May, January, July 1971.

Capitol Reporter (Jackson, Mississipi newsweekly), April 1979-August 1981.

Chicago Defender, May-June 1970.

Chronicle of Higher Education, September 1969-June 1970.

Daily Herald (Biloxi, Mississippi), February-March 1972.

Delta Democrat-Times (Greenville, Mississippi), May-August, 1970; February-March 1972.

Detroit Free Press, May-June 1970.

Hattiesburg American, May-August, 1970.

Jackson Advocate (black newsweekly), May-June 1967; May-June 1970.

Jackson Clarion-Ledger, March-April 1961; June 1963; February 1964; April-June

1967; August 1967; November 1967; May 1968; May-June 1969; September 1969-October 1970; February 1972-March 1972.

Jackson Daily News, March-April 1961; June 1963; February 1964; May 1967; August 1967; November 1967; May 1968; September 1969-October 1970; February 1972-March 1972.

Jackson State Times, March 1961.

Kudzu (underground newspaper in Jackson), September 1968-August 1970.

Los Angeles Times, May-June, August 1970.

Louisville Courier-Journal, May-June, August 1970.

Memphis Commercial-Appeal, May 1967; April-August, 1970.

Meridian Star, May-August, 1970.

New Orleans Times-Picayune, May-June, August 1970.

New York Amsterdam News, May-June 1970.

New York Times, March-August 1970; February 1972-March 1972; April 1979-January 1984.

Northside Reporter (Jackson newsweekly), Februry-March 1964; May-June 1967; May-June 1970.

Southern Sentinel (Ripley, Mississippi newsweekly), May-June 1970.

Tupelo Daily Journal, May-August, 1970.

Voice of Blackness (Jackson State College underground newspaper), May 7, 1970.

Washington Post, February, May-June, August 1970.

White and Purple (Millsaps College student newspaper) January-May 1970.

Unpublished Papers and Documents

Bell, Jimmy, and Walter Pascal. "Causes and Consequences of the Violence at Jackson State College," Jackson, July 8, 1971. Mimeo.

Gibbs, Phillip. Letters to Dale Gibbs, November 10, 1968; January 6, 1970; n.d. In possession of Dale Gibbs Thomas, Chattanooga, Tennessee.

Jackson, Mississippi. Common Council minutes, March 13, 1973, p. 292. Jackson City Hall, Jackson, Mississippi.

Jackson Peace Coordinating Committee. "4 Are Dead," Mimeographed handbill, May 1970.

Mississippi Department of Archives and History, Jackson. Mississippi Council on Human Relations collection. Reverend Kenneth L. Dean, notes on the May 11, 1967 shooting of Benjamin Brown on Lynch Street.

National Archives, Washington, D.C. Records of Presidential Committees, Commissions and Boards. Record Group 220. Governor John Bell Williams, texts of televised speeches, May 21, 1970 and June 4, 1970.

______. Judge William Harold Cox, "Federal Grand Jury Charge," June 20, 1970; Judge Russel D. Moore III, "Hinds County Grand Jury Charge," July 6, 1970.

Peoples, John A. "A Message from the President," Jackson, May 14, 1970. Mimeo.

______. "A Report of the Events at Jackson State College Beginning Wednesday

Evening May 13, 1970, and Extending Through Monday Afternoon, May 18, 1970." Submitted to the State Board of Higher Education, Jackson, May 19, 1970. Mimeo.

St. Paul's United Methodist Church, Ripley, Mississippi. Funeral service program of Phillip L. Gibbs, Sunday, May 17, 1970.

Salamon, Lester Milton. "Protest, Politics, and Modernization in the American South: Mississippi As a Developing Society." Ph.D. diss. Harvard University, 1971.

Stringer (M. W.) Masonic Temple, Jackson, Mississippi. Funeral service program of James Earl Green. Friday, May 22, 1970.

Tougaloo College Library, Tougaloo, Mississippi. *Burton v. Williams* collection. Mississippi Highway Patrol, "Log of Activities Regarding Jackson State College," May 13, 1970; Mississippi Highway Patrol, "Radio Station Log," May 14-15, 1970; Jackson Police Department, "Radio Log," May 14-15, 1970.

Young, Aurelia N. Address on the Jackson State killings, given before the National Institutes of Health, and the Society for the Study of Social Problems. Jackson, August 1970. Mimeo.

Major Collections

Jackson State University Library. Gibbs-Green Memorial collection, 1970. Jackson, Mississippi.

Mississippi Department of Archives and History. Mississippi Council on Human Relations collection. Jackson, Mississippi.

National Archives. Records of Presidential Committees, Commissions and Boards. Record Group 220. U.S. President's Commission on Campus Unrest, 1970. Working papers on Kent State University and Jackson State College. Washington, D.C.

Tougaloo College Library. Lawyers' Committee for Civil Rights Under Law, 1970. Burton vs. Williams collection. Tougaloo, Mississippi.

Interviews

Abraham, Richard. Draft counselor in 1970s. Jackson, Mississippi, January 6, 1981.

Abram, Tresia. Hinds County Grand Juror in 1970. Jackson, Mississippi, June 26, 1982.

Adams, Ciddie Lee. Mother-in-law of Phillip Gibbs. Ripley, Mississippi, July 21, 1981.

Anderson, Douglas. Former Jackson State instructor and state legislator in 1979. Jackson, Mississippi, July 4, 1979.

Anderson, Judge Reuben. Civil rights attorney and member of the mayor's biracial committee in 1970. Jackson, Mississippi, January 28, 1982.

Anonymous. Female companion of Phillip Gibbs on night of shootings. Jackson, Mississippi, August 20, 1981.

Baker, James. Jackson State student and witness to the shootings in 1970. Jackson, Mississippi, January 8, 1981.

Banks, Fred. Civil rights attorney and member of the mayor's biracial committee in 1970. Jackson, Mississippi, July 9, 1979 and January 28, 1982.

Bates, Eldna. Jackson State University student government president in 1980. Jackson, Mississippi, May 4, 1980.

Bingham, Alberta. Jim Hill High School English teacher in 1970. Jackson, Mississippi, January 21, 1981.

Bingham, Jessie. Mississippi Highway Patrolman in 1979. Telephone interview, July 1979.

Boone, David. *Jackson Daily News* sports writer in 1970. Telephone interview, Minneapolis, Minnesota, March 27, 1982.

Brantley, Robert. Millsaps College student in 1970. Jackson, Mississippi, August 6, 1981.

Brown, Earl. Residence director at Jackson State College in 1967. Jackson, Mississippi, August 12, 1982.

Brunini, Joseph. Roman Catholic bishop of Natchez-Jackson Diocese in 1970. Jackson, Mississippi, July 1, 1982.

Burton, Matt. Stepfather of James Earl Green. Jackson, Mississippi, January 18, 1981.

Burton, Myrtle Green. Mother of James Earl Green. Jackson, Mississippi, January 18, 1981.

Buxton, Warner. Jackson State College student government president and witness to the shootings in 1970. Quitman, Mississippi, June 15, 1982.

Canterbury, T. O. Owner of Canterbury's corner store when firebombed after 1970 shootings. Jackson, Mississippi, January 25, 1982.

Carr, Charles. Jackson State student and witness to May 13, 1970 unrest. Jackson, Mississippi, August 7, 1981.

Carr, Eddie Jean McDonald. Alexander Hall resident hospitalized for hysteria on night of slayings in 1970. Jackson, Mississippi, April 16, 1979 and August 7, 1981.

Carter, Levaughn. Jackson city policeman in 1970. Jackson, Mississippi, June 22, 1982.

Case, Bert. WJTV anchorman in 1970 and witness to shootings. Jackson, Mississippi, April 7, 1979, July 10, 1979, August 11, 1981 and July 26, 1982.

Clark, Fred. Jackson State student and witness to February 1964 campus unrest. Jackson, Mississippi, August 1981.

Clark, Robert G. State legislator in 1982. Jackson, Mississippi, June 30, 1982.
Coleman, Fonzie. Student wounded at Jackson State College in 1970. Jackson, Mississippi, July 1979.
Coleman, Judge J. P. Federal judge who ruled on the controversy over repairs to Alexander Hall in 1970. August 5, 1982.
Collins, Joe. Alleged victim of police brutality in 1979 in Mendenhall, Mississippi. Mendenhall, July 1979.
Colom, Roland. Roommate of Phillip Gibbs. Columbus, Mississippi, July 25, 1981.
Colom, Wilbur. Friend of Phillip Gibbs. Telephone interview, Columbus, Mississippi, winter 1983.
Cook, Martel. Jackson State student and WJTV cameraman in 1970. Jackson, Mississippi, April 17, 1979, July 20, 1979 and July 7, 1982.
Covington, Tommie. Unofficial historian of Ripley. Ripley, Mississippi, July 21, 1981.
Cox, Ellis. Relative of Phillip Gibbs. Ripley, Mississippi, July 20, 1981.
Crockett, Mamie Ballard. Student injured in 1964 campus incident. Telephone interview, Jackson, Mississippi, July 5, 1982.
Dampeer, Michael Houston. Jackson State University student in 1979. Jackson, Mississippi, July 1979.
Dantoni, Frank. Manager of Wag-a-bag corner store in 1970. Jackson, Mississippi, January 10, 1981.
Dean, Reverend Kenneth L. Director of the Mississippi Council on Human Relations in 1970. Memphis, Tennessee, July 17, 1981.
DeLaughter, Jerry. *Memphis Commercial-Appeal* reporter in 1970. Knoxville, Tennessee, September 1, 1981.
Dogan, Joann. Jackson State University student in 1979. Jackson, Mississippi, July 1979.
Doggett, David. *Kudzu* photographer and writer in 1970. Telephone interview, Los Angeles, California, July 5, 1982.
Dorsey, L. C. Delta Ministry Activist in 1981. Jackson, Mississippi, August 7, 1981.
Downey, James "Hank." Former Associated Press reporter in 1970 and witness to the shootings. Jackson, Mississippi. August 8, 1981.
Evers, Charles. Mayor of Fayette, Mississippi in 1970. Fayette, Mississippi, July 26, 1982.
Gibbs, Dondi. Alleged victim of police brutality in 1979. Jackson, Mississippi, July 1, 1979.
Gibbs, Fagin. Brother of Phillip Gibbs. Telephone interview, February, 6, 1983.
Gibbs, Nerene. Sister of Phillip Gibbs. Ripley, Mississippi, July 21, 1981 and June 21, 1982.
Gibbs, Stanley. Alleged victim of police brutality in 1979. Jackson, Mississippi, July 1, 1979.
Gilbert, Nancy. Community activist in 1970. Jackson, Mississippi, January 21, 1982.

Green, J. E. City of Jackson fireman in 1970. Jackson, Mississippi, June 27, 1982.

Green, Wesley. Brother of James Earl Green. Jackson, Mississippi, January 18, 1981.

Griffin, Karl. Student government leader in 1970. Boston, Massachusetts, March 20, 1982.

Griggins, Suzanne. Civil rights attorney in 1979. Mendenhall, Mississippi, July 1979.

Handy, N. Alfred. Lynch Street photographer and shopkeeper in 1970. Jackson, Mississippi, January 22, 1982.

Harjer, Richard. Jackson State University psychology teacher in 1982. Jackson, Mississippi, June 17, 1982.

Harvey, Constance Slaughter. Plaintiffs' attorney in Jackson State civil suit, 1970–82. Jackson, Mississippi, July 13–14, 1982.

Hayes, Emmitt. Principal of Jim Hill High School in 1970. Jackson, Mississippi, July 31, 1981.

Hayes, Gloria Mayhorn. Alexander Hall resident wounded in 1970 shootings. Telephone interview, Tupelo, Mississippi, July 11, 1979.

Haygood, Gregory. High school youth shot in 1964 incident. Jackson, Mississippi, August 17, 1981.

Hillegas, Jan. Community activist in 1970. Jackson, Mississippi, August 17, 1981.

Hobbs, Jack. WJTV newsman in 1970 and witness to shootings. Jackson, Mississippi, January 16, 1981.

James, Frank. Jackson State student in 1970 and witness to shootings. Vicksburg, Mississippi, June 30, 1982.

Johnson, Reverend Hickman. Minister in Farish Street Baptist Church in 1970. Jackson, Mississippi, January 28, 1982.

Johnson, Rhonda. Witness to alleged police brutality in 1979. Telephone interview, Tougaloo, Mississippi, July 5, 1979.

Johnson, Tommy. Graduate student at Jackson State University in 1979. Jackson, Mississippi, July 1979.

Kelly, Christopher. Attorney for Mississippi American Civil Liberties Union in 1979. Jackson, Mississippi, July 1979.

Kenter, Leroy. Student wounded at Jackson State College in 1970. Kansas City, Kansas, June 1981.

King, Reverend Edwin. Civil rights activist and former Tougaloo College chaplain in the 1960s. Jackson, Mississippi, August 20, 1981.

Kuykendall, John. Attorney and member of the mayor's biracial committee in 1970. Jackson, Mississippi, January 12, 1982.

Laurie, Stokes. Alleged victim of police brutality in 1979. Jackson, Mississippi, July 1, 1979.

Lawrence, Ken. Community activist in 1981. Jackson, Mississippi, August 17, 1981.

Levite, Howard. Student witness to 1970 shootings. Jackson, Mississippi, January 20, 1981.

Lyells, Ruby Stutts. Owner of M-L-S Drugstore on Lynch Street in 1970. Jackson, Mississippi, January 21, 1982.

McGee, Gary. Public relations officer, Jackson City Police. Jackson, Mississippi, July 12, 1979.

McMillin, Malcolm. City of Jackson policeman in 1970s. Bolton, Mississippi, January 8, 1982.

Meredith, James. Civil rights activist and Jackson State College student in 1960s. Jackson, Mississippi, January 13, 1982.

Middleton, Jeanne. Millsaps College student in 1970. Jackson, Mississippi, January 25, 1982.

Miller, Melvin. Public relations officer, Jackson State University in 1979. Jackson, Mississippi, April 1979.

Minor, Wilson. *New Orleans Times-Picayune* reporter in 1970. Jackson, Mississippi, April 8, 1979, January 19, 1981 and January 26, 1981.

Mitchell, Jerry. Self-described cornerboy in 1970. Jackson, Mississippi, January 27, 1982.

Mullen, Robert. Plaintiffs' attorney in Jackson State civil suit, 1970–82. New York City, February 1, 1983.

Murry, Climmie Johnson. Alexander Hall resident wounded in 1970. Drew, Mississippi, July 7, 1979.

O'Neill, Robert M. President of the University of Wisconsin, Madison in 1981 and co-author of an American Association of University Professors report on the Kent and Jackson State slayings. Madison, Wisconsin, June 1981.

O'Rourke, Patrick. Attorney for Lawyers Committee for Civil Rights Under Law in 1979. Jackson, Mississippi, July 1, 1979.

Patton, Amos. Co-worker of James Green in 1970. Jackson, Mississippi, January 13, 1981.

Poole, Violet. Jackson State University student in 1979. Jackson, Mississippi, July 1979.

Pope, Ray. Jackson chief of police in 1979. Jackson, Mississippi, July 12, 1979.

Price, Coney. Cornerboy in 1970. July 1, 1979.

Pyle, William. Attorney and member of the mayor's biracial committee in 1970. Jackson, Mississippi, Janaury 14, 1982.

Reeves, Bennie. History Department chairman at Jackson State University in 1982. Jackson, Mississippi, July 27, 1982.

Rhodes, Lelia. Historian of Jackson State University in 1982. Jackson, Mississippi, June 24, 1982.

Rogers, Brenda. Friend of James Green. Jackson, Mississippi, August 6, 1981.

Ross, James. Jackson State University student in 1980. Jackson, Mississippi, May 4, 1980.

Rusk, William. *Kudzu* reporter in 1970. Jackson, Mississippi, January 22, 1981.

Russell, Dorothy. Jackson State University student in 1979. Jackson, Mississippi, July 1979.

Sallis, Charles. Millsaps College professor of history in 1970. Jackson, Mississippi, January 8, 1982.

Sanders, D. B. Father of Patricia Sanders, an Alexander Hall resident wounded at Jackson State. Oxford, Mississippi, July 21, 1981.

Shamwell, Joseph. Instructor of music, Jackson State University in 1981. Jackson, Mississippi, July 26, 1981.

Shirley, Dr. Aaron. Civil rights activist and pediatrician in 1970. Jackson, Mississippi, January 5, 1982.

Simmons, Mattie. Relative of Phillip Gibbs. Ripley, Mississippi, July 20, 1981.

Sims, Jerry. Alleged victim of police brutality in 1979 in Mendenhall, Mississippi. Mendenhall, July 1979.

Smith, Davis. Attorney and former *Jackson Daily News* reporter in 1970. Jackson, Mississippi, August 2, 1981.

Spight, F. Leon. High school principal of Phillip Gibbs. Ripley, Mississippi, July 22, 1981.

Spinks, Stella. Student wounded in 1970 shootings. Telephone interview, Chicago, Illinois, April 17, 1979.

Steiner, Allison. Civil rights attorney in Mendenhall, Mississippi in 1970s. Telephone interview, Hattiesburg, Mississippi, July 1979.

Taylor, Reverend Wendell. Pastor, Central Methodist Church in 1982. Jackson, Mississippi, January 22, 1982.

Thomas, Dale Gibbs. Widow of Phillip Gibbs. Chattanooga, Tennessee, June 11, 1982.

Thompson, Bennie. Supervisor of Hinds County District 2 in 1982. Bolton, Mississippi, Janaury 14, 1982.

Thompson, H. M. Grand Master of the Stringer Masonic Lodge in 1981. Jackson, Mississippi, July 31, 1981.

Thompson, Henry "Degecha X." Jackson State activist in 1970. Hattiesburg, Mississippi, July 20, 1982.

Tomlin, Ian. Civil rights activist in 1970. Jackson, Mississippi, January 18, 1981.

Tutwiler, Milton. Mayor of Winstonville in 1979. Winstonville, Mississippi, July 1979.

Waites, Alex. Field director of the Mississippi NAACP in 1970. Jackson, Mississippi, August 7, 1981.

Walker, Margaret. Poet, novelist, and retired Jackson State professor. Jackson Mississippi, July 11, 1979.

Weakley, Vernon. Student wounded in 1970 shootings. Jackson, Mississippi, January 8, 1981.

Welch, Queenie Stokes. Alexander Hall resident and witness to 1970 shootings. Jackson, Mississippi, August 16, 1981.

Whitehead, Tuwaine Davis. Student wounded in 1970 shootings. Jackson, Mississippi, January 28, 1981.

Williams, David. Jackson State University student in 1980. Jackson, Mississippi, May 4, 1980.

Williams, John Bell. Former governor of Mississippi. Brandon, Mississippi, January 7, 1982.

Williams, Nathaniel. Alleged victim of police brutality in 1979. Jackson, Mississippi, July 1, 1979.

Williams, Samuel. Jackson State University student in 1980. Jackson, Mississippi, May 4, 1980.

Wilson, Redd. Student wounded in 1970 shootings. Jackson, Mississippi, April 16, 1979.

Young, Aurelia. Instructor of music at Jackson State College in 1970. Jackson, Mississippi, July 26, 1981.

Young, Gene "Jughead." Jackson State College student in 1970. Telephone interview, Peoria, Illinois, February 10, 1983.

INDEX

Adams, Dale. *See* Gibbs, Dale Adams
Agnew, Spiro, 29, 31, 35, 139
Aiken, George, 25
Alabama, University of, student demonstrations at, 28, 116–17
Albany (Ga.) State College, black student protests at, 29
Albuquerque, N.M., student bayonetings in, 28
Alcohol: as factor in Jackson State miniriot, 40; and Mississippi, 55
Allain, William, 165, 173
Amherst College, student strike at, 26
Anderson, John, 142
Anderson, Reuben, 91, 121
Antoine, Gregory, 88–89, 92
Arizona, University of, student protests at, 25
Armistead, Rex P., 122; civil trial testimony of, 165–66
Augusta, Ga., murder of blacks in, 34
Austin, Robert, 170

Ballard, Mamie, 12
Baltimore, Md., student protests in, 116
Bank of America, 23
Banks, Fred, 91, 120
Baton Rouge, La., 1970 violence in, 23
Bayh, Birch, 138
Beasley, Truitt, 46, 65, 73, 75–76; testimony of before committee, 96–97
Beckwith, Byron de la, 12
Berkeley. *See* California, University of (Berkeley)
Bilbo, Theodore, 41
Biloxi, Miss., 154
Bingham, Alberta, 145
Bingham, Carol Maie, 98
Birmingham, Ala., police brutality in, 8
"Black codes," 1
Black nationalism, 14
Black Panthers, 22, 23, 26, 27
Black People's Unity Movement, 16
Black Power, 26
Boone, David, 65–66; testimony of before committee, 129–30
Boston College, student strike at, 26
Bowie State College, cancellation of classes at, 117
Bowling, Francis, 91, 97–98, 126, 131
Boycotts, 8, 9, 115, 116
Branson, Dr. Herman, 139
Braun, Joseph, 166
Bray, Donald, 167
Brennan, William, 175
Brooke, Edward, 143–44
Brown, Benjamin, 16–17; murder of, 44

Index

Brown, H. Rap, 14
Buchanan, Marion, 98
Buffalo, N.Y., student demonstrations in, 28
Buffalo State College. *See* New York, State University of (Buffalo)
Burton, Matt, 146, 148–49
Burton, Myrtle Green, 143–44, 146, 148; civil trial testimony of, 159–60
Butler, Jerry, 167
Buxton, Warner, 30, 35, 38, 151, 152, 153; as CORE worker, 38

California, University of (Berkeley), student strike at, 26
California, University of (Los Angeles). *See* UCLA
California, University of (Santa Barbara), student/police confrontation at, 23
Cambodia, 19; civil war in, 23–24; U.S. invasion of, 24–25; U.S. invasion of as fuse of campus explosions, 25–27, 30, 35, 56, 133
Canton, Miss., tear-gassing of marchers in, 43
Carmichael, Stokely, 14
Carr, Charles, 20, 40, 45, 51
Carr, Eddie Jean McDonald, 60, 98
Carswell, G. Harold, 139
Carter, Hodding, 54
Carter, Levaughn, 47
Case, Bert, 39–40, 50, 66–67, 70–71, 74, 76, 95, 97, 128, 129, 151; as typical white Mississippian, 117–18; civil trial testimony of, 172; testimony of before committee, 117–23
Chicago, University of, Jackson State memorial rally at, 116
Chimneyville. *See* Jackson, Miss.
Church, Frank, 25
Cincinnati, University of, student protests at, 25, 117
Citizens' Council, 54
City University of New York, Jackson State memorial at, 117
Civil Rights Act of 1875, 1
Civil Rights Commission, U.S., represented at James Green funeral, 142
Civil Rights Division, U.S. Dept. of Justice, 138
Civil rights movement, 8–13, 18. *See also* Black nationalism; Black People's Unity Movement; COFO; CORE; Freedom Summer; Mississippi United Front; NAACP; SNCC; Southern Christian Leadership Conference
Claremont College, Jackson State memorial rally at, 116
Cleaver, Eldridge, 14
COFO (Council of Federated Organizations), 11–12. *See also* CORE; NAACP; SNCC; Southern Christian Leadership Conference
Coleman, Fonzie, 97–98
Coleman, J. P., 136–38, 152
Colgate University, student strike at, 26
Collins, Corris, 52
Colom, Roland, and Phillip Gibbs, 103, 105, 106, 108, 109, 110–12, 113–14
Colom, Wilbur, 103, 106
Colorado College, student demonstrations at, 28
Columbus, O., student protests in, 23. *See also* Ohio State University
Concerned Students of Jackson State College, 136
Congress of Racial Equality (CORE), 11
Conyers, John, 142
Cook, Martel, 49–50, 51, 67–68, 71, 118
Cooper, John Sherman, 25
CORE (Congress of Racial Equality), 11
Cornell University, student/faculty protests at, 25
Cornerboys, Lynch Street, 3–4, 14, 15, 17, 33, 144; during May 13 miniriot, 48–49; role of in May 14–15 violence, 60–62, 68, 88
Council of Federated Organizations (COFO), 11–12
Court of Appeals, U.S., Jackson State survivors before, 175
Cox, William H., 155
Cravaith, Swaine and Moore, 156
Creekmore, Rufus, 162, 173
Cronkite, Walter, 90

Index

Daniel, Claude, 167
Dantoni, Frank, 144, 147
Davis, Jefferson, 20, 154
Davis, Montie Rose, civil trial testimony of, 164
Davis, Russell, 44–45, 46, 50, 51, 58, 64, 66–67, 118, 130–31, 171, 182; friction between Jackson police and, 91
Dean, Rev. Kenneth, 16, 77
DeLaughter, Jerry, 152
Delta Democrat-Times, 54
Dennis, David, 11
Detroit, Mich., 1967 ghetto uprising in, 14
D'Floure, Tom, 18, 31
Diggs, Charles, 142
Dinkins, Gladys, 98
Doar, John, 143
Dowdy, Lewis C., 139
Downey, James ("Hank"), 66, 67, 70, 74, 119, 129, 130; testimony of before committee, 127–29
Draft, 22, 27, 30
Duke University, student strike at, 26

Eagleton, Thomas, 142
Earth Day, 22
Edwards, Emmit, 167
Environmentalism, 22
Ethridge, Tom, 16, 56
Evers, Charles, 12, 61, 149, 150, 151; in Jackson after shootings, 85, 88–89; at James Green funeral, 148; as mayor of Fayette, Miss., 43
Evers, Medgar, 61; assassination of, 9, 10, 12, 46, 116 (*see also* Beckwith, Byron de la); firebombing of home of, 9; funeral of, 143
Evers, Sheila, 61

Falkner, William C., 100, 104, 114
Faulkner, William, 100, 104
Fayette, Miss., 43
FBI (Federal Bureau of Investigation), 98, 136, 150, 152, 153; civil trial testimony of, 172; as "Freedom of Choice" chaperones, 105; and investigation of Jackson State killings, 98, 133; Jackson office of, 98, 116; report of on Jackson State killings, 181–82. *See also* Mitchell, John
"Freedom of Choice," 103, 105
Freedom of Information Act, 182
Freedom Riders, 11; in Jackson, 43
Freedom Summer (Mississippi Summer Project), 11–13; Jackson police reaction to, 11–13; in Ripley, Miss., 102–3

Gadfly, The, 58
Georgia, Jackson State dead remembered in, 116, 134
Georgia State University, Jackson State memorial rally at, 116
Gholson, Claude, 95
Gibbs, Dale Adams (Dale Adams Gibbs Thomas), 105, 106–8, 109, 112; civil trial testimony of, 162
Gibbs, Louise, 101
Gibbs, Mary, 111
Gibbs, Nerene, 102, 105, 106
Gibbs, Ozell, 101
Gibbs, Phillip, Jr., 107, 109, 162
Gibbs, Phillip, Sr., 84, 86, 99–114, 155; death and burial of, 97, 99–100, 113–14; Jackson State memorial to, 176; as Jackson State student, 105–13, 162; as observer of May 13 miniriot, 110–11; precollege life of, 101–5; wife and family of, 106–8, 109. *See also* Colom, Roland; Gibbs, Dale Adams; "Royce, Diane"
Grant, Ulysses S., 1
Green, James Earl, 84, 86, 97, 155; death and funeral of, 97, 134, 137–38, 140, 141–44, 145–46, 148–49; Jackson State memorial to, 176; life of, 144–48; posthumous respects paid by Pres. Nixon to, 143
Greensboro, N.C., and 1960 sit-in, 5
Greenville, Miss., 54
Griffith, Joseph David, 98

Handy, N. Alfred, 3–4
Hanoi, 22

Harriman, Averell, 142
Harvard University: antiwar protests by students of, 23; cancellation of classes at, 117
Haverford College, student strike at, 26
Hayden, Tom, 26
Hayes, Emmitt, 145
Haygood, Gregory, 13
Haynsworth, Clement F., 139
Head Start, 42
Hederman, Robert, 54
Hederman, Thomas, 54
Hederman press, 54–56, 129, 188–89; on Jackson State slayings, 83–84, 116. See also *Jackson Clarion Ledger; Jackson Daily News*
Henry, Robert, 54
Highway Patrol, Mississippi, 43, 62–65; assault of on Jackson State campus, 68–73, 88–89, 121, 125, 130; and Canton, Miss., tear-gassing, 43; integration of, 177; and May 13 miniriot, 41, 42, 43–52; during Ole Miss desegregation riots, 43; and 1967 Lynch Street shootings, 15–16; refusal of to cooperate in Jackson State investigations, 91–92; civil trial testimony of, 164–68; warned by Att'y Gen. Mitchell, 133; withdrawal of after Jackson Street shootings, 74–75. *See also* Armistead, Rex P.; Jones, Lloyd ("Goon"); Latham, Thomas
Hill, Jim, 9
Hinds County, Miss., consideration of Jackson State violence by Grand Jury of, 155–56
Hobbs, Jack: and coverage of Lynch Street story, 66–67, 70–71, 74, 76, 90, 118–22, 128; deposition at Jackson State civil trial, 172; and report of sniper, 74, 85, 97, 192; testimony of repudiated by President's Commission, 156; as witness before committee, 123–27
Holderfield, Edward, 94
Hoover, J. Edgar, 98
Hughes, Harold, 142

Inouye, Daniel, 142
Itta Bena, Miss., 23

Jackson, Miss., 1–21; black police officers of, 36, 47; and bloody aftermath of Medgar Evers murder, 9–10; boycott of white businesses of, 115, 116; churches of, 86, 116; civil rights movement in, 8–13, 18; civil trial testimony of police of, 169–72; Freedom Riders in, 43; and Freedom Summer, 11–13; hospitals of, 76–78, 86; investigation of police of after Jackson State slayings, 91–98; Jackson State and Millsaps College students demonstrate together in, 32; during James Green's funeral, 141–49; Mayor Davis and police of at odds, 91; and mayor's biracial investigating committee, 91–98, 117–31; in 1970, 20–21; and 1961 sit-in, 7; police of, 7–8, 14–16, 32–52 passim, 62–75, 89, 125, 177 (*see also* Beasley, Truitt; Lee, Charles; Magee, Warren; Pierce, M. B.); police-black confrontations in, 17; police of versus May 13 minirioters, 42–52; reaction in to Jackson State shootings, 115–16; after Jackson State violence, 82–89, 91–98; sit-in at Municipal Library of, 7; survivors of Jackson State shootings *v.*, 155–74; today, 175–76; walkout of black schoolchildren of to protest shootings, 115. *See also* Davis, Russell; Jackson State College; Lynch Street
Jackson Clarion-Ledger, 17, 53–56; on Jackson State slayings, 83; on James Green's funeral, 141; on Phillip Gibbs, 100; on police misconduct, 195; with praise for Jackson police, 16
Jackson College. *See* Jackson State College
Jackson Daily News, 54, 55, 83–84, 85; on Jackson State shootings, 116; on James Green's funeral, 142; on Kent State shootings, 55; with praise for police "coolness," 13. *See also* Boone, David
Jackson Peace Coordinating Committee, 3
Jackson State College, 2, 4–5; administration of, 56–58 (*see also* Peoples, Dr. John; Reddix, Jacob); aftermath of shootings at, 80–98, 115, 134–74, 175–80; Att'y Gen. Mitchell's visit to, 132–33; and Cambodian protest meeting, 30–31; campus of, 5,

Index

6, 34 (*see also* Lynch Street); campus unrest at, 12–13, 35–41; closing of, 82, 84, 90; dead and wounded of, 72–78, 84, 97–98, (*see also* Gibbs, Phillip; Green, James Earl); efforts of state to remove evidence of violence at, 134–35, 150–53; events of May 14–15 at, 60–79; FBI report on violence at, 181–82; federal grand jury investigation of violence at, 155; fraternities of, 34, 59; life at, 34, 59–60; litigation relative to slayings at, 155–74, 175; mayor's investigation of violence at, 117–31; May 13 miniriot at, 35–52, 53; memorial to slain students on campus of, 176; and Millsaps College joint activism, 32; national reaction to shootings at, 90–91; 1967 student/police confrontations at, 14–16; Phillip Gibbs as student at, 105–13; report of President's Commission on Campus Unrest on shootings at, 156; today, 175–76; and Tougaloo College joint activism, 10; and "town and gown" friction, 4 (*see also* Cornerboys, Lynch Street); underground press of, 35, 58
Jackson State Times, 184
"Jacktwo," 98. *See also* FBI, Jackson office of
James, Frank, 36
Jenkins, Rev. W. L., 136
Jersey City, N.J., ghetto rebellion in, 11
J. H. (1919 lynch victim), 56
Johnson, Climmie (Climmie Johnson Murry), 69, 72–73, 98; civil trial testimony of, 163
Johnson, Lyndon B., 22
Johnson, Walter G., 56, 171
"Johnston, Janine," 110, 111
Jones, George, 37
Jones, Jerry, 167
Jones, Lloyd ("Goon"), 16, 43–46, 48, 63–65, 73–75, 94, 121, 182, 188; civil court testimony of, 167–68; as sheriff of Simpson County, Miss., 178–79; singled out by Charles Evers, 89; and shooting of Benjamin Brown, 43–44; trial of, 155–74
Justice, U.S. Department of, 138. *See also* FBI; Mitchell, John
Kenter, Leroy, 77, 97; civil trial testimony of, 161
Kent State University: black student protests at, 29; demonstrations by students of, 25; Jackson newspapers' reaction to slayings at, 55, 56; Jackson State student reaction to slayings at, 30–31; and memorials to Jackson State dead, 117; national reaction to slayings at, 27–31; report of President's Commission on Campus Unrest on shootings at, 156; represented at James Green funeral, 142; shootings on campus of, 17, 18–19, 26–27, 34, 35, 116
Kentucky, University of, student demonstrations at, 28
King, Rev. Edwin, 10
King, Rev. Martin Luther, Jr., 14, 32, 78; assassination of, 17, 46; funeral of, 142
Knoxville College, cancellation of classes at, 117
Krause, Allison, 18
Kudzu, 190
Ku Klux Klan, 43, 178
Kuykendall, John, 91, 128, 131
Kyles, Ernest Lee, 156

Langford, Charles, 167
Latham, Thomas, 164–65
Lawyers Committee for Civil Rights under Law, 158
Lee, Charles, 46, 47, 65, 75–76, 97; testimony of before committee, 95–96
Leonard, Jerris, 150–53
Lincoln University: cancellation of classes at, 117; student protests at, 29
Little, Charles, 98; testimony of before committee, 94–95
Lynch, John Ray, 1, 17, 177, 180
Lynch, Judge Charles, 1, 56
Lynching, 56
Lynch Street, 1–5, 17; as civil rights headquarters, 8–13; Congressional delegation on, 142–43; death on, 16, 71–73; John Mitchell on, 132–33; looting on, 14; police/black confrontation on, 15–16 (*see also* Brown, Benjamin); 1968 and 1969 mini-

riots on, 17; renamed J. R. Lynch Street, 180; student violence on, 33, 36–41; today, 175–76, 179–80; white hooligans on, 14. *See also* Cornerboys, Lynch Street; Jackson, Miss., police of; Jackson State College

McAfee, Ralph, 156–57, 159, 160, 164, 165, 167–68
McComb, Miss., 11
McDonald, Eddie Jean. *See* Carr, Eddie Jean McDonald
Mace, 29
Maddox, Lester, 34
Magee, Warren, 42–52, 62–76 passim, 95, 118, 130, 167, 168, 182; civil trial testimony of, 170–72; testimony before mayor's investigating committee, 92–94; trial of, 155–74; and written report on Jackson State violence, 97
Magee, Miss., 178
Mandel, Marvin, 25
Marshall, Thurgood, 175
Maryland, University of: civilians versus protesters at, 29; student protests at, 25; student shootings at, 28
Mayhorn, Gloria, 69, 72, 76, 98
Memphis, Tenn., Thompson's Tank on loan to, 46
Memphis State University, Jackson State memorial rally at, 116
Meredith, James, 7, 8, 30, 43, 179; shooting of, 43
Michigan, University of, civilians versus protesters at, 29
Michigan State University, anti-military student demonstrations at, 26
Mikva, Abner, 142
Miles College, black student protests at, 29
Millsaps, Reuben, 4
Millsaps College, 4, 19; and protest of Jackson State shootings, 86–87; and protest of Kent State shootings, 30, 86; solidarity of students of with Jackson State students, 32, 137, 138
Minor, Wilson, 15–16, 44, 151
Mississippi, state of, 19–20; civil rights activity in, 11 (*see also* Freedom Summer); colleges of, 30; and Head Start program, 42; labor conditions in, 179; Prohibition in, 55; public school system of, 34–35, 102 (*see also* "Freedom of Choice"); student protest in, 30–32; survivors of Jackson State shootings *v.*, 154–74; today, 176–80
Mississippi, University of: black and white students in confrontation at, 30; desegregation of, 7, 43, 179. *See also* Meredith, James
Mississippi Summer Project. *See* Freedom Summer
Mississippi United Front, 115
Mississippi Valley State College, student protests at, 23, 186
Mitchell, John, 98, 150, 155; in Jackson, 116, 131–33; on student unrest, 133
Molotov cocktails, 62, 63
Mondale, Walter, 138
Moore, Russell D., III, 155
Moran, Kevin, 23
Morgan State College, Jackson State memorial demonstrations at, 116, 117
Moses, Robert, 11
Mother Jones, 178
Mullen, Robert, 171–72, 173
Murry, Climmie Johnson. *See* Johnson, Climmie
Muskie, Edmund, 138; at James Green funeral, 134, 141, 142
Myers, John, 167
My Lai, 19

NAACP (National Association for the Advancement of Colored People), 11, 90; Mississippi branch of, 9, 12, 61, 87–88, 115, 135; represented at James Green funeral, 142
Nance, M. Maceo, 139
National Guard, Mississippi: alerted by Jackson officials, 15; and May 13 miniriot, 42, 52; on standby in Jackson, 56, 58, 66, 67, 118–19, 138; and sealing off of Jackson State campus, 78
National Guard, New Mexico, student demonstrations and, 28
National Guard, Ohio, 18; and Kent State

Index

slayings, 23, 26–27
Nationalism, black, 14
National Student Association, 25
National Student Strike, 26, 27, 28
Nevada, University of, student demonstrations at, 28
New Haven, Conn., Black Panthers on trial in, 23
Newsweek, 142
New York, N.Y.: hard-hat demonstrations in, 29; public schools of closed to honor Jackson State dead, 134; racial unrest in, 22
New York, State University of (Binghamton), student protests at, 25
New York, State University of (Buffalo), black student protests at, 29; police/student confrontation at, 28
New York, State University of (Stony Brook), and student memorials to Jackson State dead, 117
New York Amsterdam News, 142
New York Times, 91; on invasion of Cambodia, 25; on Kent State/Jackson State slayings, 116; on Phillip Gibbs, 100–101
New York University, Jackson State memorial rally at, 116
Nichols, Robert, 157–58
Nixon, Richard, 21–22, 28, 30, 31, 35, 56, 131, 139; on college protesters, 29; and invasion of Cambodia, 24–25, 133; and observation of James Green funeral, 143; official reaction of to Jackson State slayings, 116; and President's Commission on Campus Unrest, 156
Nixon, Walter, 156–57, 163, 174
No Heroes, No Villains (O'Neil), 183
Nol, Lon, 24
North Carolina A&T, death at, 139
North Carolina State University, Jackson State memorial rally at, 116
Northeastern University, student strike at, 26
Northern Illinois University, cancellation of classes at, 117

Ohio State University: black student protests at, 29; police/student clash on campus of, 23
Ole Miss. *See* Mississippi, University of
O'Neil, Robert M., 183
Orangeburg (S.C.) State College, protesters' death at, 139
Oxford, Miss., 1962 riots in, 43

Parchman, Miss., 23
Patton, Amos, 144, 147
Payne College, black student protests in, 29
Pell, Claiborne, 142
Pennsylvania, University of, National Student Strike at, 26
Penson, Carl, 170
Peoples, Dr. John, 56–58, 69, 82, 84, 90, 135, 176, 189; conciliatory efforts of, 58, 135, 173; in conference with Pres. Nixon, 139; at death scene, 78–79; meeting between John Mitchell and, 131–33; report of to the State College Board, 182
Percy, Charles, 142
Perkins, Rev. John, 188
Philadelphia, Miss., civil rights activists murdered in, 11
Philadelphia, Pa., 1964 ghetto rebellion in, 11
Pierce, M. B., 7, 45–68 passim, 171
Powell, Adam Clayton, 142
President's Commission on Campus Unrest, 156
Princeton University, antimilitary student demonstrations at, 26
Prohibition, in Mississippi, 55
Pyle, William, 91, 130

Ray, James Earl, 46
Rayfield, W. D., 39
Reagan, Ronald, 29
Reconstruction, 1
Reddix, Jacob, 7, 10, 57
Reese, Andrea, 98
Reserve Officers Training Corps. *See* ROTC
Reuss, Henry, 142
Rhodes, James, 29
Ripley, Miss., 99–105, 113–14, 178; partial

desegregation of, 102–3
Rochester, N.Y., 1964 ghetto rebellion in, 11
ROTC (Reserve Officers Training Corps), as symbolic campus "red flag," 28, 64–65; at Jackson State, 5, 35, 38–39, 41, 46–60 passim, 163; at Kent State, 26, 27–28; at Ohio State, 23; at University of Maryland, 25
Rowzee, Billy, 170
"Royce, Diane," 110–13
Rutgers University: civilians versus protesters at, 29; student strike at, 26

Sallis, Charles, 86
Sanders, Pat, 163
San Diego, University of, Vietnam War protest at, 28
Santa Barbara, Calif., student violence in, 23
Scranton, William W., 156
Seale, Bobby, 14
Seattle, Wash., 1970 violence in, 23
Sevareid, Eric, 22
Sherman, William T., 20
Shirley, Dr. Aaron, 115
Shotguns (dwellings), 2, 147
Simpson, Wayne, Jr., 170
Sit-ins, 5, 8; in Jackson, 7
Smith, Davis, 44, 55, 84
SNCC (Student Nonviolent Coordinating Committee), 11
Southern Christian Leadership Conference, 11. *See also* King, Rev. Martin Luther, Jr.
Southern Mississippi, University of, Jackson State memorial rally at, 116
Spight, F. L., 104–5
Spinks, Stella, 77, 80, 98; civil trial testimony of, 163–64
Stanford University, student protests at, 25
Stringer, M. R., 38, 41, 47
Student Nonviolent Coordinating Committee (SNCC), 11
Students for a Democratic Society, 26, 31
Sumrall, John Otis, 14
Supreme Court, U.S.: black survivors of Jackson State violence before, 175; and ruling against segregated public schools, 34

Syracuse, N.Y., racial unrest in, 53
Syracuse University, student strike at, 26

Taylor, George, 158–59, 162, 169, 173
Taylor, Jimmy, 167
Teach-ins, 22
Temple University, student protests at, 25
Thomas, Dale Adams Gibbs. *See* Gibbs, Dale Adams
Thompson, Allen, 9, 11, 14, 44; on Jackson State campus, 14–15. *See also* Thompson's Tank
Thompson, Henry, 18–19, 31, 37, 58
Thompson, Lonzie, 98; civil trial testimony of, 163
Thompson's Tank, 12, 42–52 passim, 62–71 passim, 93–98, 119, 123, 129, 158, 169, 178; on loan in Memphis, Tenn., 46. *See also* Little, Charles; Thompson, Allen
Thurmond, R. J., 104
Till, Billy Dwight, 169–70
Till, Emmett, 102
Time, 142
Tougaloo College, 7, 9, 10; civil rights activism of students of, 5, 7, 9–10, 86–87
Truman, Harry, 41

UCLA (University of California at Los Angeles), student strike at, 26
United States: campus revulsion at Jackson State slayings across, 116–17; ghetto uprisings in, 11, 13–14; and invasion of Cambodia, 24–25; reaction of to Jackson State slayings, 90–91, 134
Utah, University of, Jackson State memorial rally at, 116

Vardaman, James K., 41
Vaughn, Dell, 90
Vietnam Moratorium Committee, 22
Vietnam War: and bombing of North Vietnam, 26; and Cambodia, 24–25; as focus of student unrest, 14, 17, 22–23, 30–32, 35; Pres. Nixon's defense of U.S. role in, 21–22; Jackson State students in opposi-

tion to, 30–32; U.S. casualties in, 24
Villanova University, student protests at, 25
Vinson (Mississippi Highway Patrol inspector), 167
Voice of Blackness, The, 35
Voter registration drive, in Jackson, 11

Waites, Alex, 88, 115
Ward, Jimmy, 55
Warren, Earl, 90
Washington, D.C., August 1963 March on, 55
Washington, University of, and memorials to Jackson State dead, 117
Washington Post, 91; on invasion of Cambodia, 25; on Jackson State/Kent State shootings, 116; represented at James Green funeral, 142
Washington State University, civilians versus student protesters of, 29
Wayne State University, Jackson State memorial cancellation of classes at, 117
Weakley, Vernon, 38, 69–70, 71–72, 74; civil trial testimony of, 158–59
Weather Underground, 22–23
Whitehead, Tuwaine Davis, 173; civil trial testimony of, 160–61
Williams, John Bell, 35, 41–42, 83, 92, 116, 136, 138, 140, 150, 151, 155; and May 13 Jackson State miniriot, 41; on Northern attendees of James Green funeral, 142
Wilson, C. R., 43
Wilson, Redd, 98; civil trial testimony of, 163
Winne, George, 28
Woodward, Willie Lee, 98
Wright, Charles, 94
Wright, Richard, 9, 104, 187

Yale University, demonstrations at, 23, 25–26, 29
Yarborough, Ralph, 142
Yarbro, Cecil, 151, 152, 153
Young, Gene ("Jughead"), 78–79
Young, Whitney, Jr., 141